Scribe Publications
THE LONGEST DECADE

George Megalogenis spent eleven years in the Canberra press gallery, from 1988 to 1999, before returning to Melbourne as a senior feature writer for *The Australian*. He has a degree in economics from the University of Melbourne, and is the author of *Faultlines* (Scribe, 2003).

For AM & BC

The Longest Decade

GEORGE MEGALOGENIS

SCRIBE
Melbourne

Scribe Publications Pty Ltd
PO Box 523
Carlton North, Victoria, Australia 3054
Email: info@scribepub.com.au

First published by Scribe 2006

Typeset in 12/15 pt Granjon by J & M Typesetters
Cover design by Darian Causby
Cover photo by Mike Bowers, Fairfax Photos
Printed and bound in Australia by Griffin Press

National Library of Australia
Cataloguing-in-Publication data

Megalogenis, George.
 The longest decade.

Includes index.
ISBN 1 920769 79 X.

1. Keating, Paul, 1944- . 2. Howard, John, 1939- . 3.
Australian Labor Party. 4. Liberalism - Australia. 5.
Australians - Attitudes. 6. Australia - Politics and
government - 1990-2001. 7. Australia - Politics and
government - 2001- . I. Title.

320.994

www.scribepub.com.au

Contents

Introduction

AT SOME POINT during the 1990s we overloaded on information and income, and our attention span shrank. Paul Keating and then John Howard bombarded us with change, and broke a few promises along the way. But we stopped caring because prosperity had given us the licence to retreat to the lounge room or the local coffee shop. 'Kath & Kim' nailed the era when Kim told Kath, 'I want to be effluent'.

The most boring game today is the one that forces you to choose between the architects of the Australian condition: Keating and Howard. Are you a member of the Keating fan club, or are you a Keating critic? A Howard hugger or a Howard hater? The idea that only one of these politicians holds the codes to our national soul is inherently absurd, but it informs much of what passes for political analysis in the media and the book trade.

I won't play by those rules, because there is more to learn about Australia by looking at the two of them together — their consistency on economics, as well as their conflict over national identity. Keating and Howard have split the past 30 years of power between them, almost evenly, as treasurers and prime ministers. Each stint was informed by the one before it: treasurer Keating cleaned up the mess that treasurer Howard had made of the economy at the start of the 1980s; Howard as prime minister was given a mandate to repair the society that had been divided by his predecessor, Keating, in the 1990s.

This book looks at Keating and Howard together, as part of a bigger Australian story, with a bias towards their terms in the Lodge. Both men agreed to be interviewed by me extensively on the issues that shaped their respective governments. Both have admitted errors that may surprise their supporters. And I give Keating and Howard the chance to criticise each other at the end, in the interests of balance, and for what their words about the other say about themselves.

For the sake of simplicity, I will refer to them by their positions at the time of each engagement. The Keating personas are easily recognisable: treasurer Keating between March 1983 and May 1991, and prime minister Keating from December 1991 to March 1996. There are two Howards before he became prime minister. Howard Mark I covers the lean years in opposition between March 1983 and December 1994, when he was one of the most ridiculed, and misunderstood, politicians going around. Howard Mark II tracks his resurrection as Liberal leader in January 1995, after an absence of five-and-a-half years.

The mundane truth about politicians is that their ability to shape the real world falls somewhere between two delusions. They are not as powerful as they'd like to think. But some are not as useless as the public, in their apathy and sarcasm, want to believe. Keating has a dual claim on the nation. The policies he introduced as treasurer set the economy on a trajectory it had never known before. The payoff was only clear after he had gone, when Australia was able to side-step the financial meltdown in Asia in 1997–98, and then avoid the world recession in 2001. The argument that prime minister Keating triggered about who we are as a people also lingered long after his demise. The more easily quantifiable of these legacies is the former, the economic, and for reasons he might regret. The low-inflation recovery that Keating bequeathed Howard in 1996, with its dichotomy of an upwardly mobile working class and an expanding underclass, reduced the national dialogue to the question of whose property was worth more, and the debate on Australia's identity from 'we' to 'me'.

Howard used power differently to Keating, but to the same end —to tell his version of the national story. Howard's Australia is confident, perhaps even a little too smug. But it also became what Keating had wanted—a pin-up for globalisation—because Howard happened to agree with him on that score.

Yet for each change that Keating and Howard imposed, the nation snapped back and forced them to adapt. Deregulation meant that politics had less control of the public. The Australia of Keating and Howard was neither ours nor theirs. It had become too complex to be labelled as blue collar, egalitarian, and laid back. Australia is a more interesting place today because there are so many more of us laying claim to the mainstream.

I want to tell two intertwined stories, the political and cultural, and pose the question that taunts our age: how did the Keating–Howard economy take us from growth to greed?

CHAPTER ONE

'De-spiving Australia'

PAUL KEATING could tell a very compelling story, even if it was not always strictly accurate. In private, he once insisted to me that he had seen Otis Redding in concert in 1973, six years after the Memphis-born soul singer had perished in a plane crash. I suspect the artist he really had in mind was Wilson Pickett, but Keating was not the sort to concede a point.

In politics, certainty is both a tool of the trade and an implement of self-destruction. As treasurer and then prime minister, Keating dealt with the driest of digital mediums, economics, where a fraction either way would come to mean the difference between the respect or loathing of a nation. Because it is based on statistics, economics carries the aura of precision. But the numbers only make sense months, or even years, after the event, when all the transactions in the nation have been tallied. Economics, like political journalism, is guesswork disguised as insight.

Like many who worked in the press gallery at the time, my view of treasurer Keating would fluctuate, depending on which one was talking to the nation that day — the charmer or the eccentric. Like most so-called experts, I had little understanding of how Australia would function beyond the tariff wall. My economics degree at the University of Melbourne in the early 1980s preceded deregulation. I had only two years' experience in newspapers behind me when I arrived in Canberra at the age of 24 in October 1988. As economics correspondent for Rupert Murdoch's tabloids, my first big story dealt with the slaughter of 40 million confused Bogong moths, whose seasonal migration to their summer breeding grounds in the NSW and Victorian Alps was diverted by the lighted flagpole atop the new Parliament House. Each day the creatures would take to the air, only to be drawn back that same night by the beacon of Australian democracy where they would descend like a biblical plague. The next page one I wrote in November 1988 carried the headline 'Home loan rates to soar'.

The press gallery's infatuation with treasurer Keating was fading by the time I got there. The media conferences he gave as treasurer had been rituals with no precedent in politics and which are unlikely to be repeated. To say that the journalists were in awe of him would be an understatement, but to view this as a dereliction of their duty is to misunderstand the context. There was manipulation, sure. But there was an altruism at the heart of what Keating was doing that Howard Mark I acknowledged at the time. This was the only period outside of war when a politician and the press formed a loose alliance, in the national interest. The opening of the economy was seen as a noble pursuit, and the media felt they had a role to play in educating the public. Think about the media staples today — terror and celebrity — and the 1980s and early 1990s seem, by comparison, an enlightened age of policy debate.

The competition for the support of the press was contested by both sides of politics. John Howard as Liberal leader between 1985–89, and then John Hewson in his *Fightback!* phase of 1990–93, were also preaching economic rationalism. The trick for the media was to retain independence and a healthy degree of scepticism. A common purpose did not mean partisanship. What we got wrong was to assume, as Keating had, that we knew enough about the economy to predict where it would go if this or that policy lever were pulled. The more we learned, the more we realised how little we knew.

My initial impression, nonetheless, was that the relationship with

Keating was a little weird. On a good day, even if the numbers were bad, journalists would compete like schoolroom pets for the teacher's affection. The questions to Keating were soaked in jargon. The tone was often reverential, even conspiratorial. At the end of a 70-minute session, some of the most respected pontificators in the nation would float out of the room like teenyboppers heading for the exit sign after a rock concert. Their faces beaming, they'd recite Keating's best lines to each other. When the same group had finished grilling John Howard or Andrew Peacock in the late 1980s, the heads would be shaking. 'That man will never be prime minister,' they'd say. Of course, the media can only be half right most of the time.

Keating began to lose the press gallery after the August 1988 budget. He promised to 'bring home the bacon'. He brought on a boom instead. Keating had told us to judge him by arcane concepts such at the current account deficit, which was the difference between what we bought and borrowed from the world, and what we could sell back to it. When the deficit didn't behave as he said it would, and our foreign debt ballooned to cover the shortfall, the public suddenly began to worry that the nation was going down the gurgler.

The media changed sides, from Keating's advocate to his attacker, and began the countdown to economic catastrophe. A blow-out in the deficit would be written up as the trigger for another interest-rate rise. A good number was merely a reprieve. There would be half-a-dozen different ways this debate could be re-heated before the next month's data was due for release. When interest rates were increased, the story moved, inevitably, hysterically, to the wave of anger that greeted them. We'd pull out our calculators so we could tell home borrowers how much extra a month they would have to pay, even though three out of four households weren't affected. This, incidentally, is one reason why Keating didn't hear the economy crack until it was too late. The feedback he would get from the polls, and from members of his own family, was that high interest rates weren't such a bad thing because older voters loved the double-digit returns they were collecting on their bank deposits.

But, and this is a very important qualifier, no one with any pull in the press gallery, or in the economics profession, thought in 1989 or even into 1990 that Keating's wrestle with the boom would end in a severe recession. For instance, a former colleague at *The Australian*, and a Keating sceptic, placed a $5 bet with Rupert Murdoch that unemployment would remain below 10 per cent. History was repeating itself, because the press gallery had also missed the severity of the 1982–83 recession. Blame the location, not the medium. Canberra is the nation's most middle-class city, where the gap between rich and poor is the smallest. Its main trade is politics, which is the nation's last protected market. It is not the best place from which to observe the real economy when it is heading south.

The catch was that we in the press gallery also got the recovery wrong. We had no idea when the recession came that it would unleash a tidal wave of ironies that would, in time, allow first Keating and then Howard to rise to the job of prime minister. At the end of the 1980s, the idea that either man would have a say in Australia's future seemed, at best, fanciful. Keating had lost control of the economy, and Howard had been dropped as Liberal leader.

BEFORE THE 1990s, the decades in Australia used to run to a predictable script of bust, boom, and bust. They'd commence with the economy in the pits, assume their personalities in the good times that followed, and conclude with another collapse. Conveniently, this cycle took about ten years to play out. The 1960s, for instance, were book-ended by the recessions of Robert Menzies in 1961 and William McMahon in 1971–72. The shriek that greeted The Beatles, the tumult of Vietnam, women's liberation, and full employment can be neatly slotted between these two slumps.

Drawing an economic line through the 1970s is a little harder, because there was no recovery to speak of. Labor's Gough Whitlam gave us a nasty recession in 1974–75, and the coalition's Malcolm Fraser followed up with a smaller contraction in 1977. Perhaps that's why we recall the 1970s for its politics over its popular culture. The title fight of Whitlam versus Fraser in 1975 was Australia's version of boxing's 'rumble in the jungle' between Muhammad Ali and George Foreman in Zaire. Unlike the vanquished Foreman, who left no quote to remember him by, Whitlam gave us: 'Well may we say God save the Queen, because nothing will save the Governor-General'. Later, Fraser came up with a line that proved almost the equal of Whitlam's for its ability to lodge in our subconscious. 'Life wasn't meant to be easy' summed up the 1970s better than any song or social movement.

The turn of history's page to the 1980s came with Fraser's second recession in 1982–83 and the longest dole queues since the Great Depression. When Labor returned to power in March 1983, the drought broke and the nation's optimism rose. But it was the false dawn of the sun lamp, and another bad-hair decade. Early in his term, Bob Hawke told employers that only a bum would sack a worker for taking a sickie after watching Alan Bond grab the America's Cup yacht race. This was ironic, because Bond's business dealings would come to symbolise the excesses of deregulation, which begat high interest rates, which begat another recession. Only this crash broke all the rules. It carried the name of the treasurer, not the prime minister, because the treasurer wanted applause for ending the speculative orgy of the 1980s. At first, we thought he was crazy for seeking praise, but history has validated Paul Keating in an unexpected way. The decade that followed his recession has run over time, into what the calendar said was the new millennium because we kept growing when the rest of the world shrank in 2001. Economically speaking, the 1990s are about 15 years old and still going strong.

The catch for Keating is that the longest decade belongs to John Howard. The public still associate Keating with the high interest rates that brought on the recession, and Howard for the doubling of property prices that extended the recovery. But the popular judgment is premature. The narrative will become more balanced, in time, not because Keating was right and Howard was wrong on the issues they argued over, but for the simple reason that the next recession, when it comes, will be seen as Howard's fault. That's just the way politics works.

KEATING DELIVERED the phrase that opened the decade on 29 November 1990. Earlier that morning, the commonwealth statistician announced that the economy had gone backwards by 1.6 per cent between July and September. The treasurer had handled bad numbers before, with aplomb. But this was the second quarter in a row with a minus in front of it, so it satisfied the generally accepted definition of a recession. Having spent the previous two years assuring voters there would be no recession, Keating had some explaining to do. As he left his office, and skipped across the corridor to the elevator that would take him upstairs to face the media, Keating's executioners in the press gallery were placing bets. How long would it take before he uttered the r-word? One minute, five minutes, half an hour? It is a measure of the cynicism radiating toward Keating that some journalists thought the answer would be not at all — that somehow he would argue, as he had done during the election earlier in the year, that this was another 'beautiful set of numbers'. We misjudged him. On this day, he came to plead guilty. It took him just six seconds to say the word 'recession', and barely as long again to say that he meant every bit of it:

> Well, I'll just give you a few comments on the national accounts. And the first thing to say is the accounts do show that Australia is in a recession. The most important thing about that is that this is a recession that Australia had to have. That the spending we had in the two years up to now was unsustainable. That we couldn't go on spending and consuming at the rate we were, carrying the imports we were, and the debt we were and, of course, the erosion of our gains on inflation.

The collective memory has cribbed that statement to 'the recession we had to have'. Something about this crash made it linger longer in the national psyche than most of the others that preceded it. The only comparison is the Great Depression, which was still shaping attitudes 30 or even 40 years later. But the Depression generation was frugal. They saved more than they spent during the consumer boom of the 1950s and 1960s. Their children, the baby boomers, were raised in prosperity but with the spectre of nuclear war hanging over them, so they partied.

Keating's recession generation, the boomers and their children, were hardened by the international economy. It was part of the bargain of deregulation: take nothing for granted. But where the Depression generation sought security through having money in the bank, or in a shoebox under the bed, Keating's recession generation spent what it earned, and then some. Where the Depression forged a stronger sense of community, Keating's recession would have the opposite effect, dividing the nation between two versions of Australia, the open and the closed.

The notion of a deliberate recession jarred with everything Keating had promised voters beforehand, which is why they never forgave him for it. 'Australia will emerge from the recent high level of spending without a recession and with its economic and social structure improving,' he had said in his August 1989 budget speech. Even as the first cracks appeared in his rhetoric, albeit after the 1990 election was won, Keating insisted that the public would be spared a hard landing. 'This year, inflation will fall further, the current account deficit will markedly improve and employment will pick up. In short, the kind of outcome the government was seeking, delivered without the misery and despair of high unemployment and a savage recession,' he said, fingers-crossed, in his August 1990 budget speech.

The numbers game of economics has played tricks with this recession. Hindsight says it didn't really happen the way politics and the media recorded it. Subsequent revisions by the Australian Bureau of Statistics have changed the date—from the middle of

1990 to the first half of 1991. On this timetable, the 'recession we had to have' press conference would not have been Keating's to hold, because the figures would have been released in the second half of 1991, when he was on the backbench and stalking Bob Hawke for the Labor leadership. None of this matters, of course, because politics, like life, is a chain reaction triggered by partial information.

Keating's recession hung in our thoughts because the recovery didn't erase it quickly enough. Employers were reluctant to rehire the blue-collar workers who had been sacked, because the jobs they were qualified to do had been made redundant by deregulation.

But, when they think about it, what exactly is it that people remember: the one million unemployed or the 17 per cent mortgage rate? Neither number happens to be mainstream, if mainstream is defined as the experience of the majority of voters. Most workers kept their positions. Even in the retrenchments capital of Victoria, only one out of every nine employees was thrown on the scrap heap. In New South Wales, only one out of every 24 workers was sacked.

What about interest rates? Well, roughly three out of four households didn't feel a thing, because they had either paid off their mortgage or were on a fixed interest rate of 13.5 per cent, the ceiling that applied on all home loans issued before April 1986. This privileged group covered 2.8 million of the nation's 3.8 million households. Also, the banks shielded the remaining one million borrowers by extending the term of the loan, so repayments did not rise every time the Reserve Bank of Australia cranked up official interest rates.

The melancholy of Keating's recession can be sourced to a more selfish concern: the absence of capital gains. The property boom ended in 1990, and house prices wouldn't resume their familiar spiral for another seven years, until after Keating had lost office.

The clue is in Keating's personal files, in a note he prepared as background for Labor leader Mark Latham before the interest-rate election of 2004. By now, Keating had been out of politics for eight years, but he remained a political junkie. Every Saturday in retirement he would repeat the ritual he observed during his parliamentary career: he would go through the articles he had clipped during the week — a speech he might have given, perhaps a letter he had received — and figure out what to keep, and what to bin. This was better than a self-serving diary, he reasoned, because future generations could see the raw materials of his period in power and make up their own minds.

At the end of the 1980s, Keating wrote, voters didn't notice rising interest rates until it was too late because the value of their property was climbing faster than the cost of the mortgage:

> People continued to borrow and banks continued to lend. Asset inflation was running at 20–25 per cent and people expected it to continue. Bill rates at 15 per cent had little impact so long as people thought that asset values would continue rising at 20 per cent-plus. This is why rates had to top 15 per cent.

The historical value of the document is in its confirmation that, after all these years, Keating is still happy to assert that his recession was a good one, because it set up a golden era of low-inflation growth. Here's a summary of Keating's thoughts on why there had to be a recession, and who was responsible for making it worse than it needed to be. The emphasis is Keating's:

> In 1989, after nearly five years of 4 per cent growth the economy was again tilting on the edge of a wages explosion, a collapse in the profit share and a return to double-digit inflation.
>
> Average weekly earnings were running at 6.9 per cent. In the boom in real estate and business investment, unions at the top end of the ACTU constituency; metals, building and oil were being *offered* wage increases of 12–15 per cent.
>
> Wages had, for five years, been held by the Accord; but the Accord was unravelling at the edges. Bert Evans of the Metal Trades Industry Association was telling everyone 'we are buggered — it's going to blow'.

Keating nominated three causes for the late 1980s boom. First, the 'immature response of the banking sector to deregulation, [with] each trying to out compete each other and to lock out the foreign banks'. Second, a sudden surge in the prices the world was prepared to pay for our exports, 'pumping a fortune back into the economy'. Third, the gift to business through the higher profits 'coming from six years of wage restraint'.

Keating didn't want to repeat the blunder of Fraser's government in 1982–83, when the boom turned to recession and inflation and unemployment each broke through the 10 per cent pain barrier. Keating wanted the public's 'expectations to be corrected quickly before the boom got totally out of control with another wages explosion'. He urged the Reserve Bank to 'deal with the boom'. Dealing with the boom meant crunching two types of inflation, on wages and assets. In other words, cash and capital gains. But the timing was out. The authorities waited too long, then overshot:

> Late in 1988, the government pressed the Reserve Bank to start moving rates up which it did, but slowly. The Bank called it 'snugging'. Such was the Bank's reticence that by 1989 even the Bank itself realised rates had to move up.

The next error, he wrote, was to leave interest rates too high for too long:

> In 1990, following the election, the RBA, then under Bernie Fraser, declared that the Bank would go on a 'monetary holiday'. Rates were cut too slowly, ending up at 13.5 per cent in December 1990. Even by November 1991 rates were still 10 per cent. The RBA was too slow on the way up and too slow on the way down. This is what made the recession bite.

But the consolation Keating draws from this period is that inflation was kept in check:

Wages were held and inflation was beaten. There was no return to [treasurer] Howard's 1982 wage explosion of 17 per cent and his 11 per cent inflation.

Australia came out of the recession in 1991 with inflation at 1 per cent.

Had a wages boom happened again at the end of the 1980s there would have been no success in the 1990s.

When Howard inherited the economy from Labor in 1996, the economy had grown consecutively for 19 quarters and growth was running at over 5 per cent with 2 per cent inflation. Howard called it 'five minutes of economic sunshine' — it was, in fact, five years. And it has gone on ever since. For fourteen years.

The job of terminating the boom, fuelled as it was by the 'crazy lending of the banks', was always going to be 'ugly', Keating wrote:

> The Reserve Bank by its timidity made it worse. But, nevertheless, despite the pain for the government and the community, *it was the turning point for Australia*. It broke, once and for all, *the dismal boom and bust legacy of wages explosions and profit crunches*. It gave us fourteen years of strong low inflation growth.
>
> It is why the government said at the time 'it was the recession we had to have', for without it, wages would have gotten away again and inflation would not have been beaten. The problem was the RBA made it a deeper and much harder landing and a far costlier one than it should have been.

The multiple facets of Paul Keating are displayed in his musings: a razor-sharp intellect, a propensity for blame-shifting, candour on the means and ends of policy and, of course, the fixation with John Howard. He showed me the document in June 2005. Six months later, Keating received the most unexpected endorsement of all, from Ian Macfarlane, the Reserve Bank governor who had been appointed by the Howard government soon after its election in 1996. Macfarlane agreed with Keating, that the recession had been worth it:

I think that some of the economic interpretations are completely wrong and, even more importantly, the political interpretations are completely wrong. The episode in Australia which returned us to a low-inflation, stable growth economy was regarded as a policy error, whereas in America it is regarded as a policy triumph.

The intriguing aspect of Keating's recession was how it resembled a firestorm, reducing some buildings to ash while leaving others untouched. Keating happened to achieve his promised soft landing for the economy in four out of the nation's six states. The largest, NSW, kept growing over the course of 1990-91 and 1991-92. The third largest, Queensland, was not far behind, with a near-perfect landing in 1990-91 and a stronger take-off in 1991-92. Western Australia, the fourth-largest economy, never skipped a beat; and even Tasmania, the nation's smallest and poorest state, remained in the black.

The recession was contained to Victoria and South Australia, respectively the nation's second-largest and fifth-largest economies. Here it was more depression than recession. Both states contracted for two years in a row, and both saw their government-run banks disappear. Victorians also had their second-largest building society, Geelong's aptly named Pyramid, collapse, leaving the state's second-largest town with a decade-long inferiority complex that would be reinforced by its Australian Rules football team, the Cats, losing grand finals in 1989, 1992, and 1994. John Cain and John Bannon, respectively the Labor premiers of Victoria and South Australia, should be considered co-owners of Keating's recession.

On the 1990 election campaign trail, Keating would say privately that he'd love to line up his Victorian colleagues and shoot them. He would flash a grin as he mimicked the rat-tat-tat of machine-gun fire. It was Victoria that stood between him and his twin ambition of a soft landing for the economy and an election win that would allow him to take over the prime ministership in Labor's fourth term. The day before the election, Keating flew to Melbourne with the transparent goal of getting his head on the six o'clock TV bulletins and the front page of the local tabloid, *The Sun News Pictorial*. The stunt involved Keating, a Sydneysider without the slightest interest in any sport, taking out a membership with the most parochial football club in the nation, the Collingwood Magpies. Down-trodden and anti-establishment, Collingwood appealed to the street fighter in Keating:

> I've found a show that sees everything in black and white, which is a one-eyed outfit, which is an underdog outfit and it just hates losing. I thought, 'That's the club for me because I just bloody well hate losing, I hate it.'

The lesson of Keating's Magpie moment was in the questions he fielded from the Collingwood faithful. The audience understood the treasurer's economic message. The problem was they loathed it, because they preferred the world as it had been, behind the tariff wall. The first question from the floor summed up the mood:

> We heard about this need for Australia to become part of the global scene. I am a Labor supporter and will be voting for the Labor Party on Saturday. However, the logical extension of your economic policies means we won't be seeing Collingwood's first match of the season here at Victoria Park, we'll be seeing it played in Tokyo in ten years.

The election result offered the strongest hint of the recession to come. Labor's stocks crashed in Victoria, where it lost nine seats. If the status quo had held in every other state, and no further seats changed hands, the rout in Victoria would have delivered government to the Andrew Peacock-led coalition. But Labor prevailed because it won five seats in total from the coalition in the soft-landing states of NSW and Queensland. At the end of the year, and a week after the recession had been confirmed, Keating boasted how Labor had won with interest rates still in the stratosphere:

Members of the opposition are still smarting over the fact that even
with 20 per cent interest rates we beat them; they cannot get over
how they did not nail the government in these conditions ... The
fact of the matter is the government won the election because it is
the only party in Australia with a policy structure.

The warping of Australia in recession poses the first riddle of the
decade. Why Victoria? The answer helps to place Keating's role in
the mess in a more forgiving context than the judgment handed to
him by politics, in which both the Howard government and Labor
opposition routinely write him off. Victoria had two chips on its
shoulders at the start of the 1990s. One was Sydney; the other,
economic rationalism. Melbourne was the city most sensitive to
Keating's game plan to build an open economy because it had a
bigger share of its workforce relying on protection for its livelihood.
Sydney, by comparison, had a services sector to fall back on when
the recession came, while Brisbane and Perth could rely on mining
for a quid.

The proof was in the number of jobs lost, which is a more
reliable measure of recession than gross domestic product. Victoria
accounts for a quarter of the national economy, but was responsible
for three out of every four jobs that disappeared at the start of the
1990s. As unfashionable and politically incorrect as the following
thought might seem, it is hard to see how Keating could have spared
Victoria, even if he had managed to call every interest-rate
movement perfectly. What was going on here cut deeper than the
economic cycle. It was Victoria being dragged, reluctantly, into the
global economy.

In the cocoon of old Australia, Melbourne was the
manufacturing capital of Australia. It made the things the rest of the
world didn't want to buy, from clothes to cars. Protection is cultural
arrogance by another name. The French prefer to make their own
wine and cheese; the Japanese, their rice; and the Americans, their
beefsteaks. Australians wanted their own refrigerators and electric
range hoods.

We can cut, shear, butcher, and dig better than most nations, so we never had to shelter our farmers and miners from the viciousness of international markets. But primary industries are the stuff of third world economies. Alfred Deakin, the nation's second prime minister and its founding advocate for the tariff wall, had said 'no nation ever claimed greatness which relied upon primary industry alone'. When the first consumer boom of the 1950s and 1960s gave an automobile to the working man and white goods to his stay-at-home wife, Australia knew only one way to manufacture these products, at a price higher than the going rate. The tariffs were needed to keep the manufacturers afloat.

This is a recurring theme of white settlement. The urge to replicate a first world manufacturing sector was the same as the one that compelled Australians to grow English-style gardens, with lush lawns, in the driest continent on the planet. Australia is the United States without the religion, climate, or critical mass of people. The carrying-capacity of our continent is only a fraction of theirs; yet, like the Americans, we assume the highest income in the world as a birthright. Unlike the Americans, we didn't feel the need to prove it in the global marketplace for most of the 20th century. The Hawke-Keating government was removing almost a century's worth of protection in less than ten years. It would have required almost supernatural powers to deregulate the economy without giving Victoria some form of indigestion.

The first thing to remember about old Australia is that it was built for blokes. Greed, when it led to recession in the past, could be explained by rampant masculinity. It came in threes: a politician wasting taxpayer funds, a business chief placing a dud bet with someone else's money, and a trade union boss gouging a pay rise that broke the economy. Every time the wages share took more than 62 per cent of the economic cake, recession would follow. But this time would be different.

What truly distinguished Keating's recession from all others before it was the absence of any fault that could be attached to working men. The wages share remained well below 60 per cent throughout the boom, because the treasurer had encouraged the trade unions to accept a cut in their real wages under the Accord in exchange for a higher social wage comprising lower taxes, additional family payments, and superannuation. But workers still paid for the recession with their jobs, because business had squandered the profits.

The recession carried Keating's moniker because his policies brought it on—not just the high interest rates, but all the reforms of the 1980s which broke the back of the blue-collar economy. But it wasn't his doing alone.

The white-shoed tycoons who epitomised the bust of the late 1980s, Christopher Skase and Alan Bond, were ready-made villains when the recession arrived. Skase fled to Spain rather than face bankruptcy charges, and Bond was jailed for fraud. It is not hard to see these men as emblems of the reckless lending practices of the banks and building societies. Keating didn't refer to any by name, but a part of him was looking forward to the recession to cleanse the economy of the speculators. A week before his 'recession we had to have' media conference, he echoed Travis Bickle in the movie *Taxi Driver*, longing for a downpour to wash away the muck off the streets:

> I feel for the decent people ripped off by the spivs. I mean, if there
> is one good thing, if there is a silver lining in this slowdown we're
> going through now, at least it will de-spiv Australia.

Yet Skase and Bond are cheap and, in some ways, misleading fall guys for the recession. The companies they ran, from five-star tourist resorts to breweries and television networks, survived the crash, as did the states from which they built their paper-thin empires, Queensland and Western Australia. Kerry Packer sold the Nine Network to Bond for $1 billion in the late 1980s, and bought it back for a quarter of the price three years later. This is not to discount the livelihoods ruined by the likes of Skase and Bond. But spivery is not a feature unique to an ailing economy. It is a major artery of capitalism, in sickness and in recovery.

Blaming corporate cowboys for the recession misses the point. The true culprits were the government, the bureaucracy and, most notably, the banks that lent to the spivs. In any case, business chiefs become, on most indicators, more grasping the stronger an economy gets. How else to explain the seemingly exponential rise in executive salaries, and the emergence in the 1990s of the reward for failure, the eight-figure golden handshakes for those who left their companies in a worse state than they found them? Two of the financial institutions that passed through the recession seemingly unscathed became exhibits for greed in the recovery. The life office AMP gave its imported American CEO, George Trumbull, a $13 million payout in 1999. The company was happy to be rid of him after he oversaw the doomed takeover of fellow insurer GIO. But $13 million? The National Australia Bank went from the recession's saint to the recovery's sinner, losing billions in overseas ventures. The only financial player to hold its nerve in both the recession and the recovery was Keating's bank, the government-run Commonwealth. He might have made a fine banker.

When recession became unavoidable, Keating swapped his rationale for high interest rates, from targeting imports and foreign borrowings to the very domestic concern of inflation, which had been cursing the economy since Gough Whitlam's days. This became one of the defining moments of the 1990s, when Keating said, in effect, 'Bugger it, I didn't mean for there to be a recession, but I might make something of it'. He announced the shift in a speech in February 1991: 'I don't want to just bend the inflation stick a little and then see it spring back. I want to snap the inflation stick and bring Australia back to the community of its [developed world] partners,' he said.

Fighting inflation first was a recipe for prolonging recession, and Keating knew it. So was the decision the following month, in March 1991, to execute a further round of tariff cuts. This was the apotheosis of economic rationalism, and the final round of changes to carry the joint by-line of Hawke–Keating before the two men began brawling over the Labor leadership. The most publicly identifiable victim of the policy was Nissan, which announced the closure of its car-making plant in the south-eastern suburbs of Melbourne less than a year later, in February 1992.

All roads to recession in the 1990s led to Victoria. The 1980s boom had created a false sense of security for the home state of manufacturing. Victoria was the only state to have brought unemployment below 5 per cent, and it had an interventionist Labor government keen to push it lower still. Victoria's premier, John Cain, an ideological opponent of the Hawke–Keating brand of economic rationalism, believed in protection and government-run businesses at a time when federal Labor was preaching competition and privatisation. Neither side could be certain which view would prevail because, as the economy continued to grow in 1988 and 1989, Cain pumped up the state further, while Keating pushed interest rates higher. Both assumed a recession could be avoided. They were mistaken, of course, but Victorians took it out on Cain, not Keating. Cain quit as premier soon after the March 1990 federal election. Keating, by contrast, managed to turn the recession into a promotion for himself … to the job of prime minister.

'You're terrible, Muriel'

HIS RECESSION was supposed to de-spiv the nation. What Paul Keating's new economic disorder did, instead, was unman it. Australia knew only one identity before the 1990s, that of the laconic male. He had a couldn't-give-a-stuff nature to him that set him apart from other western men. The squatter, the digger, the bronzed surf lifesaver were the same person. When Australian men weren't enough to fill the public space, a horse such as Phar Lap would appear. With Simpson and his donkey, we had the ultimate two-for-one package.

Other nations have indulged in the cult of the common man. Think of John Steinbeck's Tom Joad in the US dust bowl of the 1930s, and his post modern heir, the New Jersey-born rock star Bruce Springsteen. Plain talking and generous, they could have been Aussies. But they were a touch too earnest and a little too eager to wrap themselves in the Stars and Stripes. The only thing the Australian male would drape over himself was the arm of his mate.

The cinema is normally the last place you would look for a window into the nation's soul. Of all the celebrities the first world fixates upon, the actor is the one that has the shortest cultural hang-time. Australians don't watch Australian movies. As a measure of our lack of interest, the film industry views any year when 'Australian films gained at least 10 per cent of the local box office' as a very good year. On this count, that last good year was 1988.

The blockbusters of the 1980s tell an interesting story in themselves. There was no perceptible change in the plotline either side of the 1982–83 recession. The top film at the box office in 1981 was *Gallipoli*; the following year it was the *Man from Snowy River*. In 1986, *Crocodile Dundee* pulled the number-one ranking. Two years later, at the bicentenary of white settlement, Australian films charted first and second, but we'd seen them before — namely *Crocodile Dundee II* and the *Man from Snowy River II*. It is hard to imagine a more masculine run of subjects: Australians in uniforms, on horseback, and in the outback.

The opening decade of deregulation did not dispose of our larrikin identikit. The switch came in the 1990s. To appreciate the difference, watch the DVD of the first *Crocodile Dundee*, then the number one ranked film of 1992, *Strictly Ballroom*: the blue-eyed, bronzed Paul Hogan versus the brown-eyed, olive-skinned Paul Mercurio. *Strictly Ballroom* was the last Australian movie to beat the foreign competition. It grossed $18.7 million, $5.6 million more than the second-placed film that year, *Basic Instinct,* though this would not be enough to get the local industry's total take above 10 per cent.

The last year when two Australian movies made the top 10 was 1994. *The Adventures of Priscilla, Queen of the Desert* finished seventh, one spot ahead of *Muriel's Wedding* in eighth. They featured drag queens and daggy women. The outback became the setting for an extended rock video, and the suburbs were reduced to their banal essence.

Film critic Lawrie Zion says *Muriel's Wedding* is the greatest Australian movie of all, and I agree. It satirises every conceivable corner of the Australian psyche — suburbia, celebrity, sport, and marriage — but without the sanctimoniousness of most modern art. There are few, if any characters that command sympathy, and the script is explicitly dark. But this is an endearing film.

Muriel is both bullied and a bully, though mostly she is clueless. She grows up on Queensland's concreted coastline, steals money from her family to go on a tropical holiday, moves to Sydney, then marries someone she doesn't know because she wants to be a bride. Muriel makes a friend along the way, Rhonda, but later snubs her. In American hands, Toni Colette's character would either dissolve into a bitch-from-hell, or find true love, whatever that is. But the final scene has Muriel and Rhonda reunited and waving goodbye to Porpoise Spit, the property developer theme park they grew up in.

Muriel boasts one of Australian film's few political gags that won't date. Muriel's dad, Bill Heslop, is a local councillor, a failed candidate for state politics, a friend to businessmen, and a philanderer. At his ex-wife's funeral, he grins as a telegram of condolence is read out on behalf of Bob Hawke and his second wife, Blanche. It doesn't really matter if Bill has faked the note, because the snigger that went out in every cinema across the nation said that Hawke was yesterday's man.

Hawke is the last prime minister to resonate as the typical Australian male. He was Hoges in a pinstripe. A renaissance man in the loosest sense of the term, he played cricket, drank beer, and had a prodigious IQ. He was the last Australian leader with a nickname —Hawkie—that was used with affection. His successor, Paul Keating, was the Grim Reaper. John Howard, whom Hawke beat at the 1987 election, was Little Johnny. Hawke made sense in the 1980s, but looked out of time in the 1990s.

Come to think of it, Keating didn't make sense in the 1990s, but then neither did Howard. Keating was an early-model metrosexual. His after-hours obsessions were classical music and architecture. The lasting impression of Howard will be his ordinariness, the early-morning power walks in a logo-heavy track suit, and the certainty that night-time would find him in front of the television transfixed by the cricket.

There are two numbers that explain why *Muriel's Wedding* had to happen in the 1990s. They deal with the place of men and women in the nation. Behind the tariff wall, Australia had been a 60–40 society. Men had more than 60 per cent of all the jobs in the workforce, while 60 per cent of women of working age were at home, most of them raising young children. That left working women with only 40 per cent of the jobs, and only 40 per cent of women working. This was the male domain of Hoges and Hawkie.

The recessions of 1982–83 and 1991 wiped out a generation of blue-collar men, and had sent them into the political arms of Pauline Hanson by the second half of the 1990s. By 1991, only 58 per cent of all jobs belonged to men; by 2005, the figure had fallen to 55 per cent. Women were rising in their place, only they weren't taking the positions of the displaced men because their manufacturing jobs were gone for good. The women were being employed in the growing services sector, at both ends of the income ladder, as lawyers and accountants and checkout girls and waitresses. Unlike the men, who went backwards in 1982–83 and 1991, women did not lose ground during either recession.

The female employment rate — which is a better bullshit detector than the unemployment rate because it measures all those of working age with jobs — had been a touch under 40 per cent throughout the 1960s and 1970s. It crossed 40 per cent for good in 1984, 50 per cent in 1998, and is now at 54 per cent. By this measure, Keating and Howard can count themselves as SNAGs, because they created jobs for the women of Australia, if not the men.

The male employment rate, by contrast, has been falling since the start of the 1970s. When Howard delivered his first budget as treasurer in August 1978, it was 74 per cent. He left it to treasurer Keating in 1983 at 69 per cent, who handed it back to Prime Minister Howard in 1996 at 67 per cent. Today, it remains below 69 per cent. In other words, no real jobs have been created for men in the Keating–Howard economy. The women, on the other had, have seen their worker ranks rise by 14 percentage points. Translated into human beings, that is about 1.1 million extra women with jobs thanks to deregulation.

Australia beyond the tariff wall is a 55–45 society. Men hold 55 per cent of the jobs. And just under 55 per cent of women work. We were ready for *Muriel's Wedding* in the 1990s, in part because the nation had become more feminine at its centre. By 2005, we even found a mare to compare to Phar Lap, when Makybe Diva became the first horse to win three straight Melbourne Cups.

CHAPTER TWO

Placido Domingo versus Fangio

PAUL KEATING'S Placido Domingo speech has become the political version of Woodstock. For every person who attended the gig, another 50 have a fevered opinion about what it meant. The context has been lost in the retelling. But the context matters, because much of what happens in politics is improvised, not planned.

The first thing to get straight is that Keating didn't mean to launch a leadership challenge on 7 December 1990. The address to the annual press gallery dinner came just eight days after his 'recession we had to have' press conference — hardly the ideal time to take on Labor's most successful leader, Bob Hawke. For the media, the function sat in the middle of a blur of farewell parties and Christmas drinks. The air was thick with the stench of retrenchment. One newspaper group, Fairfax, had gone into receivership; another, News Limited, had just completed a round of redundancies and was preparing to start sacking those who hadn't taken the hint. In television land, the Nine Network had reverted to its previous owner, Kerry Packer. Christopher Skase had left Seven in a hole, and the Ten Network was also in receivership. These were dog days for journalism, our period of structural adjustment.

The day before Keating rose to his feet at the National Press Club, the secretary of the Treasury Department, Chris Higgins, died of a heart attack after completing a mini-marathon.

Keating was deeply affected by Higgins' death. It loosened his lips in a dramatic and unexpected way. The substance of Keating's speech would have been inspiring in another forum, but that night it was laced with ego and aroused a sense of incredulity. Did the chap who had just shrunk the economy really believe he had a say in where the nation was heading?

The speech deserves requoting for Keating's view of what he felt Australia should become. It was his first rough sketch of the big picture. Australia, he said, had more going for it than the two big economic success stories of the 1980s, Japan and Germany. The Japanese lived in 'dogboxes', and the Germans had seen their environment ruined by acid rain. But this was also an Australia that had never had a great leader:

> We've got to be led, and politics is about leading people. Now we've got to the stage where everyone thinks politicians are shits and that they're not worth two bob and all the rest of it, and everyone kicks the shit out of us every time we get an increase in our salary. But politicians change the world, and politics and politicians are about leadership and our problem is — if you look at some of the great countries, of the great societies, like the United States — we've never had one great leader like they've had. The United States had three great leaders, Washington, Lincoln and Roosevelt, and at times in their history that leadership pushed them on to become the great country that they are. We've never had one such person, not one.

Size wasn't the issue, he said. The Americans weren't a nation of 230 million people 'when Thomas Jefferson was sitting in a house he designed for himself in a paddock in the back end of Virginia writing the words, "Life, Liberty and the Pursuit of Human Happiness".'

> They weren't 230 million when they were getting the ethos of their country together, when they were getting their great architectural heritage together, when they were rooting their values into the soil.

They had leadership, and that's what politics is about. It's about leadership, and that's what politicians are about.

He connected the absence of a Washington, Lincoln or Roosevelt to Australia's very suburban outlook:

A decade ago, the national ethos of this country was the 35-hour week. You work 35 hours, you've got the house you wanted, the Commodore in the drive, the weekender. That was it. Well, it wasn't enough. It wasn't enough. I don't know why we were in that position. It was probably because of the bounty of our resources and our minerals. But we never laid it all down in a constitution — well, we did at the turn of the century with the signature of the British parliament on it — [but] we never said this place is ours and we're going to run it ourselves and we're going to sit down, we're going to write a constitution which a couple of hundred years later could be as fresh as the day it was written. These things we never had ... It might have been our convict past. God knows what it was, or whether it was the rip-off merchants that came with free settlement. But we missed out somewhere.

The question was, could Keating shape the future. Clearly, he thought he could:

But we're now gathering our pace and we're gathering our people, and we're now 17 million and we're a more interesting society and we're well-placed in the world and we do occupy a continent. You've heard me say before that when the party ended on the British Empire, everybody went home. But they didn't go home from South Africa and they didn't go home from Australia. Except in South Africa there are more blacks than whites and here there are more whites than blacks. And the result was we dominated our population in this continent. So we're an accident, we're in South-East Asia. We occupy a continent and we're one nation and we're basically a European nation, changing now to adapt to the region.

Keating misjudged his audience. The speech was meant to be off the record, but words this electric couldn't remain secret for long. Keating had given variations of this pep talk before to those of us in the press gallery who had been on the receiving end of a briefing. His mistake was to assume that a group of 150 journalists, many unfamiliar to him, some of whom he didn't like, and who, in turn, felt the same way about him, would keep his confidence. The senior journalists in the room agonised over how they would cover the speech, but they were spared the ethical dilemma when some who didn't attend got wind of what he had said and made it page-one news.

Yet Keating didn't mean to signal a challenge. In fact, he was surprised when it was first suggested that he had done just that. His mood at the time said the opposite — that the recession would force him to surrender his ambition. Barely a fortnight earlier, for example, Paul Kelly had written in *The Weekend Australian* that Keating was 'reconciled to the possibility that he might never become PM':

> Short of some dramatic change, he won't challenge Hawke because such a contest would be absurd. It would pulverise the Labor Party and leave Keating covered in the political blood of a successful leader. If he lost, Keating would be finished; if he won, Keating would never recover, in the public's mind, from the exercise.

This received wisdom also happened to be shared by virtually all in federal parliament, and anyone in the public who bothered to think about these things. Keating had no plan to knife Hawke that night. If anything, he seemed a touch self-destructive, a man pleading a cause he feared was lost. The bravado about being the Placido Domingo of politics was Keating saying, brutally, and without a trace of humility, that he could beat the new opposition leader, John Hewson:

> You all regard him [Hewson] as a fresh face, and good on him. In political terms he is. He has only just been here a couple of years.

But he will never lift economics and politics to an art form. There is no Placido Domingo working within.

Keating, on the other hand, saw himself as the ultimate performer, 'trying to stream the economics and the politics together — out there doing the Placido Domingo'. He had self-confidence to the power of infinity, the very thing that voters couldn't stomach as the recession cast its pall over the nation. But Keating wasn't seeking a pat on the back. He was making a prediction, that he could tell a better story than Hewson at the next election:

> If you don't think that kind of panache, that kind of experience, matters in the transmission of economic ideas. I mean enough of you write me down, and good on you, and a few of you have let me down hard. But I'm still around after eight years and I'm still walking over those bloody people opposite, and I'll keep doing it.

By the time Hawke had digested a version of the speech, the partnership that had seen Labor win four federal elections in a row was as good as over. Of course, Hawke could have chosen to laugh off the incident as harmless. That he didn't said more about the prime minister's insecurity than he realised.

Hawke told the public he would serve a full three-year term if re-elected. For a moment, he seemed to be safe. On 17 January 1991, Australia went to war, sort of, as part of the multinational force that drove Iraqi dictator Saddam Hussein out of Kuwait. We supplied ships, but no ground troops. The war was over in less than six weeks, after a land battle that lasted barely 100 hours. In March, Hawke and Keating launched their last economic statement together, demolishing the final pillar of old Australia with the slashing of tariffs. But with another budget ahead of him, this one framed in recession, Keating was weary. At the end of May, he snapped and called the first of his two challenges for the leadership. There was an almost maniacal rhythm to the contest. On the weekend before the first ballot, a Keating supporter dared me to print the joke that was doing the rounds of parliament. 'The caucus has a choice between a cunt and a lunatic. The problem is they keep changing positions,' he advised. My then employer, *The Herald Sun*, obliged by running the quote in full, but with the c-word encoded as four dots.

Hawke won that ballot, by 66 votes to 44, and Keating went to the backbench. But a time bomb was ticking. Hawke, the undisputed face of the 1980s, looked hopelessly out of touch in the new decade. Keating had exposed both of them as liars by revealing the Kirribilli agreement they had struck in 1988 for Keating to take over the prime ministership after the 1990 election. But it was Hawke, not Keating, who suffered.

Yet all Hawke had to do was hang on to the leadership until Christmas, a mere six months away, and his challenger would likely have retired. Keating would have left the stage like one of those twenty- or thirty-something artists that flame out before their time, with a healthy corpse, a back catalogue, and a myth to be nourished by what-ifs. A Gram Parsons or a Sylvia Plath. But there was a brutal, inescapable logic to Keating's claim for the top job. The new opposition leader, John Hewson, made Bob Hawke seem old.

The recession had turned politics upside down. Following the 1990 election, the coalition broke with its habit of brawling like drunks at closing time and became a unified, even dignified, team under John Hewson. The rivalry between John Howard and Andrew Peacock, which had crippled the Liberals in the 1980s, was over. Now it was Labor's civil war that had the nation gripped in fascination and revulsion. Hewson behaved, and was, in turn, treated like a prime minister in waiting.

Hewson was the first of half-a-dozen or so political meteorites that flashed across the 1990s. Dazed and confused by deregulation and recession, Australia had become, paradoxically, easy prey to an economic hard-head. The community wanted an outsider who was not corrupted by the previous decade's false hopes; a plain-speaking politician who would admit the gravity of the national crisis, then apply the medicine without fear or favour. If Hewson hadn't existed, someone would have found an economist who looked plausible in front of a television camera and turned him into a prophet.

Hewson was two years younger than Keating. He had grown up in Sydney's south; his father was a fitter and tuner. But that's where the working-class connection ended. Hewson was a prototype aspirational voter, a self-made man who devoted his life to acquisition, from university degrees to luxury cars. Hewson listed the formula-one ace Fangio as his favourite sportsman, and became known as the Ferrari-driving politician.

Hewson had been an adviser to treasurer Howard in the Fraser years. When Labor took office in 1983, he went into merchant banking to make a truckload of money. But one job was never enough. He doubled as an economics commentator, which gave him a media profile ahead of his entry into parliament at the July 1987 election.

It was a measure of the Liberal Party's talent deficit then that Hewson was promptly catapulted into the shadow ministry as finance spokesman in September 1988, with only a year's experience in politics. There was a hidden agenda to his elevation. Howard Mark I needed Hewson on his front bench to diminish the profile of his shadow treasurer, Peacock. He wanted the press gallery to seek out Hewson for expert comment.

When Peacock challenged Howard in May 1989, Hewson voted for the loser. But Peacock couldn't afford to punish Hewson. He needed a shadow treasurer who was credible, to assure the press gallery that this time he was serious about economic policy, and about winning government. Voters rejected Peacock, but they liked what they saw of Hewson in the 1990 campaign. This, plus the deep-seated animosity toward Howard from the Peacock camp, made Hewson the logical, though improbable, candidate for the Liberal leadership after the election defeat. He'd had three promotions in three years; it was too quick, of course, but it seemed like a good idea at the time.

Hewson was a workaholic in the most debilitating sense of the word. He never stopped. He jogged for an hour before his early-morning telephone hook-ups, then his day would run over time. He'd be late for everything. Every appointment stretched longer than he had planned, because he always had something more to say. Early in his ascent, I was slotted to interview him between 5.00 pm and 6.00 pm. I waited outside his office for about 40 minutes. There was no mistaking what was going on behind the door; he was engaged in a telephone shouting-match with a shadow ministerial colleague. I figured that he'd reschedule his chat with me, because he had to get to the airport. But an apologetic Hewson eventually came out and said he'd pushed the flight back. We began talking. One-and-a-half hours later, he said he really had to go.

The way Hewson and many in the media saw it when he became leader, national salvation lay in a new tax on every transaction in the economy. Unlike Labor's floating of the dollar, financial-sector deregulation, and the removal of protection, which would only yield higher living standards after years of pain, Hewson's goods and services tax combined sacrifice and reward in the one transaction. It appealed to the fastidious side of the political class; the money raised from a single rate of tax on every good and service could be used to fund lower income tax.

I must admit a conflict of interest here. The GST helped me become a well-paid senior journalist, because tax was one of my specialities in the press gallery. Every decent wage rise I received from reporting federal politics came on the back of tax-based elections in 1993 and 1998. But the GST was accountancy masquerading as nation-building. It devoured seven years of public debate, from 1990 to 1993 and again from 1997 to 2001. These were seven years that taught voters to view their relationship with government in strictly commercial terms, because the political parties began to think and talk like telemarketers. The GST created a self-fulfilling cycle of segmentation, which may take another generation to break. Voters were divided into blocs so they could be told what their tax cuts would be worth. But no one could be satisfied. Each group wanted what the other was having.

There is an iron law to electioneering in Australia, the cookie jar commandment: thou shalt not be bribed two campaigns in a row. Promises that win one election inevitably break the budget afterwards, making the next election a more frugal affair. The elections of 1993, 1998, and 2004 all involved big tax cuts. But the contests in between — in 1990, 1996, and 2001 — were handout-lite because the budget cupboard was empty. Without greed to propel these campaigns, fear took over.

Hewson managed to combine the two, greed and fear, in his *Fightback!* document. He gave with one hand and whacked with the other. Personal tax cuts were offset by the GST, reductions to government spending, and the introduction of user-pays for health services.

There was an innocence to Hewson's manifesto. It made no effort to sugar-coat its intention. Hewson wanted the creed of competition to dominate every aspect of Australian life. Those who shirked the challenge would be punished. The opening paragraph set the tone for the next 600 pages:

> The overriding purpose of the Liberal/National program for reform is to achieve a generational change in policies and attitudes that will give individual Australians greater control over their own lives. We aim to achieve this goal by creating more incentives and opportunities for all Australians to work harder and be rewarded for it, to save and to invest.

The role of government was defined by the extent of its reduction; the place of the individual in society was determined by his or her willingness to make money. The role model for *Fightback!* was Hewson himself. He saw his personal story as the best side of the Australian spirit, self-reliant. He viewed Hawke and Keating as the dark side of our character — dealmakers, sell-outs, politicians who wouldn't level with the public.

It was the final paragraph of *Fightback!*'s introduction, the fifth, which bet the coming election on the single issue of tax policy. The

nation faced 'serious economic and social problems', and the
solution was the GST:

> Reform of the taxation system is a fundamentally important focus
> of our reform program. It is vital to reduce tax and simplify the tax
> system if the energies, talents and initiative of the Australian people
> are to be encouraged and fulfilled.

A year-and-a-half in the making, *Fightback!* drove the stake
through Hawke's leadership. With Keating brooding on the
backbench, Hawke and his ministers suffered a form of group
lockjaw. They were numbed by the size and ambition of the
document. On 20 November 1991, the day before its formal launch,
a worker at the Canberra printing firm that the coalition had hired
to produce *Fightback!* swiped a partial copy and passed it on to Labor
officials. They then leaked it to the press gallery, hoping to embarrass
Hewson. What Labor achieved, instead, was two days' worth of
flattering coverage for the opposition, not one. Hewson smiled and
thanked the government for giving his package a free plug.

The coalition was enjoying a ten-point lead in the polls at the
time. After *Fightback!* was released to rave reviews, the gap widened
to 18 points, 53 per cent to 35 per cent. Hawke cut a surreal figure in
his initial response to the package. Normally, the prime minister
would use the so-called blue room next to his labyrinthine office to
give his considered thoughts to the nation. But he wasn't in the mood
for scrutiny on the day *Fightback!* came out. He chose, instead, the
hit-and-run device of the doorstop interview to put a few words on
camera for the television news bulletins, and for radio. The problem
was he had nothing to say — only that the government would be
checking the *Fightback!* numbers to see if they added up.

Misstep became stuff up. A few days later, the deputy prime
minister, Brian Howe, ended a press conference he had called to
attack *Fightback!* by opening the door to a cupboard. While he
didn't walk into it, the vision of Howe not knowing where he was
going was enough. The most painful gaffe of all came from John

Kerin, Keating's replacement as treasurer. On 5 December, the national accounts for the September quarter were due for release, which marked the first anniversary of the 'recession we had have' GDP number. Kerin was expecting proof that the hard times were over and that the recovery was finally underway. What he got was another minus, and the shock was written all over his face. He stumbled over an economic acronym, the GOS, or gross operating surplus — which means, simply, the profit share. He asked a journalist for help, and in that instant his career was over. Hawke sacked him the next day, but it was too late to save his own leadership. Less than a fortnight later, on 19 December 1991, Keating toppled Hawke in their second ballot by 56 votes to 51.

It was an unusually sombre Keating who fielded questions from the media on the night of his victory. 'I'm very greatly honoured and more than a little nervous at the great responsibility the Labor Party has entrusted to me,' he said. He made three commitments: to give everything he had to the job and to the nation; to 'tell the truth'; and 'to fight the battle against unemployment and for economic recovery with all the energy I can muster'. The pledge about telling the truth, while genuine, showed that Keating had some serious making-up to do with the public. 'In tough times, of course, the temptation is always to gild the lily. I'll be resisting that temptation as much as is humanly possible.'

The two most revealing comments related to *Fightback!*. He didn't rate it, but he admitted it had revived his leadership ambition just when he was about to give it up:

> Dr Hewson has proposed what he believes is a plan for Australia. But it's the wrong plan; it's the wrong plan. It's a plan about making a tenth-order issue, about whether you tax income or expenditure, as a first-order issue, when we know, all of us, that the first-order issues are employment growth, investment, maintenance of low levels of inflation, further production, change in the workplace, enterprise bargaining, national economic efficiency — they are the first-order issues.

The GST, Keating said, 'amounts to no more than a shift in income to the wealthy at the expense of the low-paid'.

Keating felt Hawke had missed the point by seeking to rebut *Fightback!* on technical grounds. It required a political attack. 'If the government had been able to respond more fulsomely to the opposition's consumption tax package, then the likelihood of this matter [the Labor leadership] being debated before Christmas would have been remote.' What Keating was hinting at was that he had been preparing to quit politics altogether in the new year if Hawke had survived to Christmas. He had already planned for life after parliament by purchasing a half-share in a piggery, an investment that would come to haunt him later. But, for now, the 1990s had the cataclysm it craved—a contest between Keating and Hewson to decide how much more reform should be administered before the economy could grow again.

Jumping the Picket Fence

AUSTRALIA BROKE three social picket lines in the 1990s. Each move posed a question for the nation's self-image. Are women smarter than men? Can the children of immigrants count themselves as true Australians? Have we become a nation of entrepreneurs? The numbers that follow are all officially sourced; the interpretations are my own.

In 1991, Generation X women began to surpass men at the top of the labour market. This was the first year in our history when more women under 30 held tertiary degrees than men in the same age bracket. A mountain of angst would be unleashed by the realignment. Would there be enough eligible men to partner all these brainy women, when men preferred to marry down? Would these women get to climb the corporate ladder and become bosses? Would one of their sisters make it to the Lodge? The answers were: no, no, and perhaps not for another decade, at least. By 2000, the qualified female majority covered all those under 45. This process will reach its inevitable conclusion in 2010, when women with tertiary degrees will dominate every year up to age 65. If John Howard is still prime minister then, at 71, he will represent the only demographic in which men can still claim to be better educated than women.

Here's a dirty secret of deregulation. The more women enter the workforce, the easier it gets for capitalism. It doesn't suit politicians to view sexism as a variable of prosperity because wages are supposed to be set by the merit of market forces. But the open economy has shown an almost surreal ability to have it both ways. It favours women over men, yet it pays women about 10–15 per cent less to do the same jobs as men. This transaction is one of the X-factors that helps explain Australia's longest boom, and it has nothing to do with politicians.

I wish I'd had these numbers for my first book, *Faultlines*, but they fit here just as well, because they confirm a rip-off at the heart of the Keating–Howard economy. Behind the tariff wall, when the jobs were divided 60–40 between men and women, the share of the economic cake that went to workers as wages hovered around the 60 per cent mark. As I noted in chapter 1, a recession would follow whenever it crossed 62 per cent. Today, women hold 55 per cent of the jobs, wages happen to be 55 per cent of production, and profits are at record levels. A coincidence? I doubt it. The price that capitalism has placed on the heads of women, and their willingness to take the work despite the short-changing involved, has helped to underwrite the boom.

The women of the open economy were the policy gift of the former Labor prime minister Gough Whitlam, who scrapped university fees in his first term. Throw into the mix the contraceptive pill, which went mainstream in the 1960s, and women had the means as well as the motivation to delay childbirth until much later into their twenties, until after they had established their careers.

THE ASCENSION of working women coincided with the maturation of the post-war immigration program. By the 1990s, the Australian-born children of immigrants had reached their twenties and thirties. When the Howard government counted up all the winners and losers in 2002, it found, to its surprise, that the children of non-English- speaking immigrants were better qualified and had better jobs than all the others in their peer group. They exceeded the locals, the Australian-born of the Australian-born, as well as the Australian-born of English-speaking immigrants.

Generation X is a term of incomprehension deployed by baby boomers. I prefer Generation W, for women and 'wogs', because this is the social revolution that changed the face of the nation in the 1990s.

New Australia defied categorisation because its attitudes and make-up were more complex than the boomers had been in their day. It was more feminine and cosmopolitan, because the shape of the workforce was being altered by the daughters of old Australia and the Australian-born sons and daughters of non-English-speaking immigrants. Women and wogs have the shared experience of leap-frogging their parents' generation. They also have in common the outlook of the overachiever and the outsider. But they are not necessarily the same person. They are, instead, two unique additions to the national matrix.

MEANWHILE, THE men of old Australia were undergoing their own makeover, from trade unionists to entrepreneurs. This is the head-to-head that Prime Minister Howard likes the most, and it has been informing his final years in office. In 1993, the ranks of organised labour outnumbered those who worked for themselves by more than 800,000: 2.38 million versus 1.54 million. By 2002, the tables had turned. The self-employed had grown to 1.88 million while the trade unionists had shrunk to 1.83 million.

These are the men whom Keating turned Tory. The Victorian Labor Party had a term for the lost blue-collar worker, 'Economan', because he used his redundancy cheque from Telstra, or the state electricity monopoly, or a medium-sized manufacturer, to buy an Econovan and begin a second career as a handyman. These defectors became coalition voters, first because of the recession, which they blamed on Keating; then because of the recovery, which they thanked Howard for. Keating blames the Labor Party of Kim Beazley, Simon Crean, and Mark Latham for turning its back on upward mobility. Labor in opposition stuck with the trade unions, when it should have been branching out to embrace Economan.

'What's happened to the Labor Party since 1996?' Keating asks me during one of our interviews. 'It has gone back to the old anvil. It's walked away from financial innovation, from the opening up of the economy and the whole meritocracy model of widening its own appeal to single traders, to sole operators of business, small business.'

Howard says the small-business person is, at heart, a conservative who would never warm to Keating's reconciliation and republican agendas: 'They're a natural fit for me. The thing is, a lot of those people are socially conservative, they don't like all this trendy stuff.'

Yet most Australian workers belong to neither category. In 1993, trade unionists and entrepreneurs combined formed 51 per cent of the workforce. By 2002, their collective weight had been reduced to 40 per cent. The remaining 60 per cent were those with regular jobs, with no loyalty to either creed, left or right.

It is tempting, nonetheless, to view the entrepreneur class as comprising groovy young things from Generation W, working from home on their laptops with the speakers of their sound systems blaring. But the reverse is the case. The new entrants to small business happened to be baby boomers. Four out of every five people who decided to work for themselves in the 1990s were aged 50 or over, and most were handymen. They were the workers we had to have to do our renovations and landscaping in the second half of the decade.

But there is another side to the story of the self-employed, a wog perspective, that stunned and amused me when I figured it out. In 2002, the Paris-based Organisation for Economic Co-operation and Development produced a table that ranked 23 developed nations for entrepreneurs. Australia came in third, with 15.8 per cent of the labour force self-employed on the OECD's measure. We were comfortably above the United States and the United Kingdom, which returned figures of around 10 per cent each. Guess which country topped this list? Italy was second, with 18.5 per cent of its labour force counted as entrepreneurs, while Greece was first with 19.1 per cent.

You can do whatever you want with this ladder. I asked an academic contact who runs courses for the tax office why Australia's entrepreneurial ranks were closer to the Italian and Greek economies than the American and British. It was an obvious question, but I needed the quote. 'That's the cash economy,' he giggled.

Translation: the first-generation migrants to Australia from southern Europe have as little in common with their tertiary-educated children as the grey voters have with the professional woman. The olive waves and the grey voters have merged into the same person, the small-business operator with a hand in the cash economy, leaving Generation W to become the worker of new Australia. This happens to be a form of assimilation, only it is based on age and qualifications, not race or culture.

CHAPTER THREE

King Jeff

THE PRIMARY ROLE of government in peacetime is to correct for market failure. But unlike intelligence agencies or police forces, governments aren't in the game of prevention. They step in only after the market mucks something up. Politics errs on the side of enterprise, because the main parties agree that more voters make more money that way. At least that's how the role of government has been seen in the federal sphere since deregulation.

Three state Labor premiers thought differently in the late 1980s, and their examples spooked all jurisdictions in the 1990s. Brian Burke in Western Australia, John Bannon in South Australia, and John Cain in Victoria saw deregulation as an opportunity to dabble in business. It took a few billion dollars before they realised they were out of their depth. Victoria and South Australia lost their state banks in the lending frenzy, while Burke went to jail.

Labor's BBC of the 1990s, Steve Bracks in Victoria, Peter Beattie in Queensland, and Bob Carr in New South Wales, were determined that history would not repeat itself when the next boom came around. They ran budget surpluses and repaid the debts of the previous decade by moving as many responsibilities as they could off their books and onto the private sector. The tollway became the symbol of their stinginess and their double standards. Freeways that were promised before elections suddenly became tollways afterwards. Bracks broke his word after his second victory in 2002. Carr did so after his first election win in 1995.

The Liberals have a different take on government. They think it should be run like a business, on behalf of business, but not be in business itself. The distinction is important, although a little counter-intuitive. The first rule of commerce is growth. Companies are supposed to expand their customer base and increase their profits. But conservatives would prefer that governments were made smaller, and that the savings be handed back to the shareholders, namely the voters, as tax cuts. Yet this is a zero-sum game, because the tax cuts have to be spent in the private sector on services that governments no longer supply, like education, health, and transport. Ever wonder why voters never thank governments for giving them tax cuts? Because it's their money, and it doesn't buy what it used to.

In the early 1990s, Victoria elected a conservative premier. Jeff Kennett immediately set out to provide Australia's only full-blooded case study of political leadership done the corporate way. He ruled the state much like those American CEOs who were imported to repair the balance sheets of large Australian companies in the aftermath of the recession. The principles of cutting overheads and reducing debt when applied to government means sacking public servants and selling public assets. This became Kennett's calling card, and the rest of the nation looked on in admiration and bemusement. He gutted the bureaucracy, closed schools, introduced market incentives to the public hospital system, deregulated shop-trading hours, allowed drinks to be served in the city well into the night, and built a casino by the banks of the Yarra River. He also retrenched an entire generation of politicians through the forced amalgamations of local councils. But when the time came to return the spoils of all that belt-tightening to voters, he refused to spend the surplus. So they sacked him, and returned Labor to office, just as the Victorian economy was being confirmed as Australia's gold standard.

Kennett spices the story of the 1990s because he was the only premier to influence national debates. His rein coincided with Paul Keating's final term and John Howard's first. Kennett managed to get close to both men, which places him in the tiniest of minorities. He was an advocate for Keating's big picture, and he pushed Howard to revive the GST. By finding things in both men that he liked, Kennett is the closest thing to the decade's political adjudicator.

Kennett's friendship with Keating began without anyone noticing, in November 1992, one month into the Victorian revolution. Kennett went to Canberra to ask Keating for $1.6 billion. The transaction was straight out of the corporate manual, from the chapter headed 'downsizing'. Kennett needed the money to pay for the redundancies of about 7000 public servants. He would soon double that number to 15,000, and make two further visits to Canberra, asking for an extra $400 million and then another $1.3 billion. Kennett told Keating at their first meeting that Victoria's budget needed to off-load public servants before it could hope to return to surplus. The only problem was that the state already owed more than $30 billion, thanks to the profligacy of the previous Labor government.

Keating had the power to deny the request for more funds. He could have forced Kennett to balance the books by raising more taxes, to make voters pay for the public service redundancies. He also had the true believers to think of, the trade unionists whom he had enlisted to slay John Hewson at the upcoming federal election, then just four months away. But Keating had no interest in playing politics. Why give Victorian Labor a break, when they had made the recession worse than it needed to be, Keating thought. Kennett tells me the first meeting surprised him, because Keating was onside:

Keating had no time at all for John Cain, there was no love lost between them. He did have a lot more respect for Joan Kirner. He blamed all of Labor's travails down here on Cain rather than Kirner. And I'll never forget Keating's words. He said, 'I won't give you any money, and I won't lend you any money, but I will not oppose you raising an extra billion through the Loan Council', which the Commonwealth could have stopped us doing. 'And we very much support what you are doing and if we can give you any further help we will.'

Keating then asked the two treasurers, John Dawkins and Victoria's Alan Stockdale, to leave the room so he could talk privately with Kennett. 'We sat down for an hour and yapped about politics,' Kennett says. 'And that was the start of a remarkable relationship.'

It was not necessary for handshakes. It was not necessary for contracts per se. If we gave an undertaking to each other, it was honoured. We met many times during the course of his period in office. We invariably dispensed with our business, then we got on to ruminating about the world, the country, and personalities. I know we're both from different sides of the political fence, but I think we were both fairly much focused on big picture rather than small, on outcomes rather than politics.

When Kennett assumed power in October 1992, Victoria was a basket case. More than 75,000 of its residents were packing up each year and heading interstate to start new lives. Barely 53,000 were coming the other way. Between 1991 and 1995, the state would shed 111,000 citizens in total, mainly to Queensland and NSW. For three of those years, between 1992 and 1994, not even the overseas migration program could cover the shortfall. The rate of defections broke the record set during the Great Depression in 1935.

Victoria's share of the national economy shrank accordingly. Before the recession, in June 1990, it accounted for 27.2 per cent of Australia's GDP. By June 1993, it had lost a full percentage point, or $4.26 billion of the national cake as it then was, with the spoils being shared between NSW, Queensland, and Western Australia.

Kennett freely admits that Labor lost the 1992 state election. 'We didn't win it.' He also says it was a blessing in disguise that Cain had beaten him narrowly at the previous campaign in 1988: 'Had we won then, we would have lost because we weren't as well prepared.'

Yet the idea that Kennett could become a poster boy for reform was hard to get used to at first. In the 1980s, he had been written off as a boofhead. He lost two elections, in 1985 and 1988, and was punted from the Liberal leadership in 1989 before reclaiming it two years later. My earliest memory as a junior state political reporter in Melbourne, for the old *Sun News Pictorial*, was of Kennett as a topple-toy. The state media would slap him, but he'd come bouncing back with a Luna Park smirk frozen on his face that seemed to say, 'Come on, hit me, again'. The suspicion back then was that he might be a rook short of a chess set. One time, he launched the opposition's policy for mandatory reporting of child abuse. But Kennett fumbled with the term mandatory. Asked to explain how the policy would work, he contradicted his press release by saying, 'We would rather work with a voluntary code.' The cartoon in *The Sun* the next day had Jeff, foot in mouth, telling voters, 'It is mandatory that I volunteer a gaffe.'

There was also the small matter of his notorious car phone conversation with Andrew Peacock after the state Liberals had won a by-election in March 1987. Surely no politician could ever survive the broadcast of that tape with its f-bombs and c-words? Kennett told Peacock that he had just rubbished their mutual enemy, John Howard, then the opposition leader. *The Sun* published a transcript of the conversation, leaving the readers to guess the swear words that had been deleted:

> *Kennett*: I said to him, 'Tomorrow I'm going to bucket the whole lot of you'.
> *Peacock*: Oh no, don't do that, Jeffrey.
> *Kennett*: I said, 'Tomorrow John'. He said, 'I know where your sympathies lie'. I said, 'I couldn't give a [expletive]. I've got no sympathies anymore. You're all a pack of [expletive].' I said, 'Tomorrow I'm going berserk'. Well, he went off his brain and I said to him at the end of it, 'Howard, you're a [expletive]. You haven't got my support, you never will have, but I'm not going to rubbish you in the party tomorrow but I feel a whole lot better having told you you're a [expletive].

Peacock: Ah, [expletive].

Kennett: Ah, the poor little fella didn't know whether he was Arthur or Martha.

I moved to the federal press gallery after the 1988 state election. The next time I saw Kennett, in 1993, he was on a nationwide tour giving briefings to politicians and selected journalists on the Victorian miracle. This was Super Jeff, and the federal Liberals were wondering, privately, if he should be drafted as their leader.

'Jeff Kennett was not in anyone's top 100 most desired people,' he confessed to me when I spoke to him in 2005. 'I wasn't seen as a leader in real terms before 1992. I mean, I had been ridiculed. I was foot-in-mouth and all of that stuff. But that was part of my make-up, that was part of my relief valve. I used to make a lot of jokes, mainly about myself. I used to get criticised a lot and I made a few blunders. But all of that was part of the training process.'

Kennett had a bully's radar for the vulnerable. Sometimes he would pick on colleagues to see if they'd crumble or stand up to him. Then he would confound those in the latter camp by becoming civil, even chummy, towards them. Kennett was arrogant and optimistic, sarcastic and self-effacing, charming and cruel. He was also the nearest thing Australia had to an elected dictator.

The key to his initial success, and his eventual demise, was that voters gave him control of both houses of parliament in October 1992. There was no one to compromise with, which suited Kennett's personality. Impatient by nature, he liked to make decisions quickly. He wasn't one to agonise or analyse. He had the main planks of his reform program in place before Christmas 1992.

Like many things, the switch has got to be turned pretty quickly if you are going to change the culture. I called in the public service heads and I think I removed 14 of them. I spent three minutes with each, 'You're staying; thank you very much, you're going'. That immediately sent out a message that change was on its way. The union movement didn't understand it was coming as comprehensively until probably late December, when we got those bills pushed through.

Kennett demanded military discipline. At the first meeting of the parliamentary party, he asked his backbench to view their first term together as a epic battle:

These young men and women had no idea what they had struck. To enter parliament and be confronted with all this reformist zeal was an extraordinary learning curve. I said to them, 'Whatever you do, imagine yourselves as group of Roman centurions and you are all there with your shields. If you lock those shields together, no one will get at you. But the first one who breaks puts us all at risk.'

He told them to ignore the opinion polls in the short run. 'I promise you, by the third year we'll be back on track, and I'll get you back into government at the second election.'

Kennett had a ready-made excuse for his hard line. The budget deficit was almost twice as large as the Kirner government had told voters during the election.

Within a month of being elected, Kennett sacked one in 20 of the state's public servants and cut the wages of the rest by removing their 17.5 per cent holiday pay loading. Private-sector employees lost their penalty rates for working weekends. He took with one hand, and took some more with the other. Electricity, gas, and water charges were raised by 10 per cent, and motor vehicle registration fees doubled. In fact, he ran out of taxes to increase, so he invented a new one, the so-called 'deficit reduction levy' which took another $100 a year from each household.

The story of his government can be told in three frenetic days at the end of his first month in office. On 28 October 1992, the mini-budget with all the sackings and taxes was released. The following day came the industrial relations reforms. Then, in the early hours of 30 October, Kennett rushed in a naive piece of legislation to deliver generous pay rises to senior government members, including a $160-a-week bonus for the industrial relations minister, Phil Gude. With this trio of decisions, the Victorian government was officially a business, with retrenchments, cost-cutting, and higher executive salaries. Kennett was forced to cancel the government pay rises, and Keating headed-off the changes to industrial relations by offering Victorian workers the shelter of the federal award system. But Kennett had made his point:

> We decided to take each of the areas that needed reform at the same time, head on. That was important because it meant that those who were involved in the administration of each area, in particular the unions, were all going to be fighting their own battles and couldn't coalesce around what we were doing in health, or what we were doing about education, or what we were doing about construction.

It was *Fightback!*, but without the pre-election manifesto. Voters had no idea that Kennett would be so bold. But Kennett and his team had been quietly drafting their policies in opposition. The opportunity that a landslide victory presented was too juicy to pass up.

Kennett deployed the cadence of commerce. It was muscular and mechanical. He talked about recurrent outlays to impress the credit-rating agencies. He chided Victorians that they needed to become more competitive. Yet he didn't paint eloquent word pictures like Keating to explain his reform program. Kennett was a salesman, not an intellectual. He governed on gut instinct, and mixed the hard-nosed with the populist. He poached the formula one motor car grand prix from Adelaide, and streamlined the building code so Victoria could be the first out of the blocks when the property cycle turned up again. But his propensity to misspeak remained. A year into his term, opposition leader John Brumby was probing Kennett about his family advertising agency, KNF. Kennett had said previously that he didn't work for KNF when he was opposition leader. Brumby was suggesting otherwise. Kennett exploded. 'The answer is no, absolutely no. Say it outside the House. You are the most gutless politician. That's like me saying in here that I know you sleep with boys. Do you?' Later, he would call Brumby and his deputy John Thwaites, 'the two girls from Melbourne Grammar'. 'If you can't get a girl, get a Grammar boy.' Keating was never this coarse; Bob Hawke was never this macho. But Victorians loved Kennett for it, at least for a while.

Keating saw in Kennett a fellow traveller. Party loyalties prevented either man from admitting it publicly. But they had more in common with each other than Keating had with the Victorian Labor opposition and Kennett had with the federal Liberal opposition. This did not prevent them from brawling when it suited. Keating blocked Kennett's industrial relations reforms before the 1993 election. After it, he felt like wringing Kennett's neck when the Victorian premier led the revolt against Keating's native title package. Keating couldn't understand why Victoria, the state with the smallest area of Crown land affected by the Mabo judgment, would play hardball. But these spats were the exceptions that proved the rule. They never stopped the next deal from being struck, the next private chat about what made Australia and the world tick.

The story of their symbiosis was only confirmed in Keating's final year in office in 1995, when he and Kennett double-teamed the other state premiers to introduce competition policy, probably the most misunderstood reform of the decade. Keating worked on the Queensland Labor premier Wayne Goss; Kennett, on the Western Australian Liberal Richard Court. Goss thought Keating was screwing the Liberal states; Court thought Kennett was giving Canberra a black eye.

Competition policy would become a dirty word throughout the second half of the 1990s for the wrong reasons. The idea was simple, really. There were a number of sectors in the economy that had escaped treasurer Keating's 1980s reforms because they had no rivals, either locally or overseas, to force them to lift their standards and lower their prices to consumers. They included the state monopolies in electricity, gas, and water; the rural marketing boards, from wheat to eggs; and the professions, most notably the doctors, lawyers, and accountants. They should have been soft targets.

But the politics of backlash hit the decade late, once the recovery was underway, and after Keating and Kennett had left office. Pauline Hanson added competition policy to her list of gripes, alongside Aboriginal welfare and Asian immigration. That made it harder to get the deal implemented. Five years into Howard's gargantuan term, in 2001, it was the turn of the dairy industry to reform. Milk was to flow across state boundaries for the first time in Australia's history. This happened to be a Victoria-friendly reform because its dairy farmers were the most efficient in the nation and couldn't wait for interstate competition. However, NSW and Queensland were not so sure because the old rules gave them guaranteed markets within their respective state borders. Deregulation was put to a national vote and a majority said yes. When the Howard government sat down to write the cheques for those who would be forced off their farms, the spectre of Hanson loomed. This was before the *Tampa*, at the nadir of Howard's popularity, when the coalition feared it would lose office. So what did the government do? It announced a $2 billion handout to all dairy farmers, the winners as well as the losers, just to make sure no one was left unbribed.

Kennett disagreed with Howard on the role of government. He thought surpluses should be used to repay debt, and to act as a buffer against bad times, not to redistribute to swinging voters. 'Politicians treated public monies as though it was public monies and not their own,' Kennett says of life before he came to power. 'We made the decision that we were going to treat public monies as though it was our own, but because it was public we had to treat it even more cautiously.' But once Kennett lost office, politics reverted to the old school of handouts—not only at the state level, but federally, where Howard saw Kennett's defeat in 1999 as an omen. He told Kennett he should have given voters back some of the surplus, instead of hoarding it for a future Labor government to enjoy.

It's worth fast-forwarding to this point to appreciate what the Kennett years meant, ultimately. Kennett waltzed into the September 1999 election with a margin of 14 seats in the 88-member parliament. A haircut of a few seats was the worst case. So confident was he of re-election that Kennett promised to 'bury Labor'. He also gagged his troops during the campaign. They could not make any comment to the media unless it was first vetted by his office.

Labor had only recently replaced its leader, John Brumby, with his good friend Steve Bracks. When Newspoll predicted a cliff-hanger, Bracks said: 'I hope it's right, but I think *The Australian's* on drugs.' Both Bracks and Brumby were country boys: Bracks was from Ballarat; Brumby, from Bendigo. Brumby had been quietly whipping up a revolt in the coalition's more vulnerable seats in country Victoria, but Kennett didn't appreciate the risks. Looking back, he applauds Labor's spunk. 'We didn't lose in the city, we lost in the bush.'

> I really attribute much of our loss to John Brumby, and give him credit for it. He did a lot of work in country Victoria for months before the election, years before. He had that wonderful ad with the tap, with a huge amount of water, this is what Melbourne's getting, and this is what country Victoria is getting, drip, drip, drip. Very, very effective.

Kennett only saw the ad after the election campaign. 'It had never been brought to my attention; now it might have been too late.' But he completes the thought with an unexpected compliment for the man he once called a girl from Melbourne Grammar:

> I have a grudging respect for John Brumby. I think he would have made a good treasurer in my government, where he could have actually worked on those projects that he believed in.

Kennett didn't lose the election on the night, but he had lost his majority. Labor picked up 12 seats, and another two went to independents. The result was in limbo because the vote in one of the government's seats had been suspended when a candidate had died during the campaign. Kennett continued to govern as the re-election for Frankston East was conducted. When that seat fell to Labor, it was over. Though Kennett still had one more seat than Bracks, 43 to 42, the three independents who held the balance of power sided with Labor.

Conservative commentators dubbed it as a protest gone wrong, as if Victorians didn't really mean to be rid of Super Jeff. An air of bewilderment hung over Kennett's farewell press conference. He said Labor had not beaten him:

> It's not that they have won government; they have no mandate. They are a minority Labor government supported by three individuals, one of whom hasn't even been sworn in as a parliamentarian, one of them would do us all a better service perhaps if she just rejoined the Labor Party, and the third who has indicated that he didn't believe the Labor Party had the experience to govern. So be it.

Once voters got the taste of life without Kennett, they didn't want to go back. After Kennett retired from parliament, his seat of Burwood, in Melbourne's leafy east, fell to Labor in a by-election. Labor also picked up the former deputy premier Pat McNamara's seat of Benalla. Bracks won the next general election, in 2002, by a record margin, taking the upper house as part of the deal. It was as if Kennett had never happened.

The final word on the Kennett era should be left to the numbers. By 1998, Kennett had reversed the people drain, and Victoria was receiving more settlers from interstate than were going the other way — which was a luxury it did not enjoy behind the tariff wall. It also began collecting more people from NSW, as the exiles from the Sydney property market outnumbered the Victorians heading to the nation's global city.

Yet the state's economy did not fare as well as the hype would suggest. Kennett left Victoria with its share of the national economy half a percentage point smaller than when he found it. (Victoria contained 26.2 per cent of Australia's GDP at the end of its recession in June 1993. It fell to 25.5 per cent by June 1999, and held its ground after that.) NSW, by contrast, was steady during the Kennett years, but lost its way after it hosted the 2000 Olympics.

Under Kennett, Victoria beat NSW just twice in the annual economic growth race, in his first and last years, in 1992–93 and 1998–99. It was left to Kennett's successor, Steve Bracks, to claim the spoils. Victoria's gross state product rose faster than NSW's in each of the four years from 2001–02 to 2004–05. In other words, Kennett, like Keating, lost power before he could put his name to the recovery. The two men have been regular luncheon companions since. 'Tell Paul, the next time you see him, that it's his turn to buy lunch,' Kennett said at the end of our interview.

Keating as Book Critic

THE TWO INSIDER ACCOUNTS of Paul Keating's 13 years in power, by economist John Edwards and bleeding heart Don Watson, paint their boss as burned out by the time he got to the Lodge. On one level, they were observing Keating as he had always seemed, a contradiction of emotions: moody, inspiring, vicious, detached, sentimental, and a hypochondriac.

Edwards wrote:

> He worried about light, germs, cancers, draughts. He thought mobile phones emitted harmful rays. He drank mysterious potions and performed silly exercises. He resented attempts to determine his schedule, he grew weary of people quickly, he got to bed too late and got up too late, he was evasive and dishonest in small ways rather than surrender his freedom or hurt other people's feelings. He was above all a performer with the performer's ability to rise to the occasion and to drop in languor and weariness afterward.

Watson put it this way:

> Without the heat of battle, Keating's pulse slowed. Years of death-defying struggle had given him the metabolism of a cornered rat — he could not get excited until the stakes were very high, preferably a matter of life and death ... At other times he found it hard to even sound interested ... After a while, you would swear from the polls

and the radio that the people sensed it as well, as if they knew his moods and when he didn't care.

The most caustic summary of Keating as he faced off against John Hewson came from former finance minister Peter Walsh, one of Labor's straightest shooters: 'The man who had kicked, scratched and gouged to become prime minister was a bit like the dog which chased cars, finally caught one, and didn't know what to do with it.'

Keating shakes his head when he is reminded of these pen portraits. It is easy to imagine that at other times he might have felt less charitable, that he might have matched the views of Edwards, Watson, and Walsh with a few razor-sharp character assessments of his own. Keating measures his words carefully as he accedes to my request to reply to his biographers. He says his prime ministership 'had all of the comprehension that a great grand project has':

> In my terms, the project began in 1983, and by 1991 I had seen into place most of, but not all, the considerable bits of it, that was the internationalisation of the economy. But I had yet to do the product and the labour markets — which, of course, had been left undone for 100 years.
>
> In terms of the product markets, the seminal changes to the labour market in 1993, the setting up of superannuation, the breaking of the back of inflation, these things had to be done in the years of the Keating government, not the Hawke and Keating government, the Keating government. So I was doing the economic and doing the other things, I hoped, as well. As prime minister, there is only one of you, and you have got to do a lot of this thinking for yourself. In the end, it is your personality out there, your policies, and so I tried to do that as best I could.

The big picture, as he saw it, began with the collapse of the Berlin Wall in 1989:

I knew that Australia had a real chance to do something, that the Americans did not know what to do, that they cried victory and walked off the field. Australia was in a real position to shape western policy, certainly in respect of our own region of the world. I thought that what I then had to do was to move quickly into the void, to advance Australia's interest — which, of course, I began doing on New Year's Eve 1992 with president George Herbert Bush at Kirribilli House, within ten days of me becoming prime minister. There I began the discussion about APEC and the APEC leaders' meeting.

APEC, the closer relationship with Indonesia, native title, and the republic were 'all part of a matrix', but his biographers only saw their part of it, not the whole:

> You had to be with me through the period to properly understand it. I don't think John Edwards, for instance, who wrote about my economic work, understood the prime ministerial work, and I don't think Don Watson, who tried to write about the prime ministerial work, understood my economic work. In contrast, Don Russell, for instance, understood it all perfectly because he understood the schematic.

Keating pauses to make his next point about what he sees as the dichotomy of Australia, a nation too small to be noticed in its own right, yet big enough to matter if it makes the right noises:

> Where does a middle power go unless it is efficient, competitive, and dextrous? You have no unearned weight of size as the United States does or China does or India does. You can rely only on your own ingenuity and, for better or worse, you know, you are given these positions of power and you either dispense them in what is truly in the national interest, or you don't. And I wanted to make Australia independent, open and stronger, fairer and therefore

more powerful, and then let it make its way in the new post-Cold War world in the region around us.

Keating and Watson stopped speaking in 2002, after Watson's book was launched by Keating. When they first met on 9 January 1992, in the prime minister's office, Keating told Watson of his fatigue. He had wanted the leadership badly three years earlier, in 1988, when Bob Hawke had denied it to him, 'but now he was tired':

> You 'use up a lot of horsepower in these jobs'. But the truth was most of the work had already been done. Most of the big changes had been made. The rest was mainly management and fine tuning and not letting it slip. Some micro reform, but there wasn't a lot more that needed doing.

This is a passage worth mulling over. Keating had said often in the 1980s, when he wasn't burdened with the top job, that leadership was about being right, not being popular. He also said good economics is good politics, that the tough love he administered to the electorate would, eventually, yield a return in votes for the government because the public respected leaders who did things. Keating can be excused for being over-awed when his ambition was finally achieved, and for feeling just a little fatigued. But it is troubling to think that he would see his job as 'mainly management and fine tuning'. To believe this at the bottom of recession, as Keating seemed to suggest to Watson, hinted that he was already beyond his prime. This was true in one respect. Hawke had clung to power too long, which meant that Keating took over too late. But it is a misreading of Keating to think that his tank was empty.

His prime ministership had moments of inspired politics, the 1993 election, and five very good policy ideas. They were, in order of importance to the decade: labour market reform, universal superannuation, engagement with the Asian region, native title, and competition reform. Keating's model for an Australian republic would have been number six, if it had got up on his schedule, by the turn of the century. But the first five changes survived the transition to John Howard, which is a mark of their strength. The first and last were shared platforms, while superannuation and native title prevailed despite Howard, though not in the forms that Keating intended. And engagement with Asia became a surprise example of Keating–Howard bipartisanship. But not so fast. To get there, Keating had to beat John Hewson when virtually nobody thought he could, or deserved to.

CHAPTER FOUR

Keating as de facto Opposition Leader

THERE WAS SOMETHING a little unhealthy about John Hewson's attitude to Paul Keating. He hated him, or at least gave the impression that he did. In his office, he hung up a weird painting of Keating leering over a family that had just lost its home to high interest rates. It was the sort of caricature that nations in wartime use against the enemy soldier. When Keating spoke in parliament, Hewson, seated across him in the bully pit, would lean forward and hiss in a voice too low to be caught by the microphones: 'You're weak, you're a loser, you're finished.' Hewson compared Keating's political tribe, the NSW right of the Labor Party, to a criminal gang. 'We should never forget that the NSW right is the nearest thing this country has to the mafia in decades — the NSW right stretches from our jails, in certain parts of Australia, right through to the top office in this land, the prime minister.'

Hewson was deploying the tactic of the football tagger. He would give Keating a short, sharp poke to the ribs, when the umpire wasn't watching, then wait for his opponent to over-react. Every moment Keating showed his angry side, the voters ran the other way. Keating obliged, because he knew no other approach to politics. 'Down hill, one ski, no poles' was his motto.

Keating mocked Hewson's speech pattern, which would take a word beginning with the letter 'r' and turn it into a 'w'. So whenever Hewson predicted a 'double-dip wecession', Keating would mimic the phrase and the media would try to suppress its grin. His funniest line was to dub Hewson the 'feral abacus'. It was hard, though, to figure out who was putting on the aggro for effect, and who was certifiable.

Beneath the posturing was a serious, often crazy, debate about economic and social policy. Keating and Hewson offered themselves to the electorate as fortune-tellers. They engaged in Australia's first political contest by document. It was, in a way, a communist moment, because the manifestos they developed bore an uncanny resemblance to the five- and ten-year plans that Joseph Stalin or Mao Zedong would issue in the former Soviet Union or in China. They contained visions of a worker's paradise, built on heroic production targets. Keating and Hewson were responding to the public's craving for a plan to guide the nation out of recession. The word 'plan' was repeated and reinforced in countless focus-group polls that the major parties conducted. Keating and Hewson took this mood as a licence to alter the body clock of Australian politics by scrapping the convention that promises, once made, had to be delivered quickly before they were forgotten.

Hewson offered tax cuts in two bites, to apply in October 1994 and in January 1996. He also painted a picture of Australia in the year 2000. Some 2 million new jobs would be created and the unemployment rate would be halved to 5.2 per cent, he said. Keating replied with two rounds of tax cuts of his own, to be paid across a similar time-line to Hewson's, and a promise of 800,000 new jobs by mid-1996.

Hewson set his proposed GST at 15 per cent, and applied it to everything except health, education, charities, exports, and the airfares paid by incoming tourists. The GST would collect $27.2 billion a year, and would be used to abolish the federal wholesale sales tax, petrol excise, and state payroll taxes.

Massive cuts to government spending complemented the new tax on consumption. Chief among the targets was Medicare. The government-funded health-care system was introduced by Labor in

1984. It was popular, but open to abuse. To the coalition, it was a form of creeping socialism and a contradiction of Keating's professed attachment to economic rationalism. *Fightback!* couched its rhetoric carefully. The free hospital bed that people had taken for granted would be restricted to pensioners and welfare beneficiaries. The rest of the population would be encouraged to take out private health insurance, and middle and higher earners who didn't would be penalised with 'a surcharge approximately equal to the cost of basic private health insurance' on top of the existing Medicare levy. Bulk billing, the system that allowed GPs to provide free consultations by sending the tab back to the government, would also be restricted to the needy. In keeping with its policy of honesty, *Fightback!* admitted that the majority of the population would have to pay every time they saw a GP.

The unemployed were also in Hewson's sights. He said he could strip almost $750 million from the government's dole bill in his first term by removing the benefit from those who had been out of work for more than nine months. The theory was that the long-term unemployed needed to be jolted out of their lethargy. But it didn't make sense. With unemployment heading towards 11 per cent, punishing those who could not find work, when no work existed, became a symbol of Hewson's political autism, his faith in textbook theory over the real world.

Buried on page 314 of *Fightback!* was a chart summarising the swings and roundabouts. The tax cuts were put at $12.5 billion a year by 1995–96. They were funded by two sources, 'gross expenditure savings' of $9.7 billion and 'tax bracket creep' of $3 billion.

There is such a thing as too much honesty in politics. Bracket creep is a tax rise by stealth, the extra money that governments pocket when a worker receives an inflation-linked pay rise. In using bracket creep to fund one dollar in every four of the tax cuts, Hewson was admitting, between the lines, that *Fightback!* was just another tax bribe — not reform, but the handing back to voters of the money previously taken from them by inflation. Two could play this game, Keating decided.

The youth card that Keating played against Hawke could not work against Hewson, because Hewson was the fitter man. Keating would have to paint Hewson as a zealot. His task, put bluntly, was to make Hewson seem like an even bigger bastard than he was.

Keating had just two months to prepare his response, which placed him at an immediate disadvantage because Hewson had spent the past year-and-a-half on *Fightback!*. Budgets normally take twice as long to develop. Yet Keating had the luxury of the counter-offer. *Fightback!* allowed him to promise tax cuts without a GST because *Fightback!*'s tax cuts were funded, not by the GST, but by spending cuts and bracket creep. Keating didn't want to match Hewson's spending cuts; they'd be more valuable to him as material for Labor's scare campaign. So he had just bracket creep to play with.

There was one small problem, though. As the recession dragged on, the budget tumbled into deficit by mirroring the rise in unemployment with extra spending on the dole, and reduced tax collections. To complicate matters, inflation was falling lower than Keating could have dreamed. This was a good thing, of course, because it helped to set up the nation's longest boom. But it didn't help Keating in the short term because inflation was also the fuel for bracket creep.

The tax cuts were the best-kept secret of Keating's manifesto, *One Nation*. The irony of the title would come years later, when Pauline Hanson unconsciously plagiarised it as the name for her political protest party. The tax cuts were built on a gamble that the economy, once it recovered, would grow by better than 4 per cent a year between 1992–93 and 1994–95, and then a little below 4 per cent in 1995–96. This would secure a revenue bounty large enough to fund an $8 billion present to voters, to be delivered in two bundles: the first on 1 July 1994, three months earlier than Hewson's opening tax cut; and the second on 1 January 1996. Although about $4.5 billion below Hewson's $12.5 billion offer, Keating's tax cut was enough to cancel the sweetest part of *Fightback!*. From here on, the argument would be about the differences between the two platforms, Keating's GST-free *One Nation* program, and Hewson's

GST- and spending-cut-based *Fightback!*.

Keating calibrated his tax cuts to deliver a larger windfall to middle-income families Australia than Hewson was offering. He wanted his government to be seen as the friend of the mainstream; he'd give them affordable tax cuts, but without a GST. Hewson, he would argue, was the ally of the rich: they'd get tax cuts, while the rest of the nation had to wear the GST.

Keating used incumbency ruthlessly. Aside from the tax cuts, he mailed a cheque of between $125 and $250, depending on the number of children, to every family that was already receiving the family allowance. This covered the bulk of the nation's 2 million families. At the time, it was written off as a shameless bribe. Nine years later, when John Howard seemed on the verge of losing the 2001 election, he borrowed the Keating tactic and was hailed as a political master.

One Nation was sold as a recession buster. On this front, Keating judged the economics better than Hewson did. From the melancholic vantage point of six months on the backbench, between June and December 1991, Keating proved to have a better fix on the health of the nation than Hewson did from the sanctuary of the extended honeymoon he was enjoying as opposition leader. This is a little-appreciated aspect of their tussle. History tries to be kind to Hewson by painting *Fightback!* as good policy, badly marketed. But his package misunderstood three things about Australia at the dawn of the 1990s.

First, *Fightback!* failed to comprehend how long it would take the economy to recover. Hewson was following the bust-boom script of the past. In fact, he worried that recovery would come too quickly, and that voters would lose their sense of crisis and, with it, their willingness to swallow his bitter formula. Yet he also warned of a double-dip recession, a contradiction between policy assumption and political rhetoric that he never seemed to grasp. The sky couldn't be both blue and falling in at the same time.

Second, *Fightback!* failed to give Keating his due as a reformer. It assumed that the blame for the recession lay in Keating's refusal to go hard enough in the 1980s. *Fightback!* prescribed more of everything that Keating had delivered in the previous decade — even bigger tax cuts, zero tariffs, industrial relations revolution not reform, privatisation, and huge reductions in government spending. Yet Keating's real blunder had been to place too much faith in market forces in the 1980s, in particular the banks, which took competition to mean a race to see who could sign the fattest cheque for corporate charlatans.

Keating's greatest insight was to understand the nature of his mistake as treasurer, which made it easier for him to communicate to voters as prime minister at the 1993 election. This allowed him to capitalise on *Fightback!*'s third and most profound flaw. Hewson proposed to wind back the public sector just when economic theory and common sense agreed that the job of government was to step in to secure recovery. Hewson was pulling away the safety net when the nation needed it most, during a hard landing.

It took some gall, of course, for Keating to switch from economic wizard to economic realist. He was seeking a mandate in his own right by opposing a consumption tax he had supported only a few years earlier at the 1985 tax summit, and by claiming a better program for recovery for the recession he had caused. Yet Keating's *One Nation* program was just as daring as *Fightback!*. There were two fetching policies in particular: one that appealed to the left; the other, to the right. The left-wing reform was compulsory superannuation. The right-wing reform broke the one-size-fits-all approach to wages. The words seemed harmless, which explains why their true meaning was missed at the time:

> The government has decided to introduce further legislative changes to underpin the shift to decentralisation and greater workplace focus in industrial relations. The Industrial Relations Act will be amended to encourage the making of workplace agreements. The government will encourage agreements that are fixed term and preclude wage increases from other sources.

This was arguably one of the biggest changes of the decade

because it helped to keep a lid on wages as the economy recovered. Workplace agreements would run for up to five years, which would lock-in low inflation. It didn't matter if trade unions were involved because employers held the whip hand.

When Keating released his counter-offer to *Fightback!* on 26 February 1992, he was thinking only of bridging the 18-point gap that existed between Labor and the coalition in the opinion polls. Labor trailed 34 per cent to 52 per cent.

Yet the public was prepared to give Keating the benefit of the doubt, at least early on. *One Nation* lifted Labor off the floor. By the end of March, Labor was back in the game, trailing by just one point, 43 per cent to 44 per cent. Keating had reason to be confident, but his recovery proved to be a mirage. Scandal and a stubborn economy saw the polls turn nasty over winter. Energy was wasted defending cabinet minister Graham Richardson, who had become embroiled in one too many controversies. And no amount of effort, it seemed, could lift the mood of the nation. By early August, Labor found itself no better off after eight months of Keating than it had been at the end of Hawke's term. The deficit on the primary vote was back to 12 points, 36 per cent to 48 per cent.

As winter approached, Keating first confessed to cabinet colleagues that the economy might not be generating enough growth, and with it the revenues, to pay for the *One Nation* tax cuts. It was 20 May 1992, the day that cabinet's razor gang was advised by treasurer John Dawkins that the budget deficit had expanded by almost $2 billion, which covered a quarter of the size of the tax cuts being offered. Health minister Neil Blewett recorded a tense exchange in his diary. Finance minister Ralph Willis said, 'We should have known the revenue estimates were astray' earlier in the year, when *One Nation* was being prepared. 'Keating claimed that if he had been aware of the revenue shortfall at that time, he might well not have advocated tax cuts.'

One Nation was sold as a 'four-year plan'. What Keating got wrong was the first year; it was far weaker than he had bargained for. The economy was supposed to grow at 4.75 per cent; it turned out to be 3.2 per cent. This wasn't enough to create any new jobs over the course of 1992–93, so unemployment rose to 11 per cent rather than dropped to 10 per cent as had been hoped. On the bright side, inflation and the current account deficit were running lower than had been predicted. Inflation was supposed to hover at 3.5 per cent until 1995–96; it turned out to be half that rate. This is the guts of why the tax cuts proved to be unaffordable — there wasn't enough bracket creep going on. Here, incidentally, is the reason why Keating's, and Ian Macfarlane's, claims that the recession was a policy triumph should be seen as a partial rewriting of history. Labor and the Reserve Bank hadn't meant to be this efficient on the inflation front. It was only because the recession had been worse than they had planned that inflation was able to fall so low, and stay down once the economy turned the corner.

There were other paths open to Keating for income-tax relief. He could have reduced spending or raised indirect taxes to cover the shortfall. But that would have made him no different from Hewson. *One Nation* proved to be spot-on for GDP and jobs growth from 1993–94 to 1995–96. But Keating received no thanks because the jobs were not going to those who had been retrenched in the recession.

However, this did not make Hewson the innocent party. *Fightback!* also relied on bracket creep to pay for its personal tax cuts; so it, too, faced a funding hole as inflation was vanquished. Yet somehow the press gallery did not see it this way: it mostly gave Hewson the benefit of the doubt. Scrutiny was aimed almost exclusively at Keating because he had disappointed us so many times before. The press gallery is difficult to broad-brush because it contains roughly the same mix of misfits, maniacs, and mild-mannered souls as the broader community. The majority are diligent and sober; the long lunch died with the 1980s. Only a few political journalists could be called partisan, but no one pays attention to them in any case. Yet there is an unmistakable mood in the place that affects the tone of reporting. It doesn't necessarily make sense. The pack barracked for Andrew Peacock when he took on John Howard for the Liberal leadership in 1989, and for Keating over Hawke in 1991. But sympathy in a challenge rarely extends to the election campaign. Most journalists preferred Hawke over Peacock in 1990, and Hewson over Keating in 1993. It had nothing to do with politics; rather, it was a reading of the public mood.

To lose from where the polls had placed him in August 1992, barely six months from the election, Hewson had to give voters more reason to dislike him than the prime minister who couldn't dig them out of the recession. Keating had played the recovery card with *One Nation*, but it proved to be a bluff. The August 1992 budget belled the cat on the revenue crisis with an oblique reference buried at the back of the document:

> The revenue to GDP ratio is estimated to decline slightly on a no policy change basis over the coming years and on the basis of current projections, the budget deficit in 1995-6 would be around 1.25 per cent of GDP.

In the weasel-words of bureaucracy, this was one of the most priceless of the decade. Just six months earlier, *One Nation* had said that the budget would be restored to surplus by 1995–96. Now it would be in deficit. In raw dollars, about $4 billion, or half the value of the $8.6 billion *One Nation* tax cuts, had gone missing from the books because there was a hole in the revenue base.

Hewson could have sealed his election campaign on this between-the-lines admission that *One Nation* didn't add up, and that the tax cuts were at risk of being cancelled after the election. Instead, an amazing disconnection emerged. Hewson took his position in the polls as an excuse to present an even harsher face to the public. He attacked every lobby group in the nation, from the car-makers to the churches. When he'd finished with the vested interests, he began tarring entire voting blocs with tough-guy talk that began to spook even his most ardent admirers. 'In any street, of course, it's always easy to tell the rented houses ... They are the ones where the lawn isn't mowed, the plants aren't watered and the fences aren't fixed.' Zap. With this half-smart line, Hewson had defamed one-third of all households in the nation. That was 31 August 1992. Earlier that month, Hewson had given a speech to parliament that Keating had been waiting for, had been baiting him to give, ever since the opposition leader aroused the nation's interest in early 1990.

It was Hewson's set-piece reply to the budget, the only occasion outside an election campaign when the opposition leader gets to speak to the nation without interruption from ads, media commentary, or the counter-argument of the government. There were some powerful lines in his address on the recession. As Hewson was bringing the speech to a roaring finale, Keating broke with convention that the opposition leader be heard in silence with an interjection:

> *Hewson*: For far too long, we have kidded ourselves that you can constantly knock your country and denigrate your flag without destroying national pride. Your concept of compassion …
> *Keating*: You are the one who has done that.
> *Hewson*: You should listen to this because it is very important. Your concept of compassion is to compensate people to whom you have denied choice, freedom and opportunity as a result of your policies. I remember you saying not long ago that when they fall off the pace you will reach back and pull them up. What you mean is that you will pull everyone else down to the lowest common denominator.

This was scripted, and politically suicidal. Don Watson observed that nothing Keating said against Hewson in 1992 'was as good as this':

> The Prime Minister would never quote it back in the awkward form of the original. He would say 'John Hewson says if you reach back for them, they will drag you down'. Six months later he had developed such a way with the line you could sense a surge of shock and anger in the audience. Just as remarkably, you could sense it in yourself.

Hewson had confirmed himself as a creature from another planet. That planet was called America, where the poor slept in the streets, the workers did not have health cover, and the winners from the free market earned the right to live in gated communities. Hewson seemed to be thriving on the recession. Like a journalist covering a war or disaster who feels alive in the presence of death, Hewson seemed to be invigorated by the nation's pain. His solution was more of the same because, if he didn't punish the shirkers now, with the economy on its knees, they'd be let off the hook when the recovery came. Hewson was a revolutionary in the truest sense of the word: someone who saw conflict as the means to a better world, but who could never allow the community a moment's rest after the battle had been won.

Identifying the passage of time when the electorate switched from blaming Keating for the recession to fearing that Hewson would add 15 per cent to the trauma is easy in hindsight. The polls turned suddenly for Labor in the first week of November 1992, but the trouble had started back in August.

Hewson was trapped by the expectation that he would become prime minister. He had the nation's attention, but couldn't do anything to massage public opinion when things turned nasty. He couldn't hand out cash to those he had offended, because he was still only the opposition leader. With Hewson playing prime minister in waiting, Keating was able to slip the noose of incumbency. Keating was the de facto opposition leader, already written off by the press gallery and, it seemed, by the public. This allowed him to shed any pretence, and to turn the perception that he was arrogant on its head. As the underdog, Keating was allowed to be vicious because he was tearing down the tallest poppy in the nation, the know-it-all Hewson. John Howard was busily absorbing this lesson. In time, he too would play underdog to Keating at the 1996 election. Howard could say anything he wanted to Keating. All the public noticed was the petulant reply.

On 15 September 1992, fresh from an engagement at the press club in which he had mocked *Fightback!*, Keating entered parliament in good humour. Hewson stood at the dispatch and asked: 'If you are so confident of your view of *Fightback!*, why will you not call an early election?'

Keating replied with the sledge of the decade. 'The answer is, mate, because I want to do you slowly. There has to be a bit of sport in this for us all.'

Soon Howard began testing the water to see if there was a chance he could topple Hewson. Keating worried that the Liberals might come to their senses and do just that. But Howard was still too unpopular in his own party and, it must be said, the antipathy was mutual. Howard didn't get along with at least half his colleagues. 'I'm not going to let those so-and-sos get the better of me,' he would say, privately, at the time.

Hewson met the criticisms of his package, and the internal calls to modify it, with a threat to resign if *Fightback!* were changed. On 16 October, Hewson gave the nation a hint of what sort of prime minister he would become if given the chance. A little-appreciated element of *Fightback!* was the flexibility built into the GST. A series of review teams had been set up to iron out the transitional difficulties of moving from one tax system to another. The accounting firms happily provided some of their most senior brains to staff these committees, figuring that the free hours they supplied to Hewson in opposition would yield a handsome dividend in access to the government and cash from clients when Hewson became prime minister. The issues were eye-glazing, but they involved billions of dollars to business. The first of the groups to go through this procedure with Hewson was the superannuation industry. It had little difficulty striking a compromise, and the new policy, dubbed 'Son of *Fightback!*', was announced in August. That work was done earlier in the year, when Hewson was still enjoying a honeymoon in the media, and in the opinion polls. And the superannuation industry played by the rules Hewson had laid out. The negotiations did not leak.

The tourism industry was another matter. It had been given every reason to believe it would have the GST removed from tour packages sold overseas, and have tax breaks restored for business lunches. The political sympathies of this lobby were with the coalition. This was, after all, the white-shoe brigade. There was as much chance of it turning to Keating's Labor for comfort as a sea turtle would swim toward a shark. But the Hewson they faced in October was in no mood to discuss the minutiae. He was seething that the negotiations had been detailed to *The Australian* and, later, to a government minister. Any chance of compromise was over. But Hewson couldn't just say no. He had to humiliate the industry, publicly, and on its own turf. Hewson's speech to the Australian Tourism Industry Association conference marked a point of no return. It was a tantrum. 'I am not here today, or on any other occasion, to do what is popular or to buy political support. I am here simply to do what is right for Australia,' he said.

Hewson went through each of the recommendations put to him. As he said no to each, his tongue seemed to loosen a little more. 'The most blatant case of vested-interest argument that we've seen in a long time', is how he described one of the concessions sought. No self-respecting politician would have said yes to any of the demands. But Hewson had encouraged the industry to put this material up in the first place, then publicly ridiculed it for doing so.

Just in case voters didn't catch a glimpse of the manic Hewson on the television news that Friday, he set off to Sydney to give another unusual speech the following evening. 'You've got to be suspicious of a guy that doesn't drive, doesn't like kids and things like that,' Hewson said of the then NSW Labor opposition leader Bob Carr. 'When he's up against a full-blooded Australian like John Fahey, he has not got a hope.' This was the unmistakable voice of the schoolyard bully picking on the fat kid, or the kid with glasses, or the wog boy. Hewson apologised on the Sunday. Monday night, he went on the Nine Network's 'A Current Affair' to say sorry again, and to put his foot in it, again:

> I had no intent on drawing attention to the fact that Mr Carr didn't have children. In terms of my own personal experience in the last

few years, I would be the last person to raise that issue. I don't have children with Carolyn, it isn't for the want of trying, so I certainly wasn't commenting on that.

In giving the public too much information on his second marriage, Hewson would have reminded it of his first. Almost a year earlier, on 29 September 1991, Margaret Hewson appeared on the Nine Network's 'Sixty Minutes' to give her side of their bust-up. This is territory that Australian politics prefers not to cover. Keating never sought to make an issue of Hewson's personal life. But politicians don't always determine what gets into a voter's head. Margaret Hewson said her husband left her four days before Christmas 1985, telling her she couldn't 'cope' with being a politician's wife. This anecdote is not easily forgotten. It was regurgitated in the focus-group research of the main parties. At least one senior figure in the Keating government observed privately that 'Kerry Packer handed us' the 1993 election when his network aired Margaret Hewson's story.

The next snapshot that voters saw was Hewson sweating. As October rolled into November, the polls found Labor in front for the first time, by 45 per cent to 41 per cent. Behind the scenes, Andrew Robb, the federal director of the Liberal Party, was telling Hewson that the voters were turning against him, but that the election could still be won by making Keating, not *Fightback!*, the issue. To do this, the nasties in *Fightback!* had to be removed. The problem was Hewson's public threat to resign if *Fightback!* were changed. The Liberals were snookered. Unable to switch leaders because Howard did not have the numbers for a clean takeover, and unwilling to drop *Fightback!* completely, Hewson decided, reluctantly, to become just another politician.

Food was removed from the GST, the tax cuts were reworked, and the plan to cut the dole after nine months was scrapped. New handouts were announced from cradle to grave. Childcare services joined food on the GST-free list. Single mothers were given a tax break, as were self-funded retirees. Luxury cars, which were to become cheaper under Hewson's original GST plan, would now be taxed at a higher rate, so Keating could no longer say that the Ferrari-driving opposition leader was subsidising his car collection. Hewson even threw a $10 million-a-year bribe to the tourism industry to help it 'promote inbound tourism'.

More tellingly, *Fightback!* Mark II did not add up. It had a larger funding hole in it than Keating's *One Nation*, because the most basic transaction in the document, the removal of food, had no obvious counterpoint. The GST was to be $4.2 billion smaller without food and childcare in the tax base. But the paring back of the personal tax cuts would save Hewson only $2.2 billion. Given that Keating's budget already had an admitted revenue shortfall of up to $4 billion, Hewson was now offering the more dodgy package to voters. Amazingly, Keating now had the better deal on tax cuts, and without a GST.

Streams of perspiration ran across Hewson's face as he launched *Fightback!* Mark II at the National Press Club on 18 December 1992. 'We haven't compromised the integrity of *Fightback!* one bit,' he said. Asked if voters had reason to fear that he might put food back into the GST once in government, Hewson said he would resign if food were taxed.

With *Fightback!* Mark II, Hewson had signed a second political suicide note. It was one day short of Keating's first anniversary as prime minister. The wildest of political years was coming to a close with Labor in sight of an implausible re-election. And there were still three months to go before the public would get their chance to vote.

Super Pensioners

ALARM BELLS are not supposed to start ringing when politicians call on the Finance Department, in Canberra's leafy parliamentary triangle, to discuss their superannuation perk. It is a long-standing ritual for federal MPs to check on their taxpayer-funded nest eggs before they face the people. Most have a poor grasp of the detail, but all know the basics: stay in parliament for eight years, and the taxpayer suddenly becomes your friend for life. Eight years, or three terms, whichever comes first, is all it takes to qualify for a super pension.

The worst a backbencher can expect from the super pension is an indexed payment of $50,000-plus a year for the rest of their days on this earth. After 18 years' service, it can reach six figures. Former politicians can take a job in the real world or, if they wish, a taxpayer-funded consultancy, without losing their super pension. They can even go to prison, if they are unlucky, yet be consoled with the thought that the perk will continue to pour into their bank account.

Labor's Keith Wright met the Finance Department on 18 August 1992. He had been in the Queensland parliament for 15 years, rising to the rank of opposition leader before crossing to Canberra at the 1984 election. That placed him in a privileged group of ten MPs at the time who had already earned super pensions from their state service. Although their money was frozen whilst they served in federal parliament, each had a shot at a loophole.

'We have legal advice to the effect that Mr Wright could "double dip" i.e. receive a Commonwealth benefit based on both Commonwealth and State service *as well as the State benefit*,' the department advised the finance minister Ralph Willis in a confidential briefing dated 24 August 1992.

The officials had no intention of telling Wright about the loophole, but he had already figured it out:

> At our 18 August meeting, however, Mr Wright quickly raised the 'double dip' question. He indicated he had legal advice to the effect that this was possible, and for a variety of reasons needed to take whatever steps he could to make the best of his financial position.

What concerned the bureaucrats was that Wright had just four months to go before qualifying for a federal pension. What they did not know at the time was that Wright was about to be charged with child rape.

TWO MONTHS EARLIER, Paul Keating had secured one of his greatest contributions to public policy for the 1990s: a national superannuation scheme. Workers would be forced to save 9 per cent of their wages for their retirement, and the cash would come from their employers. Although the government mandated the savings, the private sector would manage them.

Australians view savings in the way that some politicians look at truth: fine in theory, but a little tough to achieve in practice. There is always another bill to pay, another gadget to buy, another trip to book. Before Keating, super was a perk enjoyed by executives and public servants. Payouts were set in advance, and based on length of service. Roughly half the workforce had super, divided between the lucky ones in so-called defined-benefit funds and the mugs in regular accumulation funds. What politicians received from the parliamentary super fund was in keeping with the defined benefit funds in the private and public sectors. The other half of the nation had no super, which meant the only cash they had to look forward to in retirement was the age pension, unless they sold their capital city home, moved into a cheaper Gold Coast apartment, and invested the difference in their favour.

Once the tariff wall started tumbling, super, like every other transaction between employer and employee, became a little more hard-nosed. Defined-benefit funds were wound up. All new workers would be put on accumulation funds, which meant they would get back only what they put in plus the interest earned, minus fees and taxes. But not the politicians. They decided to exempt themselves from the changes, even as they were imposing them on their public servants. The MPs could allow themselves this luxury because they wrote the rules for the parliamentary super scheme.

Keating's reform took aim at two national problems at once, the current account deficit and the ageing of the population. Six years earlier, in 1986, he had convinced the trade unions to forgo a 3 per cent wage rise and to take it, instead, as super. The money was meant to flow through to all workers covered by the award system. Some employers were cheeky enough to deliberately withhold the funds; others just made mistakes. News Limited forgot to pay me for one of my years in the press gallery, but neither of us realised the error until I had moved from *The Herald Sun* to *The Australian,* when the former happily corrected the error. Fancy that: the Murdoch group's economic correspondent had no idea he was being diddled, even though he covered super as an issue.

Keating's superannuation guarantee levy elevated the award payments to a legislated right. Tardy employers would be taxed if they didn't cough up. Keating set a goal for 12 per cent of wages to be going into super by 2000: 9 per cent would come from the employer; the other 3 per cent from the worker's own pocket, although this second piece of the policy never made it into legislation.

Principle collided with politics when Keating put his legislation to the Senate in June 1992. The Australian Democrats held the balance of power, but they had lost their moderate leader Janine

Haines at the 1990 election. Their new chief, senator John Coulter, a committed greenie with an aversion to economics, did not get along with treasurer John Dawkins. Their personality clash made compulsory super a sitting duck for upper house obstruction. Yet something strange happened on the way to the brawl. Coulter was happy to leave the negotiations to the party's then unknown treasury spokesperson, Cheryl Kernot. She seized her 15 minutes in the spotlight and built a ten-year career on the back of it.

Initially, Kernot suggested that the Democrats would block the legislation, but she was bluffing. What she wanted was a compromise she could use to build her own profile in the party, and to contrast her ability to bend Labor's arm with Coulter's more combative nature. In the end, Kernot and her party settled for what seemed to be fiddles at the edge of Keating's plan. The timetable for getting the employer contribution to 9 per cent was extended by two years, to 2002.

SUPERANNUATION FORMED a wedge between politicians and the public that would take the worst part of the decade to address. When Keith Wright sought to double-dip the scheme, not a word of complaint was raised by either side of parliament. The hard numbers of his case would not be revealed for another seven years.

In his opening encounter with the Finance Department, Wright had his shopping list of loopholes confirmed by the officials. Eventually, he chose to convert his Queensland entitlement, then worth $49,650 a year, into a lump sum of $496,500. This left him free to collect the federal pension, which started at $34,393.50 a year. He was allowed, if he wanted, to convert some of that amount into a second lump sum, leaving him with a part-pension. The lifetime value of his payout was calculated by officials at almost $900,000.

The motivation for the 18 August meeting only became apparent two weeks later, when Wright was charged on ten counts, including rape of a minor.

Wright met again with the officials in October to work out what he would have to do to qualify for a federal pension 'in the context of the charges'. He was told he had to remain in federal parliament until at least 1 December, the eighth anniversary of his election. Wright wanted to know what would happen if he lost his pre-selection, which did occur in the first week of December. The department said he would have to prove 'his failure to be a candidate at the next election was due to the loss of party support he genuinely sought'.

In its 1 December note to Willis, the department advised that the loophole would allow Wright to claim more money in total than the 'maximum benefit available under either of the schemes'. He stood at the March 1993 election as an independent, lost, collected his super, was sentenced to eight years in prison on 28 October 1993, and was freed on parole in June 1999.

When the details were leaked to me in early 1999, it emerged that a second politician, this time a Liberal, had also helped himself to the double dip. Wal Fife had served almost 18 years in NSW, including more than a decade as minister, and 17 years in Canberra. Mr Fife took the maximum state lump sum available to him, worth $397,449, and a federal super pension valued at $1.31 million. This explained why the main parties greeted the reports with a bipartisanship of silence; each had a beneficiary in their ranks.

One endearing footnote in the saga was the response of Tim Fischer, one of the ten MPs named in the department's 1992 files as a potential winner. The National Party leader became deputy prime minister in the Howard government in 1996, so his perk multiplied with his higher salary. He rang me before the 2001 election to say he would not be taking advantage of the 'Wright double dip'. Fischer, a serial butcher of the English language, said: 'I will be proactively denying my access to the double anomaly for which I am grandfathered.' He remains the only politician I know of who reduced his perk on principle.

PAUL KEATING's superannuation reforms connect the dots between some of the strangest political stories of the decade. Ironically, the politician who best exemplified the double standard of the super pension committed no crime and pulled no loophole. Bill O'Chee was a political tar baby. He entered parliament via the back door in May 1990, filling the casual vacancy left by John Stone, the Queensland National Party senator who retired after Andrew Peacock lost his second election. In nine years in parliament, O'Chee never rose above the backbench. He won a sole election in his own right, in 1993, then was beaten at the GST election of October 1998. In defeat, O'Chee had qualified for a super pension, and would be free to collect it at the age of 34 when his term expired on 30 June 1999. But a regular worker of O'Chee's vintage with his or her super in a humble accumulation fund would have to wait until turning 60 before claiming their nest egg. The politicians had just exempted themselves from a decision to raise the so-called preservation age at which workers could see their super from 55 to 60 years. The 26-year gap in O'Chee's favour lit up talkback radio switchboards, and eventually forced Prime Minister Howard to scrap the early-access perk for all MPs elected after 2001.

I love the tale of our youngest political pensioner. I tried to ring O'Chee before I published the scoop about him on 6 October 1998, but he would not return the call. I never did get to speak to him. But he let the public know what he thought of his payout: '*The Australian* can go root my boot. I find it a bit galling that people who didn't want to write a story about me during the campaign now want to write a story on me.' He took to the airwaves to lecture voters that his parliamentary salary was peanuts compared to what he could have earned in the private sector. He didn't get it. O'Chee was a servant of the public; they paid him. Soon after he left politics, I sought comment from O'Chee for another, related article. He supplied a quote through an intermediary: 'If you print one tiny falsehood, one tiny inaccuracy about me, I will sue *The Australian's* arse off. I'm fed up with the crap that George Megafuckhead carries on with.' He hasn't sued.

CHAPTER FIVE

Cut Down by Women, and Tax

POLITICS is a mandatory dating game. It forces you to choose between two men, even if neither comes close to your ideal of the *one*. The other fact to appreciate about elections is that they are decided by the disengaged, not the partisans. Compulsory voting means the Australian system places power in the hands of those who pay little attention to politics. But here's the rub. The quality more scarce than honesty in politics is competition. The federal system is biased towards incumbency. Sure, the media treats every election campaign as too close to call, and bathes it in the seminal cliché that the vote will decide Australia's future. But we are kidding ourselves. Australians have a phobia about changing governments. Since prosperity went mainstream in the 1950s, they have done it just four times — in 1972, 1975, 1983, and 1996. In each case, recession was the silver bullet, and the result a forgone conclusion. Yet not all recessions lead, automatically, to the fall of the government. Robert Menzies survived the 1961 credit squeeze by one seat after his treasurer Harold Holt dealt with a boom by jacking up interest rates. Paul Keating, likewise, dodged the electoral firing-squad in 1993.

The near-misses of Menzies and Keating deserve the title of contests because the results could have gone either way. Menzies lost the primary vote to Labor's Arthur Calwell by 42.1 per cent to 47.9 per cent. After preferences, the popular vote stood at 49.5 per cent to 50.5 per cent in Labor's favour. But Menzies and Calwell were combatants from another age. The 1960s belonged to neither man in a cultural sense. Of the two, Calwell was probably the crustier relic and was no match for Menzies as an intellect. The 1961 election was close only because the economy made it so.

In 1993, Keating and John Hewson were in the prime of their lives, and bidding for the right to define the nation on the cusp of its most prosperous decade. When men clash at the peak of their egos, something primal takes over that is both ugly and compelling.

Looking back, the 1993 election could easily be dismissed as an argument over degrees of deregulation. Much of *Fightback!* would eventually be picked up by Keating and then, more notably, by John Howard. The market would come to dominate our lives in the way Hewson had envisaged. The office took precedence over family, and property over community. But when Hewson presented his template to the electorate it said No. This begs the question: was Hewson ahead of his time? Or did his platform fail only because it was too honest? After all, the reforms of the 1980s were never explicitly voted for. Bob Hawke didn't seek a mandate for economic rationalism when he unseated Malcolm Fraser in 1983. The election win came first; the floating of the dollar, later. Perhaps Hewson was an unwitting Trojan Horse, the means by which Keating and then Howard would take the nation where it didn't want to go in the 1990s. Or was he just an inexperienced politician who lost an unlosable election? The truth, as it turns out, is a combination of all of the above. In the end, his personality flaws were as critical to his failure as the nature of some of his policies.

Keating finished 1992 back in the race, but the election was still Hewson's to win, as it had been the day he became opposition leader almost three years earlier. As the 1993 election approached, the coalition returned to the lead. By 10 March, with three days to go, Hewson was coasting on the primary vote, leading by 46.5 per cent to 41 per cent, according to Newspoll. The sounds that echoed across Parliament House were the screeching of packing tape and the whir of the shredding machine as Labor ministers and their staff cleaned out their offices. But, during the final two days, a penny seemed to drop in the real world. Whatever antipathy the electorate held towards Keating, it could not match its terror of Hewson.

The campaign itself ran like a jazz track: clutter, then clarity. The political memory fixates on the gaffe at the start of the campaign and the rallies at the finish. Hewson couldn't tell the Nine Network's 'A Current Affair' how the GST would apply to a birthday cake. It was one of those questions that we policy wonks of the press gallery would never have thought to ask, because it was too tabloid. But it worked:

> *Mike Willesee*: If I buy a birthday cake from a cake shop and GST is in place, do I pay more or less for that birthday cake?
> *Hewson*: Well, it will depend whether cakes today in that shop are subject to sales tax or they're not, firstly, and they may have a sales tax on them. Let's assume that they don't have a sales tax on them and that birthday cake is going to be sales tax free, then of course, you wouldn't pay, it would be exempt, there would be no GST on it under our system. To give you an accurate answer I need to know exactly what type of cake to give a detailed answer.

The choice for voters was being boiled down to whether cake mix and candles should be taxed. This was a problem of Hewson's making. He had pulled food out of the GST to save his job. Now he couldn't explain how the reform that he promised would make life easier for business would operate in practice. Keating shot back: 'If you don't understand it, don't vote for it, because if you do understand it, you certainly won't'.

In the closing week of the campaign, Hewson took to the streets. He wanted to bring *Fightback!* to the people with a series of old-fashioned rallies, where the gospel could be heard without Keating and his mates in the media interrupting. Most politicians fancy themselves as persuaders. Even the shy ones, and there are more than the public may realise, are confident they can talk you around, one on one. All they need is a minute, ten minutes, an hour of your time, to make you see the world as they see it. But only a few thousand would be exposed to Hewson the CBD preacher. The version that the television news beamed back to the millions in their lounge rooms at 6.00 pm was of the 'feral abacus'. The cameras would cut to the bit where the Liberal leader would lead the party faithful in a corny chant. 'Labor's got to go,' he'd roar. But Labor wasn't going anywhere. In fact, Labor supporters would turn up to heckle and to jostle the Liberal supporters. *Fightback!* had its apotheosis in these mob scenes. At one encounter, an egg was hurled at Hewson which, with the lightening reflex of a fieldsman at first slip, he caught and held up to the crowd. He looked equal parts boy and bully. The footage of Hewson, sleeves rolled up, seemingly electrified by the riot at his feet, gave voters another reason to stick with the devil they knew. Keating couldn't believe his luck.

Election night found all sides unprepared for the result. The quirks of daylight savings meant that Tasmania was an hour ahead of the other eastern states, so a clear picture of voting trends would be available even as the polling booths remained open on the mainland. Two Liberal seats had fallen to Keating by 7.00 pm, and a third would be added when the counting concluded a week later. The journalists in Canberra's national tally room stared at the board like children watching a jumbo jet take off, eyes and mouths agape. A colleague from *The Australian* told me that Tasmania always went against the national trend. Hewson, he predicted, would be confirmed as prime minister by 9.00 pm. He wasn't barracking. It was three years of collective press gallery wisdom speaking, and he couldn't let it go just yet. His mistake was mild compared to *The Sunday Herald Sun,* which gave the election to Hewson in its first edition. 'Hewson in photo finish' the headline screamed. Keating later signed a copy of that front page and added the words 'Oh yeah?' to the headline.

The longer the count ran, the stranger things became. Victoria followed the lead of Tasmania and yielded four extra seats for Labor; NSW, another three. But Hewson was looking good in the north and the west. Labor dropped three seats in Queensland, three in South Australia, and two in Western Australia. It was as if someone had taken a knife and made a 45-degree cut across the south-eastern corner of Australia, one slice for Labor and the remainder for the coalition.

In the final wash-up, Labor was two seats better off, and had won the primary vote by 44.9 per cent to 44 per cent, and the vote after the distribution of preferences by 51.4 per cent to 48.6 per cent. Keating had pulled off a miracle. The architect of the recession had secured a swing of 1.5 per cent to him. In 1961, Menzies, the nation's longest-serving prime minister, had endured a swing of 4.6 per cent against him.

Keating's victory offered a mixed story about the nation's attitude to deregulation. The state most likely to embrace the tax cuts attached to the GST, NSW, happened to be Keating's strongest. Sydney was already following a different orbit to the rest of the nation. It was at the start of its global-city phase, so it was the least affected by the recession. Victoria, on the other had, was at the tail end of its depression, and its embrace of Keating fits more neatly with the theory that Hewson was rejected by a reform-weary nation.

Yet Hewson claimed a majority of the two-party vote in the basket-case economy of South Australia, as well as in booming Western Australia and Queensland. Did this make the smaller states more radical than the nation's two biggest? Hardly. As John Howard would note on election night, state factors 'heavily influenced the result'. Each state that had a Labor government sided with Hewson; in those that had coalition governments, Keating prevailed. It was federal Labor's good fortune that in the nation's two largest jurisdictions, NSW and Victoria, the coalition ruled.

Keating's decision to seize the Labor leadership in 1991 was vindicated by the result. But Bob Hawke disagreed. Interviewed on election night after Labor's win was assured, Hawke said, with a trace of bitterness, that the GST should be renamed the 'Government Salvation Tax'. He also said that Howard would have beaten Keating. Labor had said the same thing after the 1990 election — that Howard would have been a more worthy rival for Hawke than Peacock. The question that can't be answered is whether Hawke could have defeated Hewson. It is hard to imagine Hawke on his own pushing Hewson's buttons in the way that Keating did. And Hawke would have been asking for a fifth election win; Keating was seeking his first.

Keating, Hewson, and Howard all agree on one thing; it wasn't the GST that decided the 1993 election.

'In the simple telling of the press gallery, it was the GST. It wasn't just the GST,' Keating says. 'Hewson had a heartless Thatcherite policy that went against the egalitarian ethos of the country. Labor won the election because people did think the whole fabric was up for grabs.'

The vote-switcher, the issue that turned lifetime Liberals into Labor voters just this once, was not the GST, but Medicare. Conservative women were appalled by Hewson's notion of user-pays. They wanted tax cuts as a reward for effort, but they didn't want to hand the bribe back whenever their children fell ill. *Fightback!* saw Medicare as a safety net for pensioners and the poor alone, which meant middle-income families would be charged whenever they visited the GP. Health policy decided the 1993 election, and the best measure of this was how women voted. For the first time in history, 50 per cent supported Labor.

Hewson never wanted to fiddle with his package. When he did, under duress, he looked like just another politician. His mistake, in hindsight, was to worry only about the GST, when it was on Medicare that voters wanted most assurance. 'We'd fought for something we'd believed in for 12 months and then, rattled by the polls, we sold out our principles,' Hewson explained five years later, in his regular column for *The Australian Financial Review*. 'I have also never believed that the GST cost us the 1993 election. It was industrial relations and a reduced credibility on health policy that were the key issues.'

Hewson blamed the Victorian premier:

The trigger for the collapse was Jeff Kennett's decision to unilaterally abolish penalty rates and leave loadings. Throughout his election campaign, Kennett had gone to great lengths, particularly in newspaper advertisements and direct correspondence to, say nurses, to guarantee that he would not unilaterally abolish penalty rates and leave loadings. And then, out of the blue, he broke that promise. This decisively undermined our credibility on industrial relations, and across the whole of *Fightback!*.

When asked about this assessment, Kennett says he hadn't read it:

I reject that entirely. He lost it because, unfortunately, the cake issue caused all the concern. The cake issue which he couldn't answer caused confusion in the minds of the electorate. And I think because it was such a radical policy, it was something like many other things that has to be tried once or twice before it actually gets up.

Howard says the issue that hurt the coalition most was Medicare:

I think the campaign on health policy did us more damage than the campaign on IR or the GST. I think we handled the health thing quite badly.

Can I say I supported the timing of *Fightback!*'s release, and I supported *Fightback!*'s content. I strongly supported the program. But I didn't think his campaigning skills, his political skills, were as good. If you are going to have a fairly reformist program, you need to have a lot of political skills. We lost in '93 because Keating was a superior politician to Hewson, that's the overwhelming reason.

IT IS SAID by his supporters that Keating forfeited the 1996 election on the night of his 1993 triumph, when he appeared a little too triumphal. Keating's staff had advised him to be humble. Instead, he appeared to rub it in to all those who had written him off:

Well, this is the sweetest victory of all, this is the sweetest. This is a victory for the true believers, the people who in difficult times have kept the faith and to the Australian people going through hard times, it makes their act of faith all that much greater.

Peter Costello thought Keating's line about the true believers was a stroke of genius. 'He's such a smart politician,' a dejected Costello said as he watched the speech from his office at Parliament House. 'He's already setting up the next election.'

There were, in fact, glimpses of humility in Keating's speech. 'Part of this victory,' he conceded, was due to voters 'spotting what they think were the dangers in the Liberal Party's policies. What I hope is that the next election, the victory is 100 per cent due to the good government of Labor'.

The moment that really soiled the final term was not the victory speech on the night of the election, but a meeting held behind closed doors the following afternoon. One of Keating's closest allies, John Dawkins, called on him at the prime minister's Sydney residence in Kirribilli. Dawkins had been the education minister who introduced user-pays for universities. In 1988, he was the first to tell Hawke to his face that he should step down for Keating. When Keating took over the leadership at the end of 1991, he promoted Dawkins to the treasurer's post at the expense of Ralph Willis. Keating thought Dawkins would be bolder than Willis, a like mind who would test the boundaries.

With the election won, Dawkins came to praise and to niggle Keating. He told his leader he would be a more 'assertive' treasurer in this term. It didn't take Keating long to realise what his ally really meant by this. Dawkins wanted to ditch the tax cuts promised a year earlier as part of the *One Nation* package. He said he would resign if Keating insisted on honouring them.

The problem was the same as it had been a year earlier: the economy was growing, but revenue collections weren't — because inflation had been defeated, and unemployment remained high. On the day after the election, Keating was advised that he had to find an extra $10 billion over the next few years to plug the hole in the budget. Every time Treasury punched another set of numbers into its computer, the deficit jumped to another don't-go-there zone.

Keating was jammed. A decade of rubbing Howard's nose in it was about to rebound on him. For years, he had taunted the Liberals about the 'fistful of dollars'. These were the tax cuts that Malcolm Fraser had promised during the 1977 election, then cancelled the following year in Howard's first budget as treasurer. One of Keating's favourite parliamentary props was the front-page headline that greeted this announcement, 'Lies, Lies, Lies'. He would pull it out during question time whenever he felt like needling Howard. Keating didn't want to become another Fraser, another Howard.

He bowed, finally, in July 1993, a month before the budget was due. Dawkins thought he had a deal to pay one round early, and defer the other until it could be afforded, which really meant never. Keating went to the National Press Club with other ideas. Both rounds would be paid, he said: the first, early; the second, 'probably in 1998', two years later than had been scheduled in the legislation. He chose to take his dose of humble pie, and to defy Dawkins, at the end of a speech about native title. Dawkins was not happy, and would settle the score at the end of the year when he resigned.

When politicians break promises, the English language is taken to some very interesting places. Keating couldn't say he had been wrong because that would make him look weak. He couldn't say he meant what he said at the time, but that circumstances had changed, because that would make him seem shifty. It had been obvious for more than a year that the economy was not recovering quickly enough to secure the bracket creep needed to underwrite the tax cuts. But to say this now would invite the obvious retort: why did you wait until after the election to fess up? Keating chose a formula that was too cute by half:

When the tax cuts were announced in February 1992, they were intended to encompass fiscal drag. The subsequent better performance on inflation now implies that they are substantially more than fiscal drag, substantially more than intended. Delaying the introduction of the second leg will bring the tax cuts back into line with what was intended and announced in February 1992, while still seeing the tax cuts paid ... in full. They will be L A W law. And what is more, they are R E S P O N S I B L E responsible law.

This last sentence made him sound like one of his favourite soul-singers, Aretha Franklin, waving an accusing finger at the press gallery that once adored him. All he was asking for was a little respect. But the wordplay was an attempt at erasing the description he had given the tax cuts during the opening week of the election campaign. 'They've been legislated,' he had said. 'They are not a promise, they are law: L A W law. And the difference between a legislated tax cut and some opposition speaker's manifesto is all the world of difference.'

Did this make him a liar, a tax cheat, as the coalition would describe him? For this charge to stick, Keating needed to have done one of two things. Either he fiddled with the forecasts for economic growth, employment, and inflation in his *One Nation* package to make the tax cuts add up; or he realised later that the numbers were too optimistic, but decided to conceal this from the electorate.

Former Treasury secretary Tony Cole has suggested that the forecasts were prepared in the prime minister's office. But Treasury had spent the first half of the 1990s expecting revenue to be stronger that it really was. It hadn't understood the change in the economy, its contradictory mix of high growth, low inflation, and high unemployment. In the second half of the decade, when Howard had taken power, the forecasts for revenue would be routinely botched the other way, with more money pouring into public coffers than the government knew what to do with.

The second question is more serious. If Keating knew the tax cuts were unaffordable before the election, he had a duty to inform the public before they voted. We now know that his economic guru

Don Russell had advised him at the start of the campaign to abandon the tax cuts. On face value, Keating sinned by saying the tax cuts were 'L A W'.

Yet Keating had been open about the risks. The 1992 budget admitted there was a revenue hole.

'There was a notion, put about by Hewson and Howard, that I cocked up, or people acting on my behalf had cocked up the estimates in *One Nation* to sort of make the tax cuts, you know, tricky and affordable without a consumption tax', Keating says:

> In truth, we hadn't, that was the Treasury's best guess at the time. All that happened was that the lags meant it was harder to pay the second round. In the election campaign, the tax cut never got a mention. In '93, you couldn't get a word for it. I'd get up and say, 'And by the way, in the *One Nation* statement we announced tax cuts last year', and they'd say, 'Oh yeah, yeah, yeah, we know about that', you couldn't get a word for it. After the election, everyone wanted to say we won the election because of the tax-cut promise. It had nothing to do with the election, it was all about Hewson's Thatcherite policy.

Of course, Keating is right. History can't have it both ways. In his regular newspaper column for his hometown tabloid *The Sunday Telegraph*, Howard mentioned the tax cuts once, when they were announced in February 1992. He said they were 'unfunded' and could not be delivered 'without major damage to the Australian economy'. But there Howard had left it, as indeed had most of the media. If the tax cuts had been given the scepticism they deserved, the public interest would have been better served. But then Hewson's unfunded tax cuts would have demanded the same level of scrutiny. That neither side was placed under adequate pressure before the election to explain their sums was a pox on all of us in the press gallery. What bothered most journalists about 1993 was their failure to pick the result. The bigger mistake was their failure to nit-pick where it mattered—on the policy detail.

But Keating can't have it both ways either. He said he won the

1993 election because of *Fightback!*, not his tax cuts. So he could have ditched the tax cuts earlier and still prevailed.

None of this would have mattered, of course, if Keating and Dawkins had not been at each other's throats after the election. The breakdown in communication was confirmed when the August 1993 budget was released. It was a document as suicidal as *Fightback!* had been, with pain being dished out, seemingly, for its own sake. The price of getting one half of the tax cuts early was increased indirect taxes of about the same order. There were also, amazingly, cuts to Medicare, the election vote-switcher that had been more powerful for Keating than the GST.

The tax rises were to apply in stages: a little this year, a little more the next. By 1996–97, they would total $3.6 billion, which would cover the bill for the first half of the *One Nation* tax cuts, which was now put at $3.5 billion. The figure had been reduced by about $500 million because there were fewer workers in jobs to give the money to. The second round of the L A W tax cuts disappeared from the budget papers. Their fate was to be settled in 1995, when the so-called forward estimates of revenue and spending would cover the financial year in question, 1998–99.

Howard says the 1993 budget sounded the death knell for Keating's government:

> It was the most lethal piece of throwing dirt in the face of the electorate that you could find. They had run this ferocious fear campaign on an indirect tax, which was going to be offset by personal income-tax cuts. They win the election and they not only cancel their own tax cuts, but then they increase all these indirect taxes. It was madness, and it was also a bit contemptuous. I think that bit very deeply amongst a lot of their own working-class supporters, who thought, 'Gee, they ran all this stuff about this monster new tax, and look what they've done.' I don't think they ever recovered.

But there was something else in the budget that didn't ring true for Labor supporters. Keating had promised to reduce the company tax rate from 39 to 33 per cent, in order to make *Fightback!*'s company tax rate of 42 per cent appear punitive by comparison. It was worthy economic policy because a lower company tax rate would encourage employers to open their payrolls and hire more staff. But there was not one vote in it for Labor.

The budget honoured the promise to business in full, even as it denied workers half their promised tax cuts. The loss to revenue would be $1.7 billion a year by 1996–97. Another $300 million a year was given to lower-income workers who had gained nothing from the original *One Nation* tax cuts. It didn't add up. If Dawkins had chosen to scrap, or defer, the company tax cut, he could have covered half the cost of round two of the personal tax cuts. At a stretch, he could have delivered this leg by pushing back its start date a year to, say, 1 January 1997. He could have sold it as a trade-off for bringing forward round one. The only people complaining would have been in business.

Yet, for all the trauma, the hole in the budget remained. The goal posts for achieving a small deficit by 1995–96 had been shifted by another year to 1996–97.

The budget papers contained a telling admission: 'Rather than achieve necessary revenue increases by cancelling the tax cuts, or deferring them until economic growth made them affordable as originally expected, the government has decided to alter the tax mix.'

Altering the tax mix was what Hewson wanted to do with his GST. Just in case voters didn't realise they had been done over by Labor, the trade unions were leading the public attacks against the budget. Their relationship with the government had been strained by Keating's push to reform the industrial relations system. This was not the first occasion that the Labor government had been at civil war. But it was the first time Keating had to fight on his own, without Bob Hawke to draw some of the flack. The tag team is the better model for a reformist government, with the treasurer as agitator and the prime minister keeping an eye on the politics. With Keating as leader, and Dawkins as his treasurer, the theory broke down. The government now had a bad cop and a mad cop. The cops were interchangeable.

Keating had promised a less political approach to the prime ministership than Hawke. More policy and fewer opinion polls was the theory. But the 1993 election win gave Keating a false sense of immortality. He had ignored the party research that told him to tone down his aggression. He remained optimistic when the polling said he was finished. After the election, he lost his edge. The 1993 budget was his nadir. To appreciate why, fast-forward two years to the 1995 budget, when the fate of the second round of the tax cuts was settled. What happened? Keating revealed his last great idea. The tax cuts were to be paid as superannuation. The government contribution would be worth 3 per cent of wages, to go with the 9 per cent already coming from employers. A further 3 per cent was to come out of workers' own pockets, for a total of 15 per cent super by 2002. Also, the company tax rate was pushed back up to 36 per cent, thus cancelling half the 1993 election handout to business.

Why didn't he think of any of this in 1993? When I ask he shrugs, and his mind jumps to another track. He rushes into the next room, flicks through his archives, and comes back with a letter he had written to the secretary of the Treasury, Ken Henry, in May 2003 seeking proof that the 'so-called "L A W" tax cuts' had, in fact, been honoured. Henry replied with copies of the relevant pages in the 1995 budget, which supported Keating's case.

The most interesting section in Henry's response, though, dealt with Keating's record as a tax-cutter.

Keating had asked: 'How many rounds of tax cuts were paid during the period I was either treasurer or prime minister? Could you have these rounds itemised as to when they were first paid and the full year cost of each round?'

Henry listed five sets of tax cuts: $2.1 billion in 1984; $4.6 billion in 1987; $4.9 billion in 1989; $2.6 billion in 1991; and the first leg of *One Nation*, which actually came in at $3.4 billion in 1993.

Notice a pattern here? Keating delivered bigger tax cuts in the late 1980s, when he was a tax reformer. The job got harder in the

1990s. The recession ended not just inflation as Australia knew it, but the free ride of jobs. With less revenue being collected, and more unemployment benefits being paid out, tax cuts were impossible to achieve without further reform. But the economy, and the electorate, were not in a position to bear the cost. It would be another seven years before the budget could afford to give voters another income tax cut. This time, it would be Howard dishing out the dough.

The Beatles versus Gladiator

THE DECLINE of the compact disc is the allegory for the 1990s. It connects the loss of community and the nation's journey from anger to avarice with the fracturing in music tastes. We can't name the latest hit on the charts for the same reason we don't join political parties, go to church, or get involved in clubs.

The shared experience that defines an era relies on two very simple things: people have to be in roughly the same place at the same time to receive a cultural or political signal, and they have to be coming from a similar place to be able to interpret it in the same way.

Deregulation dispersed Australians. It hollowed out the centre of the jobs ladder, and it added women to the mix, along with a dash of flair with the children of immigrants. Women explain the conflicting strains of new Australia: the affluence and the anxiety.

Men, in turn, are the reason the nation no longer feels as equal than it once was. Picture a jobs ladder for full-time workers with five rungs: top, upper-middle, middle, battler, and bottom. A generation ago, it resembled an egg with almost half the men sitting pretty in the middle thanks to centralised wage-fixing. (A middle income is defined as between 0.75 times and 1.25 times the median income.) Two decades of economic change have shrunk the proportion of male workers on the middle rung from 46.8 per cent to 37.5 per cent, which represents about 315,000 fewer people in the centre in real terms. Half of this group has gone to the very top rung, but the other half has slipped to the battler rung. In 1981, there were 13.9 percentage points more men in the middle than in the top and battler rungs combined. By 2001, the gap had virtually disappeared. The egg-shaped nation is now an hourglass. Deregulation doesn't really discriminate. It scatters the wages of men at the same time that is short-changes women.

Our idea of what it is to be Australian is up for grabs because there is no longer any one bit of Australia that we can agree on. Not even bricks and mortar binds us, because for twenty- and thirty-somethings the mortgage, like marriage and babies, has become just another thing to delay getting involved in.

Technology added two further twists to the dispersal. The internet radicalised the way we received our information, and accentuated the distance between people. Consumers and voters were now free to choose the cultural or political signal that made sense to them, without being exposed to someone else's idea of the mainstream. All you need do was Google your prejudice and it would appear, like magic, on the screen, with nothing else to distract you.

Technology has also loosened the grip of music on the public imagination. There are no agreed soundtracks to remind us of the doubling of property prices, or the tension between new and old Australia. 'Countdown' had gone off the air in 1987, while its US equivalent, 'American Bandstand', ceased transmission in 1989. The standard explanation is Gen X: it couldn't be marketed to, because it kept switching its fads, from Nirvana one minute to computer games the next and then on to reality TV. But Gen X, as the marketers called it, was the first group to be too smart to be pegged by a monoculture. The baby-boomer consensus which existed in the 1960s and 1970s, when all ears were pinned to the radio, and eyes glued to television, could not be recreated because Gen X had choices.

THE PRICE of CDs chewed up more time than any other political issue during the 1990s, apart from the GST. Who said Australian politicians aren't in touch with the real world? It took five cabinet meetings between 1991 and 1995 to confirm rock 'n' roll as the only sector of the economy that Labor wanted to protect from competition. It took the coalition another two years between 1996 and 1998 to decide to free up the market.

The CD saga began with a report from the Prices Surveillance Authority in December 1990 that found Australian music buyers were paying up to $12 more for new-release material than consumers in the US. The PSA was a ginger body established in 1984 as a sop to the trade unions, to assure them that business would be persuaded to exercise price restraint as a quid pro quo for the wage restraint being forced on the workers. Its chairman was the media-savvy Professor Allan Fels, and he flogged the CD story for all it was worth. But at first he wasn't talking primarily about CDs. The more popular medium at the start of the 1990s was the cassette.

The music business ran a legal racket. In each jurisdiction, from the US to Australia, the local subsidiaries of the then six multinational record labels were free to distribute whatever album they saw fit. If a title wasn't made available to retailers, tough luck, because the copyright laws prevented the same CD from being imported from another source nation. Fels said this practice kept prices higher in Australia than overseas. The $30 CD forced consumers to play it safe. More than half the top-100-selling albums on the Australia charts in the early 1990s would be greatest hits packages.

For Paul Keating, an economic rationalist and classical music buff, the argument should have been easy to resolve. But it wasn't his baby in 1991. He was on the backbench when cabinet met in July and again in October 1991. The music industry had been to Canberra, with Midnight Oil front man Peter Garrett among the stars enlisted to persuade ministers to preserve the status quo. The artists said the record labels would pull out of the Australian market if they lost their copyright. Normally, when a business tries to threaten a government, it's the chief executive who makes the call. In this instance, it was the employees, the rock stars, who were twisting arms.

The first two cabinet debates ended in stalemate. It was only at the third attempt, in June 1992, that a decision to deregulate was made, but the legislation lapsed with the calling of the 1993 election. The music industry returned for the rematch with the free marketeers. Ministers who had been for competition in 1992 were quietly changing camps in the second half of 1993. Finally, in March 1995, at the fifth attempt, Labor announced it would stick with protection.

But then Keating lost the 1996 election, which meant all bets were off. The new Howard government said it wanted to deregulate, just as Labor had initially. But another two years elapsed before the reform could be secured in a crazy all-night sitting of the Senate in July 1998, when Mal Colston blocked the full sale of Telstra, but then went home to allow the CD legislation to pass, even though the music industry thought he would stick around to vote No. The Americans weren't pleased. Bill Clinton's administration warned of retribution if Australia became the first English-speaking jurisdiction in the world to allow parallel imports of sound recordings.

While successive Labor and coalition governments dithered, the internet was sending the CD to the same place as the vinyl LP, in rock 'n' heaven. In the first full year of deregulation, 1999, prices remained steady, the industry did not pack up its recording plants, and the US did not punish us with trade sanctions. This meant no one was right — not the free marketers who thought consumers would save big dollars, or the artists who feared Armageddon. The reason was that the CD had lost its cultural monopoly.

A year later, in Christmas 2000, one of the multinational retailers, HMV, noticed that CDs were no longer the most popular item in their stores. The DVD of Russell Crowe's 'Gladiator' outsold the most popular record that month, the latest Beatles' compilation. With this head-to-head, the CD debate had been confirmed as a 'Seinfeld' moment — a discussion that ran so long it ended up being about nothing.

THE POLITICAL equivalent of the death of the CD is the decline in partisan voters. Bob Hawke's victory in 1990 had been the first in which the government was returned with less than 40 per cent of the primary vote. John Howard would have his own sub-40 per cent escape in 1998. In that election, a new record was set: the minor parties pulled more than 20 per cent of the primary vote between them.

The way Howard sees the electorate is revealing. The largest bloc today is neither conservative nor Labor. At the start of the 1990s, he says, the partisans on each side outnumbered the swingers. Now, the swingers are the largest individual bloc:

> It was 35 [per cent coalition] 35 [per cent Labor], 30 [per cent swingers]. I think 20 years before that, it was 40, 40, 20. But I think it's now 30, 30, 40. Now this is a combination of the end of the great ideological divide that the Cold War drove, it's also a product of the diminishing power of the trade union movement, it's a product of the greater level of tertiary education in the community and it's a product of the relentless march of egalitarianism.

He explains that egalitarianism used to be a value of the workers; now it is a creed that has travelled to the top of the income ladder. 'I think more affluent people now see the value of egalitarianism,' he says.

The movie and the music business has learned to play the niche, while pretending to reflect the mainstream. The record labels decided that the baby boomers, with their larger numbers and more easily predicted tastes, should receive more attention. The hits 'n' memories radio format, the greatest-hits CD, the remastered CD, and the boxed set were a form of early cultural Alzheimer's.

Politics made the same call, only it went to a subset of the baby boomers, the voters who answered to the colour codes of grey and blue-collar. These voters had time on their hands, and an axe to grind with globalisation. They were older, more likely to be unemployed, or working part-time, and probably still listening to

The Beatles. Talkback radio was their preferred medium. Australia in the 1990s was a scary place for these people, and a new brand of journalist rose to accommodate them, the shock jock. These voters broke with a habit of a lifetime and began supporting the minor parties, which propelled the main parties onto a decade-long search for a new language to bring them back, to make them feel like they were part of the nation.

CHAPTER SIX

'Rednecks with Blue Collars'

THE GREATEST CONTRAST between the Keating and Howard years is race. One prime minister tried to run ahead of public opinion, and achieved a victory of sorts on native title. The other oscillated between leading and following community attitudes, and was rewarded at the ballot box each time, even though the people would come to modify his policies in unexpected ways.

Their disagreement began with the High Court's judgment on 3 June 1992 in the case of Eddie Mabo against the state of Queensland. Mabo and four others had launched a claim in May 1982 for legal recognition of their traditional land rights on Murray Island, in the nation's far north. The Queensland government of Joh Bjelke-Petersen replied with retrospective legislation to erase those rights. The High Court ruled in Mabo's favour and, in doing so, struck down 'terra nullius', the idea that Australia belonged to no one before European settlement. Justice Gerard Brennan said: 'Whatever the justification advanced in earlier days for refusing to recognise the rights and interests in land of the indigenous inhabitants of settled colonies, an unjust and discriminatory doctrine of that kind can no longer be accepted.'

The High Court not only found that native title existed before 1788, but that it had survived in Mabo's community because no government had extinguished it in the intervening 204 years by issuing a new title to anyone else. The essence of the Mabo case was continuity. His people, almost uniquely, had not been driven off their land.

The revolutionary nature of the judgment was not apparent in 1992 because the political class was transfixed by John Hewson's *Fightback!*. Soon after the 1993 election, though, the vested interests of industry and indigenous groups suffered a collective meltdown. Miners, farmers, and state premiers began to howl, long and loud, about the supposed extremism of the judgment. Aboriginal Australians, they warned, could use Mabo to hijack mining leases, pastoral leases, even freehold titles to suburban homes. A common tactic was to place a billion-dollar sign in front of the project and say that native title would thwart economic development.

Indigenous groups threw fuel on the bonfire by preparing lands claims that were breath-taking in their reach and naivety. In one eight-day stretch in early June 1993, barely a year after the Mabo judgment, half the nation was reportedly up for grabs. Claims were made for central NSW, from Dubbo to Albury; as much as 53 per cent of Tasmania; southern NSW and the ACT; central and south-west Queensland; and the water between the mainland and Papua New Guinea. The media beat up the ambit claims, even though a balanced assessment would have dismissed many of them. But these were not balanced times.

The 24-hour news cycle had been entrenched by the time Mabo entered the media's lexicon of shrillness. Political debate would skirt seamlessly across three mediums, from the morning newspapers, to radio, to the six o'clock television news — and, for those junkies who still had the energy, late-night current affairs TV. When the afternoon newspapers in Sydney and Melbourne were closed in 1990, journalists mistook the disappearing mastheads for a decline in the reach of the media. The reverse was true. The public was having more information forced down its throat through talkback radio and the sound bites of radio and TV. The media, like politics, is a heat-seeking missile. In 1993, with the economy still in the dumps, both institutions made a scapegoat of the nation's most disadvantaged citizens.

The language of the conservatives was often wild, and that egged on the media, which can never resist the temptation to amplify and recycle a naughty word. The conservatives implied the High Court was trying to engineer a reverse invasion: black usurping white. Tim Fischer, the federal National Party leader, accused the High Court of 'judicial activism', which was true. But then he went over the top.

Fischer's most incendiary offering was a lecture on anthropology, delivered at a National Party conference on 20 June 1993:

> We need to be honest and acknowledge that Aboriginal sense of nationhood or even infrastructure was not highly developed. At no stage did Aboriginal civilisation develop substantial buildings, roadways or even a wheeled cart as part of their different priorities and approach … I would strongly make the point that rightly or wrongly, dispossession of Aboriginal civilisation was always going to happen. Those in the guilt industry have to consider that developing cultures and peoples will always overtake relatively stationary cultures.

Later, as deputy prime minister, he would promise 'bucket loads of extinguishment' in response to the follow-up Wik judgment, and wanted a 'capital C conservative law person' on the bench. Early in 1997, Sir Gerard Brennan, by now the chief justice of the High Court, was compelled to write to Fischer to remind him of the separation of powers between the legislature and the judiciary. 'Attacks of the kind you have made, emanating from a deputy prime minister, are damaging to this court,' Sir Gerard wrote. 'You will appreciate that public confidence in the constitutional institutions of government is critical to the stability of our society.'

Victorian premier Jeff Kennet warned that backyards might be open to native title claims. In July 1993, he said Mabo threatened 'everything we've grown up and worked towards in this society' and that 'every property in Australia could be at risk'. He suggested, perhaps tongue in cheek (but one was never sure with Kennett), that

Australian Aboriginals should be given the Australian Capital Territory. 'If there is one way of settling this dispute, I, for one, would be happy to hand it [the ACT] over to the community and leave the rest of Australia to the non-Aboriginal community.' Indigenous leaders replied that Kennett was talking apartheid.

Fischer and Kennett would be among the first to criticise Pauline Hanson in 1996, well before John Howard would appreciate the damage she was doing to social cohesion at home and the nation's reputation abroad. But in 1993 these moderates on race were among the majority of politicians and business lobbyists whose knees jerked the wrong way on Mabo. Faced with the uncertainty of the High Court judgment, their first instinct was to hurl a grenade at it without thinking of the consequences for Aboriginal Australians. The stereotype of the welfare bludger is the hardest one for indigenous people to shake. The reaction to Mabo reinforced it.

On the Labor side, many wanted Keating to kill the issue. They told him, privately, to hand the miners and the farmers what they wanted. Or, if that was too difficult for his conscience, perhaps he could delay the federal response to allow the states to wipe out native title in the interim. Keating had other ideas. The irony was that, in seeking the middle ground between black and white, Keating's position was the most radical of all. He wanted to give Aboriginal Australians something they never had before—and which a majority of the electorate thought he was crazy to even consider.

Two incidents shaped Keating's attitudes on reconciliation. As a child he recalls his grandmother's stories of the dampers that were left out for the Aborigines to eat. 'You know what these dampers were', he would explain. 'They were laced with poison'. In 1984, he watched Bob Hawke have his arm twisted by the hard men of Labor's right-wing faction to abandon land rights reforms. Keating abhorred the pragmatism:

> *Keating*: I've always, from my earliest days, felt as though we were, in Australia, sort of a bunch of uninvited guests.

And I always felt that there would be a point where we would have the opportunity of making good some of the hurt done to these people, making good on some of the injustices. What happened was it came up with legislative land rights in the early days of the Hawke government. Brian Burke and Graham Richardson fought Hawke over legislated land rights and Hawke capitulated, much to his chagrin.

Question: Was Hawke as genuine as you were?

Keating: The test of genuineness was to do it. I said to Hawke one day, 'Tell Richardson and Burke to go to buggery; you know, you and I are on this tram, we'll get it through, particularly in the party'. But he didn't want to stand them up, for reasons best known to himself.

I tended to always think that this issue would finally find me, as inflation found me, you know, as tariffs found me, as most other things tended to find me, that somewhere it would come.

Keating allows himself a small, self-deprecating chuckle at this point—aware, perhaps, that he might be sounding a little too caught up in his own publicity.

Mabo was when the public really noticed Keating changing topics from the economy to national identity. Sure, he had mentioned the republic during the election campaign and, before it, talked about the need to engage with our neighbours in Asia. But these weren't considered Keating obsessions before Mabo. The Keating of 1991 and 1992 defined himself by who he was not—Hewson—and by what he believed in—competition, with a safety net for the poor. With Mabo he became someone else: a hero to former enemies on the left, and a villain to older Labor voters. The public thought reconciliation with our first citizens was a good idea. But they couldn't understand why Keating was so eager to give Australian Aboriginals a right that other Australians did not have. They were suspicious of Keating's motives. Perhaps this was a diversion, they thought—a sign that Keating had stopped listening to their kitchen-table concerns. This is what the polling said, anyway.

Some in the union movement publicly accused Keating of being on Planet Mabo — code for placing the interests of Aboriginal Australians ahead of the workers. Reminded of that jibe 12 years later, he smiles:

> Planet Mabo, yeah. Well, you know, a lot of rednecks in the Labor Party have got blue collars on. I'd been in a co-operative relationship with them at that stage for ten years. That didn't mean I took any notice of them on these matters. I didn't.

The other putdown, this one muttered behind the scenes, was that Keating had been hoodwinked by his speechwriter, Don Watson. Like the 1980s accusation that he had become a creature of Treasury, it was the Labor way of saying that Keating, the autodidact, was vulnerable to intellectual manipulation. Keating bristles at the recollection:

> These claims were, of course, all untrue. No speechwriter can write a speech that a prime minister gives when a prime minister doesn't agree with the context. Let's apply the test. Would John Howard give the Don Watson text? Of course he wouldn't.

The truth about Mabo was that Keating had no choice. Native title was a googly bowled up by the High Court that Keating couldn't let go through. The court had left it to parliament to sort out the detail. If Keating had dropped the issue, as many of his colleagues implored him to, the states, led by Western Australia, would have extinguished native title, and would then have run the risk of subsequent High Court appeals reviving native title. There was a bloody-mindedness to the conservative approach that would have egged Keating on. He loathed what he saw as their opportunism. Farmers told him he should protect their pastoral leases by elevating them to freehold title.

But there was also a moral dimension that could not be ignored. 'Moral' is a big word, and I don't like using it because it denies the other side of an argument. But it applies here. The federal opposition, the state premiers, the miners and farmers were playing target politics with human beings. For most Aboriginal Australians, native title meant nothing. They lived in the cities and country towns, so they had no hope of making a successful claim. Yet the impression that formed in the electorate was of a greedy, ungrateful people. For Keating to take on this public hostility was a gusty and, indeed, honourable call.

The caricature of Keating as aloof is partly debunked by Mabo. This is not to say that he was a model of engagement throughout his prime ministership. He was often distracted, sometimes grouchy, and mostly his own worst enemy. But Mabo was an example of Keating as an innovator with a deft touch. He spent the best part of 1993 on the issue, in talks with all sides. He argued with the premiers in June. But he was learning on the job, like everyone else, and by year's end he had turned, amongst others, Kennett into a supporter, had the National Farmers' Federation onside, and created a new generation of Aboriginal Australian leaders, including a young lawyer from Cape York, Noel Pearson.

Mabo compelled Keating to confront the dark side of the electorate. On 17 June 1993, he flew to Sydney to spend an hour-and-a-quarter in the studios of radio station 2UE. The calls Keating fielded that day, from listeners in NSW and Queensland, were toxic. One exchange is worth quoting at length because the views expressed in it would be echoed in the opinion polling of the main parties throughout the 1990s:

Caller: Why does your government see the Aboriginal people as a much more equal people than the average white Australian?
Keating: We don't. We see them as equal.
Caller: Well, you might say that, but all the indications are that you don't.
Keating: I think it was implied in your question, you don't. You think that for non-Aboriginal Australians, there ought to be discrimination in their favour against blacks.

Caller: Not whatsoever. I don't see that at all. But myself, and everybody I talk to, and I'm not racist, every person I talk to …

Keating: That's what they all say, don't they? They put these questions, they always say 'I'm not racist, but. You know, I don't believe that Aboriginal Australians ought to have a basis in equality with non-Aboriginal Australians.' Well, of course, that's part of the problem.

Caller: Aren't they more equal than us at the moment with the preferences they get?

Keating: More equal? It is not for me to be giving you a history lesson. They were largely dispossessed of the land they held.

Caller: I think there is a question over that, a lot of people will tell you that. You are telling us one thing …

Keating: If you are sitting on the title of any block of land in NSW you can bet an Aboriginal person at some stage was dispossessed of it.

Caller: You know that for sure, do you?

They weren't arguing. Keating was in control of his emotions; so was the caller. They had just no way of relating to each other.

Keating had given voters fair warning with his Redfern speech in December 1992, though they weren't really listening at the time. Mabo, he said, was 'an historic turning point, the basis of a new relationship between indigenous and non-Aboriginal Australians'. The speech has been misrepresented as an expression of guilt. This was the furthest thing from Keating's mind:

Down the years, there has been no shortage of guilt, but it has not produced the responses we need. Guilt is not a very constructive emotion. I think what we need to do is open our hearts a bit. All of us. Perhaps when we recognise what we have in common we will see things which must be done, the practical things.

Yes, it was Keating, not Howard, who first coined the phrase 'practical reconciliation'. It would prove to be a goal too big for either man to achieve in office.

Almost a year on, in November 1993, as he addressed the nation to explain his Mabo legislation, Keating repeated the line about guilt. 'We have no need, nor any use, for guilt. This generation cannot be held responsible for the cruelty of previous generations.'

These passages are forgotten because of what had come earlier in the Redfern speech:

> The starting point might be to recognise that the problem starts with us non-Aboriginal Australians. It begins, I think, with an act of recognition. Recognition that it was we who did the dispossessing. We took the traditional lands and smashed the traditional way of life. We brought the diseases. The alcohol. We committed the murders. We took the children from their mothers. We practised discrimination and prejudice. It was our ignorance and our prejudice. And our failure to imagine these things being done to us.

Significantly, Keating now concedes that the High Court judgment was complicated, even confused in places. He calls it 'motley'. 'When I say that, I don't mean to imply that they were unprincipled, but motley and messy, no coherence about it. You know, just a whole lot of thoughts on which you had to glean something.' But Keating saw opportunity where most others saw threat. He was bloody-minded in his own way, but it was the stubbornness of the optimist:

> There was a black and a white judgment. The white bit was to say that any grant of an interest in land by a land manager of the Crown from 1788 extinguished any native title right. The black bit was that anything unextinguished and left in the property of the Crown was subject to native title, provided customary tradition was being maintained and there was continuous occupation. What the High Court didn't say is what the title was, and who had it and who could get it. That was left to me, but I took up the challenge

rather than leave it, and hanging the court out to dry. And I knew had I not taken it up, that the Court government in Western Australia, probably the Goss government in Queensland, and the South Australian government would legislate in some way in the interim to wipe out the native title rights.

I didn't think you could go to the region saying, 'Here we are, the new Australian nation, free of White Australia, people who have turned over a new leaf", except that we deal with our indigenes unfairly and poorly, and that's aside from the principal matter that we were all diminished by what had happened. It's not a matter of apportioning blame.

What complicated the parliamentary response to Mabo was Gough Whitlam's 1975 *Racial Discrimination Act*. All leases granted between 1975 and the June 1992 High Court judgment, including for some of the nation's largest mining projects 'were technically invalid,' Keating says, 'because Aboriginal people were neither consulted nor compensated':

> So part of the challenge of the *Native Title Act* was to find a way where we could advantage Aboriginal people while not disadvantaging them for the fact that these titles that had been issued since 1975 ultra vires of the *Racial Discrimination Act*.

Perhaps the most amazing thing about Mabo was that Keating found a way to pass his *Native Title Act* in December through the same Senate that had just held up his 1993 budget for two months. The deal was clinched when Keating agreed to validate all past leases, while making all those issued in the future subject to the *Racial Discrimination Act*. He convinced the indigenous groups to forgo compensation claims for the past in exchange for a right to negotiate for the future:

> There was a point in history here that just had to be put right, in my opinion. My problem was getting Aboriginal people to deal

with, because no one was invested with any authority to deal with them. And this was where, finally after much chiding by me, Lois O'Donoghue rose to the challenge and dragged a group together which included David Ross and, of course, Noel Pearson, Marcia Langton and others. In many respects, the native title discussions were probably the high point of Aboriginal empowerment in Australia.

It took me the better part of 12 months. The cabinet sub-committee would meet at least two or three times a week for nearly all of the year and, of course, most of the cabinet wanted me to give it up. There wasn't a vote in it.

The Senate debate was the longest in parliamentary history until that point. It has been exceeded only once since then, by the Wik amendments of 1997–98. The Mabo legislation cleared the Senate four days before Christmas 1993 to spontaneous cheering in the chamber, and in the public and press galleries. Later that evening, at a party thrown in the office of the government Senate leader Gareth Evans, I received a sneak preview of the political courtship that would undo Labor and the Australian Democrats later in the decade. Evans, cradling a bottle of red, broke into a conversation between Democrats leader Cheryl Kernot and myself. Evans threw his free arm around her and declared, 'She should be in the Labor cabinet.'

Mabo would bury Hewson's leadership. The coalition had confused ends with means, and decided to vote No at every stage of the debate, which denied it the chance to influence the Senate negotiations. There was a childishness to the coalition tactics, which Labor would mimic in opposition later in the 1990s. The theory seemed to be that mindless obstruction was the more honourable path than direct engagement.

The following morning, as the legislation came back to the lower house to be rubber stamped, Keating told Hewson this was a second strike against his leadership. '*Fightback!* a failure; Mabo a failure. Two out of two is your track record.' Hewson replied that it was 'a day of shame for Australia'.

With Mabo, Keating reclaimed, however briefly, the status of a winner with the media, and he restored the government's primary vote to the low 40s, where it had been before the August budget. By mid-March 1994, Labor was leading the coalition by 45 per cent to 42 per cent. Mabo was the 1993 election all over again, a triumph conjured from seemingly nowhere.

Mabo proved that while race cards recur, they can be beaten. Voters react to what politicians do, and to what they hear and read in the media. Initially, Keating was marked down for the uncertainty generated by native title. But when the legislation made it through the Senate, he was seen as having resolved the crisis. The other lesson is that opposition is the wrong place from which to play the politics of colour. Hewson ultimately fared no better than Howard Mark I had on Asian immigration in 1998. Race debates only work, politically speaking, if the instigator is a prime minister, because he or she can use the authority of office to create the impression they are acting in the national interest. Oppositions find it hard to disagree in these circumstances, as Kim Beazley learned in 2001 with the asylum-seeker issue. When an opposition or trade union leader challenges the government on race, they appear to be spoilers, and usually lose more voters from their moderate supporter base than they pick up from the other side.

When Howard returned to the opposition leadership in January 1995, he supported the principle of Mabo, but reserved the right to make amendments to clean up the legislation. Keating could have felt satisfied that the war had been won. But he had left an unexploded mine, and it would go off on Howard's watch. Keating's Mabo legislation clarified what happened when native title rubbed up against a mining lease. But it was silent on the question that the farmers wanted an answer to — whether a pastoral lease extinguished native title. The preamble to the legislation said that it did. But this only reflected the government's advice; it was not the law. Keating understood the distinction. He did not want to elevate pastoral leases to freehold title at the expense of native title. He figured, correctly, that a pastoral lease would have precedence in the event of any clash — which, he thought, should be enough to mollify the farmers:

> I always believed that though the High Court in those collections of judgments, motley as they were, unclear about the whole concept of the co-existence of title, I always believed, properly tested, the High Court would find, or a majority of them would find, in favour of the co-existence of title. And partly, not only because a pastoral lease was not technically a lease, and therefore a grant of it didn't extinguish anything, but rather the more general point that Indigenous people could enjoy a traditional lifestyle on these vast tracts of land and it not be inconsistent with the primary purpose of the lease.

But farmers were not ready to let Australian Aboriginals onto the properties, to conduct corroborees on the same land where the cows grazed. The pastoralists would get their chance to claw back Keating's regime nine months into Howard's prime ministership, in December 1996, when the High Court handed down its judgment in the Wik case. The Wik people were claiming 28,000 square kilometres of the Cape York Peninsula. This was a chunk of the mainland to the west of Eddie Mabo's Murray Island. The catch was that the Wik claim overlapped ten pastoral leases. Two days before Christmas, the High Court sided with the Wik people, and sent the coalition into a panic. The court found that native and pastoral titles could co-exist; but, in the event of conflict, the pastoral lease won out. Keating had been proven right, but this infuriated the coalition.

Phase two of the native title debate would be even uglier than Mabo had been. It ate up as much of Howard's time as it had Keating's. It would be 18 months before the Wik amendments made it through the Senate, at the third attempt, in July 1998. The accusation that Howard played with the politics of race haunted those 18 months.

One of the ironies of native title is that it achieved more change in the political class by transforming conservative opponents into sympathisers than it did in helping raise the living standards of Aboriginal Australians. Kennett recanted his backyard warning, and Hewson became an advocate for reconciliation and a critic of Howard's refusal to apologise to the stolen generations.

Kennett likens native title to the GST, an idea that proved less scary in practice than it seemed when it was first debated:

> There was a lot of confusion about the judgment itself. Keating was passionate and his way of handling it was different from Hawke's. If you go back to Keating and Hawke over GST, Keating said yes, Hawke said no, and Keating had to toe the line. Then Hewson comes in with the idea, *Fightback!*, and he loses the plot because he couldn't sell it. And then Howard comes along, and by that stage the public are all used to the concept, and he gets it through. It almost costs him his job, but he gets it over the line. The same happened in terms of Aboriginal land rights, in one sense. Today people are a lot more comfortable about it because they have seen it in practice, and in most cases it's working very well.

Fischer has softened, also. 'What has been unfair to the Indigenous community has been the litany of negative coverage,' he says. Yet his criticism of the High Court remains:

> To some extent, in retrospect, the High Court made the decisions X and Y on native title, [but] they didn't put down an easy way for anyone to manage it. They left so many balls in the air that it added to the burden of the situation. It was maximum mischief, notwithstanding the rights and wrongs of the core issue. There was maximum mischief in the looseness and the lack of clarity of the key judgments.

For Fischer, in particular, native title was a missed opportunity. He would have spared the nation much angst if he had offered Keating bipartisanship in 1993. The rancour generated by Mabo in 1993 led to Pauline Hanson's attack on Australian Aboriginal welfare in 1996, which led to the threat of a 'race based' election in 1998 over the Senate's refusal to pass Howard's Wik legislation.

Labor in opposition proved just as obstructive in 1998 as the coalition had been in 1993. The political class had learned nothing in five years. In this context, Keating's contribution is all the more remarkable. He established a system, however complicated, that could not be turned back. After Wik, Howard said he would amend native title, not extinguish it. Like Keating, Howard pleased no one.

There used to be a hip-pocket logic to race debates in Australia. Fear of foreigners rose whenever the economy fell into recession, then dissipated once the recovery was assured. In the 1990s, we got our backlashes back to front. Deregulation shifted the pressure points, from the regular immigration intake to Aboriginal Australians and asylum-seekers. Ordinary workers stopped worrying that foreigners would take their jobs because the Keating and Howard governments recast the program to place a greater weight on skilled immigration. These new arrivals headed to the top of the jobs ladder, where the tertiary-educated Australian worker was more welcoming. The backlash switched to our first citizens and, later, to the boat people, because the blue-collar workers who had lost their jobs in the recession feared that these non-white faces would jump them in the handout queue.

Snapshot #6

The Most Popular Nation on Earth

TRY TO FIGURE OUT this quirk in our national character. Australians look up to no one; there is no other nation we would want to emulate. We may be comforted by American power, entranced by US popular culture, and keen for a high-flying posting to New York. However, we don't like the extremes of the American settlement, its lopsided wealth distribution, its religious fundamentalism, and its embrace of guns.

Even so, Australians are insecure in a way that no other western nation can fathom. It's to do with size and location; our 20 million versus Indonesia's 200 million, and China's 1.2 billion. And youth. At a touch over 200 years, white settlement has been too brief for us to nail an Australian identity we can agree on, and to achieve an understanding with our first citizens.

But when the rest of the world looks at Australia, it sees, simply, a good life. In 2005, a respected international polling agency, the Pew Global Attitudes Project, surveyed 16 nations across the spectrum, developed and emerging, Christian and Muslim. Australia wasn't involved, but one question did bring us into the picture: 'Suppose a young person who wanted to leave this country asked you to recommend where to go to lead a good life — what country would you recommend?'

One in four nations volunteered Australia as the place to migrate to. Our fan club comprised the British, Canadians, Germans, and Dutch. We were the only country to score four votes out of the 16.

The US could muster just one ballot, India's. We were also placed second by eight others, including the Lebanese, the Indians, the Turks, and the Indonesians, which all rated us ahead of our Anglo brethren in the US and Great Britain.

Our ferocious loyalty to the United States is more complicated than the desire for a great and powerful friend to protect us. It is the plea of the little brother who wants to be acknowledged. This urge transcends party politics. Conservative prime ministers have embraced Democrat presidents, as Harold Holt did in 1967 when he greeted Lyndon Baines Johnson with the slogan 'All the way with LBJ'. Labor prime ministers have claimed special relationships with Republican presidents, as Bob Hawke did with Ronald Reagan. Hawke's speechwriter Stephen Mills wrote that, when the two leaders met, Hawke 'went joke for joke with Reagan'. He also had a rapport with George Bush senior. Hawke telephoned Bush on the eve of the first Gulf War with an offer to play peace broker. Hawke wanted to go to Baghdad to persuade Saddam Hussein into withdrawing Iraqi troops from Kuwait. Fortunately, the idea was dropped.

One of the consolations of the Keating and Howard eras is that our leaders got to play with presidents from their own side of the partisan divide; Paul Keating had the Democrat Bill Clinton and John Howard has had the Republican George W. Bush.

Yet the ideological closeness between the leaders did not necessarily make us better known as a people. In June 2005, when the survey of world attitudes was conducted, the Americans voted Australia third behind Canada and Great Britain as the nation they'd recommend for someone seeking a new home.

There is an episode of 'The Simpsons' that demonstrates better than any poll the American indifference towards Australia. Bart is perplexed when his sister Lisa tells him that water drains counter-clockwise in the Northern Hemisphere. 'Bart, water will only go the other way in the Southern Hemisphere,' she says. 'What the hell is the Southern Hemisphere?' he barks back.

Eager to debunk Lisa, Bart starts phoning nations south of the equator to ask which way their toilets flush. Finally, Bart reaches

Squatter's Crog, somewhere in outback Australia. A pip-squeak called Tobias, with an excruciating accent, accepts the reverse-charge call.

Later, when the bill arrives in the mail, the boy's father, Bruno Drundridge, refuses to pay and telephones Bart to demand compensation. 'You're all the way in Australia,' Bart chuckles. 'Hey, I think I hear a dingo eating your baby.'

This makes the Aussie dad mad. Eager to show Bart that he is no 'drongo', Bruno takes his complaint to his local member of parliament, Gus, who happens to be playing with the pigs in the backyard. Together, they march off to see the prime minister, Andy, who is sun-bathing nude on a rubber tyre in the middle of a creek. A tinny of Fosters' is in his right hand, of course. The Australian government writes to Bart, demanding an apology.

Bart and family are flown to Australia to face the music. The scene in federal parliament is hysterical. Bart says sorry, but the prime minister, now dressed in judicial gown and wig, informs him that he will suffer an additional punishment—'a boot up the bum'.

Perhaps the typecasting of an outback nation might be acceptable in a cartoon series. But surely a more sophisticated impression was made on president Clinton, who visited Australia in 1996. Er, no. Clinton's 957-page memoir *My Life* mentions Australia three times—once more than Albania, and once less than the southern-American city of Atlanta. The punch line is that Clinton was on the same page as the scriptwriters of 'The Simpsons'. What grabbed the president most about us was the fauna:

> After a meeting with Prime Minister John Howard, a speech to the Australian parliament in Canberra, and a day in Sydney, including an unforgettable game with one of the greatest golfers of our time, Greg Norman, we flew north to Port Douglas, a coastal resort on the Coral Sea near the Great Barrier Reef. While there we walked through the Daintree Rainforest with an aboriginal guide, toured a wildlife preserve where I cuddled a koala named Chelsea, and snorkelled around the magnificent reef.

CHAPTER SEVEN

All the Way with Jakarta

THE FIRST PHOTO reproduced in Paul Keating's foreign-policy memoir, *Engagement, Australia faces the Asia-Pacific*, catches the prime minister sharing a joke with Bill Clinton. It is a picture of two handsome leaders at the zenith of their power. Their eyes are smiling. They seem to have been friends for years.

Clinton's book runs to three times the length of Keating's tome. The typeface is also twice as dense. However, in the cut and paste of diary entries, essays, and recollections, Clinton found no room for even a line on Keating, though he did mention John Howard twice. He did refer to Keating's foreign-policy baby, APEC, the Asia-Pacific Economic Co-operation forum. But Clinton took the credit for himself.

It is the nature of political diaries that they are skewed by the perpendicular pronoun. Clinton made APEC happen, but it wasn't his idea. Keating had raised it first with Clinton's predecessor, George Bush senior, in January 1992. But Bush was non-committal. When Keating tried again with Clinton, he found a more receptive ear. In his book *Engagement,* Keating described an epiphany:

Luck was running with us in a number of ways, but nowhere more than in the election of President Clinton in November 1992. I wrote to the forthcoming president a letter that was more than the usual formal congratulations. I said, in effect, 'Have I got an idea for you!'

Clinton was president between January 1993 and January 2001, which made him commander in chief for the bulk of America's complacent decade, after the fall of the Berlin Wall in November 1989 and before 11 September 2001. Prior to East Timor's liberation in September 1999, Australia enjoyed an uninterrupted stretch of nine years when it didn't have to call on US muscle or was required to commit troops to a US-led war. This happened to make Keating's job both easier and harder. Keating was the first Labor prime minister in almost half a century to enjoy a full term in office that coincided with a Democrat presidency in the White House. This background is important to bear in mind when considering Keating's foreign-policy record. He was less gung-ho about the US than Bob Hawke had been; but, then again, he didn't need to be.

Clinton and Keating were like minds, even if Keating had slipped Clinton's mind by the time he wrote his memoir. Their common interest was free trade, and the second APEC leaders' meeting in Bogor, Indonesia, in November 1994, would see the region's developed nations agree to remove all barriers to each other's imports by 2010. The developing nations had another ten years, to 2020, to achieve the same end.

Remove Keating from the equation and it is likely that APEC would have happened anyway. If John Hewson had been prime minister, he would surely have received the same advice that Keating had, to seek a closer relationship with Asia. Hewson might have charmed his way through Jakarta, Singapore, and Tokyo, as Keating had, methodically collecting allies to encourage Clinton to make APEC happen. If it hadn't been Hewson, another leader in the region would probably have stepped up. This sort of speculation matters nought. Keating was pivotal to elevating APEC from a talkfest for economic ministers to a forum for the region's leaders. According to John Howard, APEC handed Australia two decent breaks towards the end of the decade. It gave us the means to secure an international peacekeeping mission in East Timor in September 1999 and a forum to co-ordinate the response to global terror two years later.

Yet Keating's reputation in the region was the mirror opposite to the reaction that his big picture was generating at home. Many voters lumped APEC in the same basket of grievances as Mabo: another example of Keating with his head in the clouds. The Liberals certainly picked this up in their polling, which is why Howard began his first term downplaying APEC.

This is where Australia's real Asian debate occurred in the 1990s: not over immigration, but engagement. Howard would use his prime ministership to deftly rewrite Keating's foreign-policy record. He accused Keating of adopting an Asian-first policy, to the detriment of our long-standing alliance with the US. This happens to be Howard's least-convincing critique of Keating. It would take the logic of a contortionist to believe that Keating loathed the US when Clinton, a fellow traveller from the centre-left of politics, happened to be the president.

But Howard's powers of persuasion, and some short memories in the media and in academe, have allowed Keating to be tarred with the Asia-first brush. The subtext is not too hard to work out. Howard wants to have it both ways: accuse Keating of selling out the national interest by placing Asia ahead of the US, while also rebutting Keating's claim that Asian leaders would not deal with Howard.

The charges against Keating must be taken seriously because many voters believed them. It is also worth scratching beneath the surface of the public's response to the Keating agenda to see if it involved some xenophobia.

There are three strands in the argument against Keating, which his critics often jumble together. They are that Keating didn't really like Australia; that he was too close to Indonesian president Suharto; and that he wanted to make us more Asian.

The most trivial of the indictments was that Keating was uncomfortable living here and that, given half a chance, he would have relocated his family to Paris. This was the macho wing of the Labor Party saying that Keating was not a true Aussie. The 2004 US presidential elections saw a variation on this theme when one of the

lines that the Republicans ran against Democrat challenger John
Kerry was that he spoke French. Translation: he wasn't a real man
like George W. Bush.

Hawke played the French card most famously against Keating
in his own memoirs published in 1994. Recounting a discussion they
had in January 1991, soon after the Placido Domingo speech,
Hawke expressed his astonishment that Keating thought he
deserved the Labor leadership even if they agreed that Hawke 'had
a better chance of winning the next election':

> I was horrified that Paul Keating was prepared to place his own
> interests above those of a Labor victory. As disturbing at this was,
> worse was still to come. Keating's 'Paris Option' was part of
> political folklore, but it was now given its ugliest formulation. The
> question arose of what he would do if he didn't get his 'turn' as
> prime minister. I said I think he should stay, but he rejoined 'We'll
> be off to Europe. We won't be staying here—the arse-end of the
> world' ... His comment will stick in my craw. It goes a long way to
> explaining why Australians will not take to a man who thinks so
> little of them and their country.

Keating rejected Hawke's version of events. Ten years after he
was booted out of office, Keating was still living in Sydney.

The second line of fire directed at Keating is that he was cowed
by a dictator, Indonesian president Suharto. The argument runs in
hindsight, and boils down to whether Keating would have acted, as
Howard did, to free East Timor. Howard has said that Keating
would have done things differently, which is a grave charge. It
presumes that Keating had allowed his thinking to be muddled by
Suharto, and that he would have lacked the ability to break out of
this mindset when Suharto lost power in May 1998. A related theme
here is Howard's rejection of Keating's defence treaty with
Indonesia in December 1995, which was negotiated in secret. When
spruiking that agreement, Keating said: 'We are not going to hock
the entire Indonesian relationship on Timor; that's what the lobby's

got to understand'. Read in isolation, it looks like Keating placed commerce above human rights. In September 1999, Howard said the East Timor crisis showed how Keating's defence pact with Indonesia 'has been demonstrated as an utter irrelevance'. On the first anniversary of East Timor's liberation, Howard said he had 'no doubt that Australia's response to East Timor would have been totally different if Mr Keating … had been running the country a year ago'.

Yet the public record offers an unusual advocate for Keating's side of the story. It happens to be his prosecutor, Howard. In opposition, Howard wanted voters to realise that Keating was not the first prime minister to discover the region. He accused said the need for bipartisanship had been acknowledged 'for many years'.

Two months later, in June 1992, Howard visited Suharto in Jakarta. On his return, he told the readers of *The Sunday Telegraph* 'that no relationship is more important to Australia than that with Indonesia'. Not even the massacre of unarmed civilians by Indonesian troops at the Santa Cruz cemetery in the East Timorese capital in November 1991 seemed to deter Howard. 'Despite the Dili tragedy and cumulative misunderstandings in the past, the relationship between the two countries remains on a very stable footing,' he wrote. Judged by today's standards, Howard had been a co-appeaser with Keating in 1992.

Howard retained the Keating policy towards East Timor on becoming prime minister in 1996. He visited Suharto six months into his first term. 'I told the president that inevitably with a change in government certain things would be different, there would be different nuances,' Howard advised journalists after the meeting. 'But there was an essential continuity in so far as the Australian government was concerned to both the depth and the quality of the relationship.'

Howard raised East Timor with Suharto, just as Keating had before him. But he didn't push it too far. And the proof for this? It was in November 1996, when Clinton visited Australia, that Howard made his most Keatingesque comment on East Timor. 'My government, and governments before mine of both political persuasions have shown a determination not to allow that issue [East Timor] to contaminate or undermine that relationship [with Indonesia],' Howard said. This was no slip of the tongue, because Howard was standing beside Clinton at a joint press conference when he spoke. It wasn't until B.J. Habibie succeeded Suharto two years later that Australia was in a position to change its policy towards East Timor. Whether Keating would have done exactly as Howard did is hard to say. What is clear is that, when faced with the very circumstances that Keating had been confronted with in office, with Suharto in charge, Howard thought East Timor not worth fighting for. That doesn't make Howard any more a lackey of Suharto than Keating had been. It only confirms that both men saw the issue in the same way.

The continuities between Keating and Howard are as important as their conflicts. On economics, they don't pretend to be at odds. But each man, and his respective supporter base, denies the other the common sense to pursue the national interest on the international stage. The Keating fan club sees Howard's approach as Asia-lite; the Howard huggers say their man was merely restoring the natural order by placing the US ahead of Asia.

The subtext of the former is that Howard is a racist. No one ever says it so blatantly, of course. Keating has never called Howard a racist, only an opportunist. But there is no escaping the left's hidden agenda in this debate.

Equally, the anti-Keating argument assumes, with a wink and a nod, that Keating loathes his own race, that he prefers cosmopolitan Australia over white Australia.

An example of the collective wisdom comes from Melbourne writer Andrew Markus in his 2001 book, *Race, John Howard and the Remaking of Australia*:

Seven days after [Pauline] Hanson's maiden speech, the prime minister undertook his first overseas trip [to Indonesia]. Addressing a banquet hosted by President Suharto he stated, in opposition to Keating government policy and in tandem with the Hanson rhetoric, that he did not see Australia as a bridge between Asia and the West. It was necessary to realise that there were fundamental cultural differences between Australia and Asia. Australia would 'yield to nobody' in asserting its 'great qualities and enduring values' of its distinctive culture and traditions. 'We don't claim to be Asian'.

Markus asserts as historical fact that Howard was the first Australian leader to say to Asians on their own turf: 'We don't claim to be Asian'.

Guess which prime minister said the following in a speech in Singapore? 'I have never believed that Australians should describe themselves as Asians or that Australia is or can become part of Asia.' It was Keating, in January 1996.

Howard wasn't claiming an original thought in Jakarta in September 1996. When asked, afterwards, about his comment that 'We don't claim to be Asian', Howard wanted the travelling media to understand that he agreed with Keating. 'I think, in fact, it's a remark that has been made in Asia by my predecessor — I think, in fact, in Singapore,' he said. 'There's nothing new about it.'

Here's another sample of Keating and Howard singing from the same hymn sheet on Asia. In that same January 1996 speech in Singapore, Keating told his audience there were aspects of Asian culture that matched Australian values:

> The values I believe in and most Australians believe in are precisely those that are often referred to in this debate as 'Asian' ... the importance of family, the benefit of education, the need for order and public accountability, the inherent value of work — most Australians would describe these as Australian values. Indeed, the word most Australians would very likely choose to describe as the core Australia value is 'mateship' — and 'mateship' expresses an ethic of communitarianism and mutual obligation, which, in other contexts is called 'Asian'.

The m-words of mateship and mutual obligation are Howard specials. Surely if Keating used them as well, perhaps these two mortal enemies would have more in common than they would want us to believe. But what about the stuff about Australian values being Asian values? Surely Howard wouldn't agree with Keating on this point? Well, yes. A year earlier, in January 1995, Howard said: 'A lot of people who've come here from South-East Asia, their values are my values—small business, the emphasis on family, entrepreneurial risk-taking, the emphasis on education.'

Keating and Howard clashed on ideas that reflected schisms in the broader Australian community. Yet on foreign policy the two men are much closer than they and their respective advocates would allow.

Another way to see this is through their dealings with Australia's prickliest neighbour, Malaysian prime minister Mahathir bin Mohamad.

If Keating was supposed to be so obsequious to Asian leaders, why did his most memorable foreign-policy quote come when he told Mahathir, in effect, to piss off? Mahathir was the only leader to boycott the first APEC meeting in Seattle in November 1993. He suggested his snub was a tactic to get the rest of the world to take Malaysia seriously. 'Sometimes you have to thumb your nose at people before they notice you,' Mahathir said. 'Perhaps that may be a strategy we will follow.' Keating was annoyed, but forgot to bite his lip when the media baited him for a response. He passed up the first two questions, then fell for the third, when asked if he would meet with Mahathir next year.

> Yes, I'll see him in his own right. Malaysia is a country which Australia has interests with and which is a neighbour and I'll see him on these terms. But APEC is bigger than all of us, Australia, the United States, Malaysia, Dr Mahathir and any other recalcitrant.

Opposition leader John Hewson knew whose side he was on. 'Keating's mouth got us into this, Keating's mouth will have to get us out.' Don Watson wrote that Hewson 'for once expressed the public mood perfectly'.

This episode reflects poorly on the coalition, in the same way that Keating's claim that Asian leaders wouldn't deal with Howard was also a blunder. How is the national interest served by one side of Australian politics giving a xenophobe such as Mahathir the excuse to escalate a diplomatic row? Mahathir had form. He was looking to prove himself as Australia's shin-kicker in the region. So eager was the coalition to damage Keating that it was prepared to live with the contradiction of accusing him of being too close to Asia, while demanding that he grovel to Mahathir.

'They broke the rules,' Keating says:

> When you're out of Australia, and your country is negotiating with another country, particularly one that is important, you don't go for cheap points. And the 'recalcitrant' debate with Mahathir was over an issue in principle. I wanted an East Asia body which included the United States and Mahathir didn't, and for that the Liberal Party attacked me. My falling out with Mahathir was over an issue of principle. What did they want me to do, agree with Mahathir so that Australia wasn't in APEC and the US wasn't in APEC? But that's the consequence of what they were saying.

The crisis ran for three weeks, with the Malaysians threatening sanctions if Keating did not apologise. 'In the end I threatened them,' Keating says. Defence minister Robert Ray was in Malaysia for an arms exhibition, and passed on a warning that if Malaysia did impose sanctions, Australia would retaliate:

> I said to Robert, 'You tell them this, I will reimpose exchange controls on Malaysia, instantly'. I mean I'm a deregulationist, but I won't have Australia's position traduced, so I'll impose it on all capital ventures to Malaysia, one. Two, I will withdraw from the five power defence agreement, because we will not, by implication, be defending this country if we are held up to ridicule and

contempt by them. They dropped off within seven days.

Howard used the early phase of his prime ministership to try to mend fences with Mahathir. Howard said Malaysia enjoyed a 'special relationship' with Australia. But Mahathir would prove to be just as stubborn with Howard as he had been with Keating. He attacked, amongst other things, Australia's role in East Timor in 1999.

Here's the scoop. Howard says he sympathised with Keating:

Mahathir was a difficult person to deal with; he had an unreasonable hostility to Australia … If you look back at the comments I made as opposition leader at the time, I don't think you'll find that I was too critical of Keating. I was very careful with what I said because I didn't accept for a moment that he [Mahathir] should be able to blackmail us like that.

The public must share some responsibility for inflaming the 'recalcitrant' debate in 1993. Voters could back Mahathir over Keating because they didn't fear Malaysia. If it had been president Suharto that Keating offended, chances are his poll ratings would have skyrocketed, and no apology would have been sought by the opposition. The electorate didn't care that Howard fell out with Indonesian president Megawati Sukarnoputri in September 2001 over the asylum-seeker issue.

Australians have long harboured a suspicion of Indonesia. The killing of five Australian journalists in Dili during the Indonesian invasion of East Timor in December 1975 was the lightning rod. Keating found the misunderstanding cut both ways. Polling that the Labor government undertook in 1994 showed two-thirds of Indonesians believed the White Australia policy was still in operation. 'On Australia's side, there seemed an equal level of ignorance about modern Indonesian society that was not much altered by decades of package tours to Bali,' Keating wrote in his book *Engagement*.

Both Keating and Howard have largely run ahead of public

opinion on Indonesia. Keating says it is easy to forget the original
context for his relationship with president Suharto:

> It's very hard to think today what life was like a decade ago, but a
> decade ago the Cold War had finished and we had a challenge in
> investing a new foreign policy for Australia, or I had a challenge,
> including one in which the Americans continued to play a role in
> South-East and North Asia. At the end of the Cold War the
> propensity of the Americans was to break off everywhere, to go
> back to economic triumphalism. Clinton won the election on 'it's
> the economy, stupid'. He was eschewing foreign adventures of the
> kind he said George Herbert Bush had been participating in in
> Iraq. Everything was up for grabs at the end of the Cold War.

Keating was looking for a way to keep the US involved in the
region:

> I could only do this with the active support of some of the locals,
> and it turned out that the person who understood this best was the
> president of Indonesia, president Suharto. This is why, in part, I
> made my first visit abroad to Indonesia, and to give Suharto his
> due as we had been advised, every foreign minister and prime
> minister had been advised, that the advent of the new order
> government had brought peace and stability to the region of a kind
> that Australia could only have hoped for in the middle 1960s.

Keating counts the favour Suharto did to Australia in the
billions. 'We got back to spending 2 per cent of GDP on defence
when we more likely would have been spending 6 or 8.' In today's
dollars, that's a difference of about $35–$45 billion:

> I was happy to say, to give Suharto an accolade, most particularly
> because it was true and I think once that was given, once he had
> been given the recognition of his understanding of Australia, he
> was prepared actually and having a strategic view himself of the

world, and knowing that Indonesia was less important to the Americans at the end of the Cold War than before, that he saw the opportunity and the importance of developing a structure. With Suharto, I was able to get Miyazawa of Japan, with him I was able to get the Chinese, and with the three of them I was able to get the new president Clinton.

Suharto fitted in with Keating's big picture, which is why Keating gets tarred with Suharto's demise. This is unfair in one respect because Howard sought to develop the same level of understanding with Suharto's successor, B.J. Habibie, whom he described as a 'friend' and a 'great' and 'strong' leader before they fell out over East Timor.

The irony for both men is that neither could claim to have the ear of the Indonesians when it mattered most. In retirement, Keating met with Suharto to try to talk him into a peaceful handover of power in 1998. But Suharto didn't take the advice. Howard couldn't get Habibie to listen to him a year later at the height of the violence in East Timor.

Australians as Warmongers

POLITICS SOMETIMES MISSES changes in public attitudes if there isn't an argument to immediately capture the feeling. We can say it now, looking back: Australians were becoming more militaristic in their outlook in the early 1990s. But it wasn't apparent at the time when the crowds at Anzac Day began to swell, and the backpacker pilgrimage to Gallipoli went from word-of-mouth to a mass movement, that something more assertive in our character was also stirring. Perhaps it was the absence of action overseas, the end of the Cold War, or the rise of Australian nationalism under Bob Hawke in the 1980s that facilitated the change. Either way, Australians had a new take on war, and it continues to shape our self-image today.

We didn't march as the previous generation had, with medals pinned proudly, or defiantly, or both. We went to the dawn services instead, which transformed Anzac Day from the divisive event it had been in the 1960s and 1970s to a ceremony more in keeping with its original purpose: remembrance. The mood shift was driven by the youth of deregulation, the teens and twenty-somethings who were born after Australia's involvement in Vietnam had ended in 1972, and who took their first job after Paul Keating's recession had ended. Who would have picked it?

Keating largely missed it, because he wasn't prime minister long enough to be forced to make a decision on war that would bring the new mood into full relief. He included World War Two in the commemorative spirit with the Australia Remembers campaign in

1995, to mark the 50th anniversary of the fall of Berlin and the surrender of Tokyo. But Anzac Day had already become too big; it was morphing into the true Australia Day. John Howard would have missed the sentiment also if a few more seats had fallen to Labor at the 1998 GST election. The man most likely to articulate the feeling would have been Kim Beazley, who had been the defence minister in the Hawke years. But 'Bomber Beazley' didn't get the chance because it was Howard who happened to be in charge when the electorate literally demanded Australia go to war with Indonesia in September 1999.

The East Timor crisis clarified two things. Australians don't mind fighting wars that don't directly involve them, provided the cause is just. And they don't like the Indonesian government, despite Keating's efforts to forge a closer relationship with Jakarta in the early 1990s.

Howard received less elite credit than was due to him for the liberation of East Timor because both left and right condemned him for the bloodshed that followed the independence ballot at the end of August 1999. Cultural enemies such as left-leaning *The Sydney Morning Herald* and the ultra-dry Sydney talkshow host Alan Jones found common cause against the prime minister because each wanted Australia to play an even firmer hand. They wanted troops in before the ballot, even if that meant offending Jakarta. Howard took no notice of either side because he had already had this very argument with the Indonesians, and lost it.

On 27 April 1999, four months before the independence ballot was due to be held, Howard met with Suharto's successor, B.J. Habibie, in Bali. They talked privately for 90 minutes. When the question of the conduct of the vote came up, the tone turned frosty:

I asked Habibie whether he would consent to a force going in [to oversee the ballot]. He said 'No'—there was no way he would agree to that. I mean, he went absolutely ballistic when I suggested it. He had General Wiranto and everybody else outside, there was no way they were going to agree to that. That was an absurd proposition that we could somehow or other have sent people in before we had a mandate from the UN, and without the consent of the Indonesians. Hello, we would have been invading our nearest neighbour.

Howard had moved quickly after Suharto stepped down in May 1998, to establish a rapport with the new president. He wrote to Habibie in December 1998 to suggest, as he explained later, 'that the people of East Timor should be given the right to vote about their future'. Howard favoured a period of autonomy before a vote on full independence. But Habibie was governing at the speed of light. In early January 1999, Habibie shocked Howard and the rest of the world when he said that Indonesia wanted to be rid of East Timor within the year:

> I was surprised at his reaction. But it is fair to say in our defence, we had a very lengthy discussion about it and we felt the time had come to urge a change of policy on the Indonesian government, so it was quite deliberate.

At the joint press conference held after their April 1999 meeting, they spoke of the friendship between the two nations. Howard repeated his advice that Jakarta should not rush its disengagement, and that the East Timorese should not seek independence too quickly. 'We believe that from everybody's point of view, that if the people of East Timor, in that free and open process of consultation, were to express support for remaining an autonomous part of the Republic of Indonesia that would be better for them, for the Republic and for the region.'

In one respect, Howard was a prisoner of events. He did not have the ear of Habibie. The day before the ballot, on 29 August, he sought an assurance from the Indonesian president about the safety of Australian observers. He also raised the matter of peacekeepers, but Habibie said he would only consider it in two months' time, after the Indonesian parliament was due to vote to separate from

East Timor. Howard called again on the weekend after the ballot, when it was clear to the rest of the world that pro-Jakarta militias had begun their rampage. Again, the answer from Habibie was not yet. As the killings escalated, Howard made a third call on 6 September. Habibie said he would declare martial law, and if that did not stop the violence, then 'he would consider inviting in a peacekeeping force'.

Howard also did not have Clinton's attention. Privately and publicly he urged the Americans to provide 'boots on the ground' to restore peace. On 7 September, he rang Clinton and said, 'Bill, we need the Yanks in this.'

Howard then asked his former political foe Andrew Peacock, who was by now the ambassador to Washington, to use his contacts in the Clinton administration and in the congress to make Australia's case for intervention. Peacock talked to twelve senators in one day. 'Much of it fell to me,' Peacock confirmed two years later. 'The president was very responsive and accommodating.'

By a stroke of luck, APEC was meeting in Auckland in the midst of the crisis. On 9 September, Howard publicly confirmed his frustration with Clinton. 'I don't think the Americans have yet put as much pressure on as we would like. I would like America to make it very plain internationally that Indonesia should have an international force. I would like the president to be saying that directly, publicly, to the Indonesian government.'

Clinton wrote in his memoirs that when he raised the idea of an Australian-led peacekeeping force with Habibie, 'the Indonesians were opposed to it, but soon they were forced to relent'. Habibie backed down on 12 September, after a week-and-a-half of brinkmanship. When Howard tried to get in touch with him that weekend, the Indonesian president would not return his call.

East Timor seemed easy in hindsight. A multinational force of 7500, led by Australian major general Peter Cosgrove, with Thai major general Songkitti as the deputy force commander, promptly restored order. With this victory, Howard learned the true extent of his leverage in the region. He could stand up to Jakarta, and not destroy the relationship. But Howard says it wasn't so simple at the time:

> Everybody looks back and says now, 'Oh, it all went very well, perhaps it was not as difficult as you might have thought.' But if it had gone badly, if we'd have had a bad encounter militarily and had a lot of people killed in a patrol ambush or something at the beginning, the whole thing could have become very, very controversial and there would have been a lot of criticism.

Keating admits he would have handled things differently. 'I would have first and foremost relied on diplomacy.' He would not have written to Habibie, as Howard had done, and he would have insisted on peacekeepers before the ballot. The three Keating positions appear to be incompatible. There would have been no ballot without the letter, and diplomacy would not have worked because Keating would have been no closer to Habibie than Howard had been. But Keating could argue that he was closer to Clinton so, perhaps, he might have won US backing to get the Australian troops in earlier than Howard had, and saved some lives. But Keating would not have secured direct US involvement with 'boots on the ground', anymore than Howard had managed to, because the Americans had no direct interests on the line in East Timor.

Where Keating is more critical of Howard is in allowing the Indonesians to junk the defence agreement between the two nations that he secured in his final months as prime minister in December 1995. 'Habibie was erratic, and he pulled down something that he could never have put in place. It was only someone with the foresight and the strength of Suharto who could have put it in place,' he tells me. Howard replies that East Timor showed the treaty was 'completely and utterly useless'.

Habibie became to Howard what Suharto had been to Keating, a friend best forgotten. But that did not stop Howard from seeking a new ally in Jakarta because, like Keating, he viewed this as Australia's most important relationship. In October 1999, Howard extended the hand of friendship to Habibie's successor, Abdurrahman Wahid, whom he said was a 'champion of tolerance and decency in public life'. In July 2001, he congratulated Wahid's successor, Megawati Sukarnoputri as a 'champion of democratic ideals'. He was the first western leader to visit her the following month, on 12 August. Neither mentioned the issue that would divide them a fortnight later: asylum-seekers.

Howard sent a double message to the region. He was a friend, yet when he spoke at home he said Australia had proved to be the 'economic strong man of Asia' because it hadn't been touched by the Asian financial crisis in 1997–98. He used the phrase repeatedly in the wake of East Timor and, later, during the brawl over the *Tampa*. Howard was asserting a brand of nationalism that no Australian leader before him had dared. He was saying that we were the toughest nation in South-East Asia.

But Howard's prime ministership was a work in progress. After the first Bali bombing on 12 October 2002, he understood the need to be onside with Indonesia again—as, indeed, Jakarta did in return. When Susilo Bambang Yudhoyono became Indonesia's first directly elected president in October 2004, Howard immediately flew to Jakarta for the inauguration. Their friendship would be sealed two months later with the Boxing Day 2004 tsunami, which claimed almost 300,000 lives in the region. Howard offered $1 billion in aid to Indonesia, and SBY said he was overwhelmed by the generosity.

But relations at the people-to-people level soured again in the new year when a 27-year-old Gold Coast beauty student, Schapelle Corby, was accused of trafficking drugs to Bali. She pleaded her innocence, and many Australians were inclined to believe her alibi that Qantas baggage-handlers were responsible for the marijuana that had been found in her boogie board. But the Indonesian courts found her guilty and sentenced her to 20 years in jail. From one perspective, it was pure soap opera because Corby was a damsel in distress. On another level, her case tapped deep-seated suspicions in Australia about the maturity of the Indonesian legal and political systems. Howard found himself where Keating had been a decade earlier: with a valued ally in Jakarta, but a local electorate still ambivalent about the relationship. Howard urged the nation to calm down, fearing the backlash would get out of hand.

Perhaps if Keating and Howard had avoided the temptation to score cheap domestic points off each other in the mid-1990s, they might have brought the voters along with them. Engagement with the region happened to be a common cause, even though they wanted to pretend otherwise.

CHAPTER EIGHT

The Search for a Contest

THREE INTEREST-RATE RISES were all it took for the governor of the Reserve Bank, Bernie Fraser, to make his friend Paul Keating unelectable. To paraphrase Albert Camus, Fraser delivered 'three sharp knocks at the door of unhappiness' for Keating in August, October, and December 1994. The rate hikes were the first in five years. Their size and their frequency came as a shock, as if some killer virus had been unleashed on the nation that the authorities were helpless to contain. The initial move was worth 0.75 percentage points, then two lots of 1 percentage points each. Fraser explained each round as a pre-emptive strike to ensure that inflation stayed down as the economy picked up. Keating admits now that they ruined his government:

> Bernie was doggedly trying to fight inflation. I knew that 250 basis points was too heavy a response to the spike in the CPI, which came off fresh food and vegetables and a few other things; it certainly did not come off wages. But when that happened, it gave Howard the hook to say, 'Ah, five minutes of sunshine, we had rates up in '89 and we have got them up again in '94'. And I don't think the government recovered from that rate rise.

Keating's mind is ticking as he recalls the dilemma:

I think the 1993 budget was very bad for me politically and the government, and the easy resort to such a high interest-rate change, 250 basis points, by the Reserve Bank in 1994, probably finished the government off. I don't think we recovered from those two things. Now I put so much of my political life into breaking the back of inflation and setting up a new wages structure, and building the Reserve Bank as an institution, I didn't want to have some kind of institutional argument going on with the bank, so I wore it, in the interests of keeping inflation down and letting the bank's gathering standing grow. But it was a very high price for me personally and as prime minister.

But he catches the thought before it sounds too accusing, making it clear that he supported Fraser in the fight against inflation:

Not saying that Bernie did it without my agreement; of course we agreed. The fact about the Reserve Bank is it always overdoes things. It's either too slow up, and then goes too high up, or too slow down. Ian Macfarlane has perhaps broken that habit. When I became treasurer, the Reserve Bank had no standing. It used to fix the exchange rate, it was fixed bureaucratically, with the secretary of the Treasury and the secretary of the Department of Finance. It was a bond-selling agent for the Treasury. Building it into an institution was a big thing, and you had to cede it institutional strength, so I did, and I was not about to change that. But there was an obligation on the part of the bank to manage this gift more propitiously than it did.

John Howard agrees with Keating that the bank went too far:

We'd had a bit of a recovery then the Reserve Bank put up interest rates by 2.75 per cent. It was unbelievable, and the impact of that was enormous. I think it was a mistake, whoever was responsible for it, because the Reserve Bank was not then totally independent. But it was a terrible mistake.

By 1994, Keating had reached a tipping point in public attitudes towards him. There was his promise at the 1990 election that there'd be no recession. There was the assurance that voters could have tax cuts without a GST in 1993. There was the recovery without jobs. All of the above came into play when interest rates moved up again. Voters equated rising interest rates with recession. The Reserve Bank was telling the public to tighten their belts, to ensure that the recovery could last. But no one likes to be told they are living beyond their means when almost one million people are still out of work, and house prices are as flat as an airport runway.

Tumult was in the air in 1994, even before interest rates began to bite. Political meteorites began to flash across the sky, and the media mistook each one for the future. There were whispers that Jeff Kennett would come to Canberra. There was talk, too, that the Liberals might get their first female leader. Senator Bronwyn Bishop had seized the spotlight briefly in 1992 when she shouted at the tax commissioner, Trevor Boucher, during a parliamentary committee hearing. Her profile ballooned after the 1993 election when the pundits began fossicking for contenders to replace John Hewson as opposition leader.

Bishop would be the prototype for the Pauline Hanson phenomenon two years later. She built her support base outside the Canberra press gallery, on talkback radio, in women's magazines, and on television chat shows. For a few months in late 1993 and early 1994, some Liberals seriously considered whether she might, indeed, be the answer. In January 1994, Newspoll said more voters preferred Bishop to lead the opposition than Hewson and Howard combined, 39 per cent versus 21 per cent and 13 per cent respectively. She put herself into contention by switching to the House of Representatives. Then, just as suddenly, she flamed out. In March 1994, at a by-election for the blue-ribbon Liberal seat of Mackellar, in Sydney's northern beaches, Bishop couldn't muster a swing. This gave her many detractors within the Liberal Party the excuse to look elsewhere for a messiah.

In the same month, on the Labor side, Carmen Lawrence, the

former premier of Western Australia, rode a wave of hype to the nation's capital. Unlike Bishop, she achieved a swing at a by-election for Fremantle, the seat vacated by ex-treasurer John Dawkins. She went straight into cabinet, and the expectation was she would be deputy prime minister, Keating's running mate, at the next election. She would prove, instead, to be Labor's political albatross.

The parliamentary gene pool was being stirred by new blood. Tony Abbott arrived on the same day as Bishop's career disappeared in a puff of smoke, as the Liberal member for Warringah, the electorate adjacent to Bishop's Mackellar. Mark Latham entered the zoo a few weeks beforehand, at the end of January 1994, as the Labor member for Gough Whitlam's seat of Werriwa, in Sydney's west. My first recollection of Latham was when he introduced himself at a bar in Canberra. 'I like the stuff you are writing about competition policy,' he said. It was the opening line of an academic.

The craving for a new era, whatever it might be, brought the Liberals to Alexander Downer, who toppled Hewson in May 1994. Downer lasted just eight months as leader. His most memorable quote was a deliberate misquote of his own work. He had released a statement of broad policy and philosophy called *The Things that Matter* on 5 September 1994. Two days later, he killed it, and himself, with the one gaffe. In a speech to promote the document, he thought it would be funny to adapt the title to some of the coalition's policies. Footwear policy should be 'the thongs that matter'; fashion policy, 'the things that flatter'. So far, his only offence was a lack of humour. But then he turned to domestic violence policy, which he said should be 'the things that batter'. He apologised the next day, but it was too late.

In economics, the turning point in a cycle is characterised by the data jumping around like preschoolers on a trampoline. For Keating, 1994 was the last chance to get out of politics with his reputation largely intact, and without the trauma of losing an election. He should have thought seriously about retiring, as he had been advised — perhaps at the end that year, after the free trade agreement was signed at the meeting of the Asia-Pacific Economic

Co-operation forum at Bogor, Indonesia, and before Downer ceded the opposition leadership to Howard in January 1995.

Another window would have been the release of the government's employment white paper in May 1994 while Hewson was still opposition leader. Fifty years earlier, John Curtin's Labor government prepared a white paper for the reconstruction of Australia after the end of World War Two, which was then still a year away. The white paper set the goal of 'full employment' for the peacetime economy, which in practical terms meant two groups of Australians would have to be demobilised. The women who had worked in the factories and hospitals to service the war economy would have to return to the kitchen to make way for the men in uniform who were coming home from battle. Full employment, as Australia understood it in the 1950s and 1960s, was a job for every man who wanted one. Women didn't enter the equation.

Keating's white paper wanted to halve unemployment to 'around 5 per cent by the turn of the century'. The *Working Nation* statement is the least scrutinised of the Keating-era policy documents because the Howard government pulled the plug on many of the training programs it contained. But it announced a new concept, which Howard would expand on in office. Keating called it the job compact. Howard renamed it work-for-the-dole.

Keating explained the job compact as a 'reform which heightens the obligations on both the government and those receiving unemployment benefits'.

'Through the compact, the government will offer a job to those who have been on unemployment benefits for 18 months or more. They, in turn, must take up the offer or they will lose their benefits.' Sound familiar? This was a softer version of *Fightback!*'s proposal to strip the dole from the unemployed after nine months. The difference is that Keating was offering both stick and carrot:

In addition, the government will take steps to identity those at risk of long-term unemployment and give them prompt assistance. Together with those who have been continuously unemployed for

12 months, they will receive individual case management to overcome barriers and be given access to relevant labour market programs. The government envisages that over half a million unemployed people will be individually case managed.

During the Great Depression, the unemployed were enlisted to dig ditches and lay bitumen. The Great Ocean Road, which winds through some of Victoria's postcard water views, was a work-for-the-dole scheme. The media loved drawing the long bow between the 'recession we had to have' and the Great Depression. But they were worlds apart. Unemployment in the late 1920s and throughout the 1930s was a shared experience. The community's sympathies were with those without work. The 1990s, by contrast, generated a public hostility to the jobless. The clue was buried at the back of Keating's *Working Nation*, on page 125. The government had set up a committee to canvass voters' attitudes ahead of the white paper. What it found were the first stirrings of downward envy:

> The public consultations revealed a strong community concern that some unemployed people are making insufficient effort to find employment, whether through reduced motivation resulting from long term unemployment, reduced opportunities during the recession, or a perception that they would be better off on unemployment allowances.

Within a couple of years, this perception would be fixed on the television screen, in the form of the Paxtons. The Nine Network's 'A Current Affair' framed the three siblings as the nation's quintessential bludgers because they had refused jobs at a Queensland tourist resort. (The family had been set up; and the jobs weren't real because the tourist operator soon went broke.)

The dichotomy of what Keating called the 'joyless recovery' was the mismatch between the new jobs being generated and those who had been retrenched. Employers preferred women to men in the recovery, and part-time and casual jobs to full-time positions. In the bust-and-boom past, the pain of the previous recession could be forgotten as soon as employers began rehiring the men they had laid off. But not this time.

The blue-collar male who felt so threatened by Mabo, by multiculturalism, and by the return of mothers to the workforce had two choices during the recession: work for himself, or go on welfare. A report to the government from the Bureau of Industry Economics, released in the same month as the white paper, put the problem this way:

> Cyclical employment losses [should], by definition, be reversed when economic conditions improve. However, because of technological change and ongoing productivity improvements, much of the labour retrenched because of the recession will not in fact be re-employed as demand improves.

Winning elections in this environment would prove to be next to impossible for incumbents of any political hue. Between 1989 and 1995, government would change hands in every state and territory bar the Northern Territory. Then it changed again between 1996 and 2002 in every state with the exception of NSW. Keating would be asking for a sixth term in a little over a year's time, in 1996. He was tempting fate by sticking around.

He was also becoming deeply unpopular. Disentangling the mood of the nation, and its distaste for all things political, from its attitude toward Keating in particular becomes harder with hindsight because of what happened to Howard in office. Each interest-rate rise in 1994 triggered a freefall in Keating's standing with voters. By the end of 1994, the score was 32 per cent satisfied and 59 per cent dissatisfied. What is remarkable about this number is that Howard found himself in precisely the same place in his first term in office. In June 1998, 28 per cent of voters were happy with Howard, while 59 per cent were not. These were hard times to be in the public eye, whether you were prime minister or a member of the Paxton family.

Nevertheless, there was a wilfulness to Keating's behaviour during his final term. The piggery he had purchased a half-share of in 1991, when he thought his bid for the Labor leadership was doomed and he was preparing for life as a private citizen, became exhibit A in the opposition's case that he was out of touch with ordinary Australians. Sure, there was a double standard here. A coalition politician was deemed all the more worthy of public office for his private assets; a Labor politician was not allowed the hint of independent wealth. But Keating couldn't win the argument by saying he was no different to the other side. The political imagery of the piggery investment was appalling. Keating couldn't be a prime minister and a businessman at the same time, especially in times of stubbornly high unemployment. Later, the Howard government hoped to find evidence of impropriety against Keating, but an investigation by the then attorney-general Daryl Williams in 1999 gave Keating a clean bill of health.

One of Keating's biggest handicaps was his moodiness. He no longer felt he needed to explain himself to the Canberra press gallery, which was an unusual call to make because no politician can choose to cut off the oxygen of media publicity without affecting his or her health. Keating wanted to punish the press gallery for writing him off at the 1993 election. Looking back, Keating admits he might have gone too far:

> I was very disappointed in the press gallery. You see, when I became treasurer, the press gallery only wrote about tax cuts, election speculation, and leadership changes. When I finished they'd talk about the current account deficit, inflation, monetary policy, you name it, everything was on. This was because I had to do those long, weekly press conferences for 30 or 40 minutes, or an hour and what have you.

Keating was peeved that John Hewson had decided not to appear at the traditional National Press Club address in the final week of the 1993 campaign, and that journalists had applauded him for taking this step. It seems a trivial reason for giving the press gallery the cold shoulder after the election. But that's the way Keating operates sometimes:

This told me something [the media's response to Hewson] that there wasn't much point in doing what I'd been doing before, and that is holding these long press conferences to convince the gallery who thought I was better off not being accountable at all. So I decided to give that away.

Question: Was that a mistake in hindsight?

Keating: Probably.

Question: Because you've got to keep communicating?

Keating: Well, I kept communicating, but I just did it in different ways. Probably it was, but then again the willing-on of the coalition with its Thatcherite program by senior press gallery people was pretty squalid really, and frankly I thought I'd been too good to them.

Question: So it was a falling out?

Keating: Yes, I thought I'd been too good to them. The Canberra press gallery bit the hand that educated them. They required accountability from me, but required no such accountability from the opposition. Howard was able to go to the 1996 election with no policy scrutiny. Fundamentally, the gallery reverted to being a bunch of worthless old tarts in search of a contest, with one or two notable exceptions.

There was also the decision to cut back his appearances in parliament. A roster system was introduced in 1994 to give Keating every second day off from question time. There was a sense of fatigue about the decision. It was not that he wanted to work less, but there were some tasks he had grown tired of:

Tony Blair does one question time a week, and he does it for 30 minutes on notice. I was doing four a week, for an hour without notice, and a lot of it was essentially abuse. The Labor speakers wouldn't take the coalition on, really, so I was carrying 80 per cent of the questions, dealing with the other side. The thing was so disruptive of the parliamentary day, the moment it was on, of course, you know you'd be on the question time brief at some earlier point in the day. Until it was well and truly over you could never get back to cabinet work. We'd gone into this sort of overdrive day, which was the four-day-a-week question time period, and it becomes sport in a sense, and I was carrying most of the burden and in some substantial measure the coalition were trying to make me the topic. So if I was there less, I was less the topic.

But he bristles at the idea that he was lazy:

How can any prime minister be part-time, particularly with my record of change? What happened is the gallery got tired of the government, that's what happened. The government wasn't tired at all; the government had done more things in 1993, 1994 and 1995 than its whole 13 years in office, but the press gallery had gotten tired; it had gotten tired of the government, amongst other things, and it wanted a contest and new people, and in a way I sort of understand that.

And yet Keating saw off two opposition leaders in 1994 — the only prime minister to claim two scalps within a year. Howard went close when Labor's Simon Crean and then Mark Latham imploded in December 2003 and January 2005 respectively.

In 1994, the fear on the Liberal side of politics was that one more election loss would spell the end of the centre-right party, with its centre and its right, the wets and the dries, splintering into two competing entities. In a two-horse race, it's easy for the one that comes second to have the odd nightmare about the knackery. The possibility of destroying the Liberals certainly motivated Keating to stay on. But his moment had passed when Howard replaced Downer in January 1995. Ten years and four federal election losses later, it would be Labor's turn at the wheel of self-flagellation.

When Keating addressed the Labor Party's 40th national conference in September 1994, he still sounded like, and was treated as, the most brilliant politician of his generation. Keating said Labor was 'stronger than ever before' and could now start planning for the 21st century. This was the meeting that was supposed to turn the Labor men into SNAGs, as they pledged to have women standing in 35 per cent of all winnable seats by 2002. They never got there.

It was also a conference that reeked of complacency. Keating seemed to be defining the national interest by the vested interests that had helped him defeat John Hewson's *Fightback!* in 1993. He replaced Hewson's checklist of winners and losers with one of his own:

> What won the last election for Labor? The things we stood for won it for us. The social policies, Medicare, the rights of Aboriginal Australians, the rights of women, the central place of the arts, the republic. We won it with our vision of Australia.

National identity, like beauty, is in the eye of the beholder. Keating's support for Aborigines, women, and artists grated with traditional Labor voters because they assumed he thought they weren't good enough for new Australia. It might not have mattered in a strong economy because the blue-collar male could always console himself with capital gain. But not now. Keating was aiming to heighten Australia's sense of self when household wealth seemed to have stalled.

Howard Mark II would prove in a little over a year that a majority of voters could be turned off Keating's causes. Howard did this by telling the blue-collar male that Keating had neglected them. Keating saw the challenge coming in a policy sense, which is where the white paper came in. But he could never bring himself to soften his presentation, to strip away the layers of his personality that turned off traditional Labor supporters. This would be the ultimate contradiction of Keating's four years and three months in the

Lodge. He had consciously switched the storyline from economic to social policy and then on to national identity. His agenda served as the perfect foil to *Fightback!*, and it helped to snatch an amazing election win from the jaws of recession. Yet Keating's non-economic persona also became a symbol of his disconnection. He was trying to motivate the nation to think about the three Rs of reconciliation, republic, and a closer engagement with the region when its mind's eye was still fixed on the kitchen table. The public believed he was talking down to them. They wanted what he couldn't promise: a return to the imagined comfort zone of the 1950s and 1960s, when Australia last enjoyed full employment. Keating's 5 per cent unemployment target would be achieved, belatedly, in June 2005, five years later than scheduled, and nine years after the electorate had sacked him. The economy was then preparing to enter its 15th year of growth, which is something that the so-called golden era never went close to achieving. But this was Howard's Australia, not his.

Keating wasn't suited to the times, even as he was shaping them. But given the choice between changing Australia and managing it, he always erred on the side of reform:

If you are in the sort of the poll-driven, focus-group business, which I'm sure the current prime minister is, and you are not into changing the place for the better, I don't regard mean-spirited workplace reforms as being change; they're just pieces of ideological bitchiness. But if you are truly into the genuine, big, big changes for the better, then they are by their essence often the antithesis of popularity — just as the remaking of the labour market was, just as the remaking of the product market was, just as native title was. And is politics about those kind of things, or is it simply a sort of survival art form where you do the tricky-poo changes your party tells you, 'Look we've done our focus groups this week, you better not talk about this, you better not talk about that, you better say this and you better say that'? Well, I couldn't put up with one minute of that, you know.

The Long Decade

PROGRESS THEN REGRESS. Mandawuy Yunupingu knows the riff. He was the leader of the band Yothu Yindi, whose single 'Treaty' is the closest thing to a modern national anthem. In March 1992, the staff at the Catani Bar in Melbourne's inner-bayside suburb of St Kilda decided that 'A-list' meant no Aboriginal Australians allowed. Mandawuy was told he couldn't drink there. The bad press bounced around the globe. Mandawuy had just been named Australian of the Year.

Three years later, on Anzac Day, an on-field scuffle between two of Melbourne's most famous Australian Rules football clubs, Collingwood and Essendon, sprang into legend when Magpie ruckman Damien Monkhurst said to the Bomber midfielder Michael Long, 'Get off me, you little black cunt.'

Long seethed for a couple of days after the clash, then spoke up. He named Monkhurst, but sanitised the offending remark somewhat by telling the media he had been called a 'black bastard'. A national debate erupted.

Australians arguably waste more intellectual energy on sport that any other people. The simplest way to get an A-list author or thinker to pen an article for a newspaper is to ask them to muse on their football team or their favourite cricketer. When the Sydney Swans made their first AFL grand final in 1996, the go-to columnist was playwrite David Williamson, the former Magpie supporter who had converted to the red and the white when he moved from

Melbourne to the harbour city. Williamson wrote again about the Swans in their glory year, 2005, for *The Sydney Morning Herald*, this time from his home on Queensland's sunshine coast. In January 2004, Don Watson led *The Age's* opinion page with a piece about Steve Waugh's retirement from test cricket, titled 'Why we loved the other PM'.

In the Howard era, every other winner of the Australian of the Year was a sportsperson: Waugh in 2004, Patrick Rafter in 2002, Mark Taylor in 1999, and Cathy Freeman in 1998. Better cricketers, a tennis player and a runner, perhaps, than the 1978 recipient, Alan Bond.

Immigrants can measure their inclusion in the mainstream of the Australian community by their absence from the public space occupied by footy heroes. The Greeks, the Italians, the Chinese, and the Vietnamese are over-represented in the professions, and under-represented in Aussie Rules and in the rugby codes, league and union. By contrast, the over-achievers in indigenous communities are wearing football jumpers, not business suits. Between 1992 and 2005, Australian Aboriginals claimed the Norm Smith medal for best player in the AFL grand final, on average, once every three years: Peter Matera from the West Coast Eagles in 1992; Michael Long in 1993; the Adelaide Crow's Andrew McLeod in 1997 and 1998; and Port Adelaide's Byron Picket in 2004. But football is the default ticket to prosperity. It conceals disadvantage at the same time as it gives white Australia a reason to cheer black Australia. At the 2001 census, there were almost twice as many Australian Aboriginal men in prison as there were at universities or other tertiary institutions.

Initially, Long divided people between those who supported his stand and those who saw him as a snitch. The AFL Players' Association issued a joint statement with independent federal MP Phil Cleary that read like it was typed on eggshells:

There's nothing wrong with sledging and we're not saying that a player who makes a remark with racist overtones is necessarily racist. However, it is our view that society's expectations have changed and that Aboriginal players such as Michael Long and Nicky Winmar have every right to expect 'white fella footballers' like the rest of Australia, post-Mabo, to be committed to the reconciliation process.

Former Collingwood premiership captain Tony Shaw disagreed, arguing that Monkhurst was the real victim. 'There are unwritten laws in football and I don't think they [Essendon] are going about things in the right way. I just hope Michael knows what he is doing,' Shaw said. Former Geelong Cats player and human headline Sam Newman wrote in the Melbourne broadsheet, *The Age* that 'Michael Long IS black. To add the word "bastard" would be extremely aggravating but probably designed to do no more than distract him from the job at hand.' Finally, Carlton supporter and cultural warrior B.A. Santamaria weighed in with a column attacking racial vilification laws as 'tripe'. He asked: 'If Michael Long had had an Italian name and Monkhurst had called him a "wog", would we have had the columns of hypocritical breast-beating which has been served up because Michael Long, one of the most brilliant, effervescent and effective players in the AFL, is an Aborigine?'. Monkhurst would put his side of the incident in perspective two years later. 'I mucked up and I accept that,' he said. 'It was a heat-of-the-moment thing. Longy was trying to squeeze a free kick out of me and I reacted badly to it.'

Long mattered to the decade. He transcended the oval-ball game, because he challenged the cop-it-sweet hypocrisy of old Australia that what was said on the playing field stayed there. He changed community attitudes in a way that leaders could never hope to, because politicians in a two-party democracy will always have at least half the population barracking for their rival. To its enduring credit, the AFL backed Long, though it did take two weeks and two attempts before he received a satisfactory apology from Monkhurst. The AFL made racial abuse a reportable offence under a new players' code of conduct.

But from another vantage point, the Long case confirmed the AFL, and the football public, as slow learners. Something similar had already occurred two years earlier, at the same stage in the 1993 season. The St Kilda Saints were playing Collingwood in an emotional game at the latter's suburban home ground, Victoria Park. St Kilda's Nicky Winmar had been taunted all day by the Magpie faithful. When the final siren sounded and the Saints had won, he pulled up his jumper, jabbed at his chest, and said, 'I'm black and I'm proud of it'.

The Collingwood club president, Allan McAlister, put his foot in his mouth a week later. 'As long as they [Australian Aboriginals] conduct themselves like white people off the field, well, everyone will admire and respect them,' McAlister said. He apologised and led Collingwood to a goodwill tour of indigenous communities in February 1994, with Magpie membership ticket-holder Paul Keating in tow.

The prime minister knew whose side he was on at that game. 'Nicky Winmar's gesture of defiance at Collingwood is destined to be legendary; in my view it was a great gesture,' he said. 'Think of what one gesture of defiance triggered: a national debate on racism in sport and a new recognition of the role Aboriginals play in Australian sport ... I truly believe the game has changed between black and white Australia.'

It hadn't changed enough yet for Cathy Freeman. The same year, she draped herself in the Australian and Aboriginal flags as she celebrated her gold-medal run at the 1994 Commonwealth Games. She earned scorn from Liberal MP Bill Taylor, who told parliament: 'I have to say I was somewhat disappointed because, as she ran across the track and accepted the accolades of the crowd, she was rather reluctant to show the Australian national flag. Instead, she seemed to be preoccupied with the Aboriginal flag.'

Australians will intuitively tolerate white male sporting rogues. Our abusive US Open and Wimbledon tennis champ Lleyton Hewitt is okay because he is a winner. And Shane Warne can be forgiven his conviction for drug cheating, and the sleazy text messages he sent to women other than his wife, because no one spins a cricket ball like Warney. Of course, it is just sport, and an argument can be made that we shouldn't care about the private person inside the athlete, or their political views. But enough Australians felt uncomfortable with Freeman because of the colour of her skin, and the flag she flew in 1994, for a politician to think he could attack her identity. The nation had grown up, belatedly, by the 2000 Olympics when she was allowed to celebrate her gold medal with both flags.

There are layers to Long's celebrity that would have stretched the imagination of a soap-opera scriptwriter. Five years on, in April 2000, Howard's government said that 'there was never a generation of stolen children' because only 10 per cent had been affected by the practice of removing half-castes from their families. Long took it personally. He wrote a short letter to *The Age* newspaper in which he called the prime minister a 'cold-hearted prick'. He described the 'trauma and abuse' of his late mother:

> My mother was taken when she was a baby, taken to Darwin and put on a boat—she had never seen the sea before—screaming and yelling, not knowing what was happening and then crying herself to sleep. I am so angry anyone could do this to a child just because their skin was a different colour.

Long closed by asking Howard to walk in his shoes:

> I am part of the stolen generation. It's like dropping a rock in a pool of water. It has a rippling effect, so don't tell me it affects only 10 per cent. No amount of money can replace what your government has done to my family.

Just before Christmas 2004, Long set out to march from Melbourne to Canberra as a protest and a plea. He wanted to meet with Howard to talk about reconciliation. The prime minister agreed and sent word back to Long, who ended his trek just before the NSW border. It was a measure of how far both men had come.

IT IS A mere fluke of the calendar, of course, but when Long stood up to Monkhurst, a player almost 30cm taller, he echoed a pivotal moment in Steve Waugh's highlights reel. On 22 April 1995, three days before the Anzac Day battle between Essendon and Collingwood, Waugh was batting on an unplayable Trinidad pitch. West Indian speed machine Curtly Ambrose was glaring at Waugh.

Ceding about the same height disadvantage as Long did to Monkhurst, Waugh told Ambrose: 'You just bowl.'

'Are you talking to me? Don't talk to me like that,' Ambrose hissed back.

He then approached Waugh, as if to challenge him to a duel. They locked eyes for another 15 seconds or so before the West Indian captain, Richie Richardson, pulled Ambrose away. As Waugh prepared to face the next delivery, he pointed to his helmet, as if daring Ambrose to brand it with the cherry-red of the new ball. At least that's how the media recorded the confrontation at the time.

What Waugh actually said, as he revealed in his autobiography in 2005, was far less heroic. 'What the fuck are you looking at?' and 'Why don't you go and get fucked' were the sledges which helped turn the Australian cricket team from easy beats to world champions. Australia lost that test but won the next, with Waugh making a double-century.

The six turning-points in the Waugh story, covering his rise, fall, rise, and retirement, mark off the years for the boom, recession, and recovery of the Keating–Howard economy.

The first round of deregulation covers the period from Waugh's mullet-haired test debut in 1985 to the false boom of his maiden century in 1989. The form slump in 1990 and his axing from the Australian team in 1991 span the 'recession we had to have'. The Bradmanesque series in the West Indies in 1995, and the first time his batting average crossed 50 in 1996, secured the recovery and the handover from Keating to Howard. Finally, the late-career surge in 2003, with a boundary off the last ball of the day to claim his 30th century, and the right to retire a winner the following year, matched the second wind of the recovery thanks to the boom in China, and

Howard's second political honeymoon. But this period also hinted at a selfishness as both men seemed to chase records for their own sake.

Waugh crept up on the nation. Each century he chiselled out from the world's best bowling attacks, and its worst, added to the increment of his legend. His eighth ton, the 200 against the West Indies in 1995, helped Australia claim its first series victory in the Caribbean in a generation. As captain, he would win more than 70 per cent of the Tests. Yet Waugh always seemed to flirt with oblivion; it was one of the traits that made his career so compelling to watch.

Waugh dealt with each reverse by reassessing his game. His most symbolic adjustment was to curb his natural instinct to play the hook shot. The attacking batsman who was prone to throwing away his wicket in his youth was remade as a pragmatic, run-making machine in his thirties. Howard Mark II took even fewer risks than the new Waugh. Howard, like Waugh, became the last man standing, not out at the end of each innings. He grafted his wins, settled his scores, and became more admired the longer he hung around.

CHAPTER NINE

More Bypasses than Lazarus

BY THE MID-1990s, John Howard had been written off more times than Kenny, the kid who gets killed in each episode of the cult cartoon series 'South Park'. The only comfort he had felt when he lost the Liberal leadership in May 1989 was that Australia had begun to turn his way. 'The irony of that time was it was just about the time the more conservative social agenda was starting to bite in the community,' he says. 'You may remember *Future Directions*? People ridiculed it at the time; the hard-heads in the Labor Party didn't. They were worried about it.'

For Howard, the frustration of the 1980s was driven by personality as well as policy. He wasn't a very popular figure on his own side. He may have been the best politician the Liberals had, as many on the Labor side conceded privately at the time; but Howard had, by his own admission, very few friends:

> The problem for me had been that I'd become leader by accident and had been deposed by ambush, and that neither event was good for the party. The party hadn't really intended to elect me as leader in 1985. What it wanted in 1985 was for me to remain as deputy leader and Peacock to remain as leader — that was the will of the party.

As opposition leader the first time around, he never had the luxury of a united team behind him. Peacock didn't respect him enough to give him that. But Howard had been no victim. He did the same to Peacock. In fact, Howard cast one of the first stones, not that it matters now. Peacock succeeded Malcolm Fraser after the 1983 election, and had an honourable loss to Bob Hawke at the early election of 1984. But Howard was spoiling for a fight. The day after Peacock fell short, Howard received a call from newspaper journalist Peter Rees, but he misheard his name. He thought Peter Rees was Peter Reith, who had just been elected as the Liberal member for the Victorian bayside seat of Flinders. 'Peacock has had his chance,' Howard said. 'We don't really know what he stands for … I don't think Andrew is ever going to be prime minister.' Howard didn't realise his error until a perplexed Rees rang back to check if he could use what he had been told. Howard was mortified. Rees agreed not to write the story until after Howard became leader in September 1985.

Howard had not meant to challenge Peacock when he did because he thought he did not have the numbers. But the two of them were not getting on, and the media was building Howard up as an alternative. Peacock tried to settle the issue by calling a ballot for the deputy leadership, hoping to bump off his antagonist. Howard thought he would lose but, when he prevailed, Peacock spat the dummy and sacked himself. With the benefit of hindsight, Howard concedes that he should have rejected the leadership. 'If we'd both been sensible we would have gone away and said, "Well, this is bloody ridiculous, the party has re-elected me. Andrew, you've got to put up with that, but I don't, you know, want [the leadership]".'

He clarifies that this was not his mindset at the time. 'I'm not saying that because I'm trying to sound wise.' The leadership opportunity presented itself and he grabbed it, unaware that it would poison his side of politics for the next nine years. The Howard who was deposed in May 1989 was so unpopular that two senior members of the press gallery hugged each other when they learned that Peacock had pulled together the numbers for a successful challenge. Howard gave his best performance in defeat.

Asked if he would have another crack at the leadership, he guffawed, 'Break it down. That's Lazarus with a triple bypass.' The Peacock forces did their best to soil their success by going on the ABC's 'Four Corners' program to reveal the inner machinations of their plot. By humiliating Howard, they gave him the licence to be bitter. When one of his factional rivals, Ian Macphee, was defeated in a pre-selection battle a few weeks later, I telephoned Howard at home for a comment. He chuckled, long and hard. I asked if I could report laughter as his response, and he said, 'Yes'.

There was an unintended prophecy in Lazarus with a triple bypass. On three occasions in the early 1990s, Howard would put his hand up to reclaim the Liberal leadership and be rebuffed each time. Twice he was told not to bother, in 1990 and 1994, because the party was keen to move on to the next generation. After the 1990 election defeat, he was certain the chance would not come again. 'I really accepted then that my future in politics lay in being industrial relations minister in a government that Hewson led.' Many politicians who see their ambition thwarted become disillusioned. Some cash in their chips on a junket. Others are placated with a sinecure. Hawke gave the Labor leader he deposed, Bill Hayden, the foreign affairs job, then made him governor-general. Howard as prime minister would give Peacock the ambassadorship to Washington.

Where Howard differed in exile was that he still wanted to slog it out on ideas, even if it was from the second tier. 'If you make a contribution in the past and you want to make a contribution in the future, you have to attach yourself to a policy, and I had hurled myself into industrial relations.' Keating was still watching his rival, but part of him couldn't compute why Howard would stick around when he didn't have the leadership to look forward to. It wasn't until Hewson lost the unlosable election in 1993 that Howard could see his fortunes improving:

> I decided to run after the '93 election because a number of people
> suggested I run who hadn't previously supported me, but on top of

that it just seemed to me absurd that John should still run because, I mean the bloke had said, 'I'll give it my best shot, if they don't like the full monty, I'll give it away'. No one really thought after Hewson defeated me in '93 that that resolved the leadership issue, and the debate went on and on and on and on.

Hewson won the ballot against Howard by 47 votes to 30. The feral abacus couldn't beat Keating in a recession, but he was more popular in the Liberal Party than Howard. The margin of 17 was identical to that of 1989, when Peacock had defeated Howard by 44 to 27. *Herald Sun* journalist Tony O'Leary, who would later become Prime Minister Howard's press secretary, wrote that defeat to Hewson was the final straw: 'Mr Howard made no apologies for making another bid for the top job, and did not rule out running again, although yesterday was probably his last chance to regain the post.'

Hindsight says this was a lucky break for Howard. If he had taken the leadership immediately after the election, it is unlikely that he would have held the party together for a full term. When the time came to knife Hewson in May 1994, Howard hit the phones again, but Peacock was backing the younger duo of Alexander Downer and Peter Costello. 'I talked to people, but there was no support,' Howard says. 'People were quite taken by the idea of it being the "dream team", the new generation. There were still elements in the party that just weren't prepared to go back to me and I accepted that. I think it's fair to say that I thought that was definitely it.'

That weekend, as the rivals Hewson and Downer were counting and recounting the numbers, there was a function in Howard's electorate to mark his 20th anniversary in parliament. It was a melancholy moment, a wake almost. Howard did not feel like celebrating because, he figured, this was the end of his ambition to become prime minister.

Costello had told Howard 'that he couldn't run and he couldn't win'. He placed their conversation on the public record for the ABC's television series 'The Liberals':

'I think there was a certain sadness. Yes, because I think John Howard has always wanted to be the leader and the prime minister. He's always had a claim on it. Circumstances conspired against his one opportunity [in 1987] and I think [1994] was the ruling-off of a long-time ambition.'

It wasn't clear at the time, but Hewson's narrow defeat to Downer marked the point when the political gods really smiled upon Howard. The Liberals were irretrievably split by the ballot, and Downer was out of his depth as leader. There would be virtually no honeymoon, which meant Howard had a chance after all. Howard decided after Hewson beat him in 1993 that he did not want to face another ballot. 'I made up my mind that the only circumstance in which I might ever come back to the leadership would be if the party, in effect, drafted me.' His colleagues thought he was dreaming. 'I used to talk to people occasionally about that, and they'd say, "Oh, you never get drafted, that's ridiculous, no such thing ever happens." And I said, "Well, Hawke did." It can happen, and it did.'

BEFORE HOWARD could reclaim the Liberal leadership, he had to beat up on his former self. To prove he had changed, he had to repudiate the politician he had been in the 1980s. The question was whether he had the self-awareness and the smarts to pin-point an aspect of his past that he could ditch without submerging his identity.

Labor seemed more adept at the makeover business than the Liberals. Hawke swore off the womanising and the boozing to shaft Hayden on his own side and then Malcolm Fraser a few weeks later at the 1983 election. A decade on, Keating managed to eschew economic rationalism long enough to slay Hawke in the caucus room and then Hewson at the ballot box. But between these two textbook examples there was the painful memory of Peacock, who seemed less credible the second time around. Keating had Peacock pegged on the day he ousted Howard. 'Can a soufflé rise twice?' Keating had asked.

For Howard, there were two pieces of baggage to shed. He had been an avowed enemy of Medicare, and he had spoken out against Asian immigration in 1988. Medicare was a no-brainer, because it had helped Keating win in 1993:

> We had to modify our position on Medicare. I did do that quite deliberately. And I think we have demonstrated since that it was a genuine change. I mean, I was against Medicare years ago, and all of those quotes that are rolled out against me then are perfectly true; I did say those things. But I came to a conclusion after the '93 election that the public liked Medicare; the public were too welded on to Medicare.

Embracing Medicare could wait, though. Howard's opening act of contrition would be on Asian immigration, which might seem surprising because the nation was on the cusp of one its nastiest bouts of xenophobia. But Howard never sought an anti-Asian immigration mandate. He wouldn't have been able to carry his own electorate of Bennelong if he had dared.

Howard placed the apology where everyone in the political class would see it, on the front page of *The Weekend Australian* on 7 January 1995. 'I was wrong on Asians, says Howard.' The headline matched the text, because it was a direct quote. 'I was wrong. The remarks were clumsy,' he said.

This was Howard presenting himself to his colleagues, and to the punters, as a multicultural man: 'I'm sorry that my remarks were seen by people, Australians, if they were seen by Australians of Asian descent as suggesting that I regarded them in any way as lesser Australians than any other Australians, then I regret that very much.'

Howard described himself as a 'tolerant conservative' who wanted Australia to become 'comfortable and relaxed'. The phrase would bob up in another context during the election campaign a year later, when he seemed to be telling voters they could pull back their Jason recliner chairs, put their feet up, and pretend it was the 1950s again. On this occasion, he was talking about how he and

Keating were really on the same page on foreign policy. 'What I want is for us to feel comfortable and relaxed about, and to derive great benefit from, our engagement with the Asia-Pacific but still to value our cultural and other links with other parts of the world.'

Downer gave up the Liberal leadership three weeks later, on Australia Day 1995, ending eight months of misery for himself and the party. Howard did not gloat. He issued a short statement, but waited until the party room had formally voted for him, unopposed, before speaking publicly. The first press conference of Howard Mark II saw him jettison much of his 1980s ideology:

> Over the last weekend, I've read acres of advice about how I should change, how I have changed, how I haven't changed enough, and even from some lamenting the fact that I haven't changed at all. Can I just say to you that anybody who's been in politics for as long as the prime minister and I have, and we've both been in politics roughly the same period of time, have made our share of mistakes and carry our baggage.

Gone were the harshest elements of his industrial-relations policy *Jobsback*; and gone, too, it seemed, was the monarchy. Howard suggested he would facilitate a republic if that was what people wanted. 'I remain a supporter of our present constitution, but I recognise that that's not the view that everybody in the Australian community holds and there is an emerging debate on that issue.'

But there were some things, he said, he wouldn't modify:

> I have always believed in an Australia built on reward for individual effort with a special place of honour for small business as the engine room of our economy. I've always believed in a safety net for those amongst us who don't make it. I've always believed in the family as the stabilising and cohering unit of our society. And, I believe very passionately in an Australia drawn from the four corners of the earth, but united together behind a common set of Australian values.

In short, he was an economic realist, a social conservative, and a multiculturalist.

The following day, Howard Mark II was asked if he planned to be a touch more pragmatic than the last time, 'maybe win first and decide policy later?' The answer would set a standard he could not keep in his first term.

'I'm going to be pragmatic but I'm not going to be dishonest. I'm not going to say one thing and do the exact opposite when I get in. I'm not going to, as the prime minister did, promise lower tax in the election campaign but deliver higher tax when he got in.' Famous first words.

The press gallery didn't really know Howard in 1995. They remembered him by his 1980s persona, the white-picket fence of *Future Directions*, and the attempt to invent a new word, 'incentivation', which was supposed to galvanise the nation but made it giggle instead. Many journalists had written him off as a relic, and hadn't bothered to seek him out for an insight into the day's events or to gather clues as to when he thought his next chance might come. Howard brought some of the misunderstanding on himself because he was a difficult person to get to know. There was an age gap he couldn't disguise.

In his wilderness years, between 1989 and 1994, he would turn up regularly at press gallery functions. He would be one of the last to leave. Howard liked a drink, but he never let his guard down. I have heard him swear just once in private. Keating never got drunk, but he would punctuate his private conversation with f-bombs. It was colourful, often coarse, but almost always amusing.

Howard fancied himself as a political commentator. He would have been a journalist if he wasn't in parliament. But where power dulled Keating's ability to hear the electorate, the absence of power for Howard would give him a hyper-awareness of what people thought about him, about themselves, and about their nation. He learned to conceal the bits of his political character that the public didn't like. Not his image, because what Labor thought a weakness was, in fact, a strength. Honest John was meant as a putdown. But there was a large proportion of the community that related to Honest John. They liked his conservative social values, his doggedness, and his lack of pretension.

The noose which Howard had fashioned for his first term as prime minister, and indeed his second, was tax. Howard made a mistake on 1 May 1995 by saying more than he needed to on the GST. He told a business luncheon that the 1993 election had been a referendum on the GST. 'There's no way that we can have it as part of our policy at the next election.' This was ambiguous, of course, because it left dangling the question of the second term, but it was no different to what he had been saying since resuming the opposition leadership three months earlier. It was the next sentence that begged to be turned into page-one news:

> As to what happens some years in the future, I don't want to, you know, I don't know. But the electorate said 'No'. And in a democracy you've got to take note of that. And what happens in the future, I don't know.

Robert Garran, *The Australian's* economic correspondent, wrote that Howard had left open the possibility of a GST in the future. It was a carefully worded article, saying no more or no less than Howard had.

Howard sensed trouble, so he shot the messenger. He fired off a four-line press release to rebut Garran's article:

> Suggestions in today's *Australian* that I have left open the possibility of a GST are completely wrong. A GST or anything resembling it is no longer coalition policy. Nor will it be policy at any time in the future. It is completely off the political agenda in Australia.

He faced the cameras that afternoon, and elevated his denial into one of his most memorable phrases:

Journalist: So you've left open the door for a GST now, haven't you?
Howard: No, there's no way that a GST will ever be part of our policy.
Journalist: Never ever?
Howard: Never ever. It's dead. It was killed by the voters in the last election.

Yet a decade on, when Keating runs off the checklist of policies he says that Howard pursued in office, in breach of the undertakings he gave to voters in 1996, the GST barely rates a mention. What annoys Keating is that Howard claimed to be someone else on Medicare and on industrial relations. Howard said he supported bulk billing, and that any changes to industrial relations would be incremental. No family would be worse off on health care; no worker would be worse off when they negotiated with their employer. To Keating, these were the bigger sins. The GST was a lower-order issue. Keating had argued for a GST in 1985, and one always sensed that an element of his campaign against it in 1993 was just politics. If he were given a clean sheet of paper and told to design a tax system from scratch, I suspect there'd be a GST in there somewhere.

They only got it in '96 by pretending they were us, right. And I made this point in the [concession] speech on [election] night, they had to say they were us to get away with it. In other words, they couldn't win on their Thatcherite policy — the community wouldn't take it. They tried various versions of it, in '84, '87, '90 and '93, and every time they came the gutser, so finally they said the only way to win this is to trick our way into power, say we're them.

Keating blames the media, not the voters, for giving Howard Mark II an easy ride:

If someone is opposed for 20 years to the principles of Medicare, who said in 1987 he'd tear it up, who has opposed every national wage increase and wants to go to a dog-eat-dog IR system, who then says within six months of becoming leader of the opposition he believes in none of this any more, is he believable? When John Howard says, 'I'm not John Howard, I'm a hedgehog', is he John Howard or is he a hedgehog? The Canberra press gallery says, 'No, no, he's told us he's not John Howard, he's a hedgehog'. So he's a hedgehog. The fact is, Howard never changed, he was always the same suburban reactionary, and he's been there long enough to see a large part of his suburban, reactionary agenda into place.

What made Howard believable to voters in the mid-1990s, when he hadn't been in the 1980s, were his social policies. His conservative agenda helped to create the impression that he was, in fact, offering to undo some of Keating's economic agenda because they talked about restoring old Australian values. Howard twigged to something that Bill Clinton understood early on in his presidency, that voters in the 1990s preferred to be told small stories. Bite-sized gestures were easier to digest than the big picture. Did you facilitate APEC or give handouts to families with young children? Obviously, governments could do both. But long-term governments err on the side of the grand program; long-term prime ministers think in terms of their legacy. The 1996 election would be a mismatch. The electorate had stopping listening to Keating and was willing to forgive Howard the odd weasel word on the way through because, of the two politicians, he had the humility they craved. They wanted Howard to be tough, to stand up to the bully Keating, but they also wanted him to bend to their will, which Keating had stopped doing.

Howard explains that his small-target strategy was more a strategic retreat than disappearing act. 'There was a limit to how small I could make myself as a target because I had some very-well defined positions like IR and family tax, and generally being seen as a socially conservative person. That, I was never going to change.'

Howard set out his values in a series of so-called headland speeches. They were deliberately light on detail. But they were deadly serious statements of intent because they confirmed that Howard wanted to demolish Keating's version of Australia. The mandate he was seeking was socially conservative and economically liberal. It was, in reality, the same mix that he had deployed in the 1980s, but with one subtle difference: this time, he would not try to position himself to the right of Labor on economics, as Hewson had. The fight he wanted to pick with Keating was on social policy, because he believed that Labor had gone further to the left after the 1993 election than the Australian community wanted.

The first of the headland speeches on 6 June 1995 set the tone. Howard said Australians were being taught to think of themselves as 'sub-groups', which was damaging 'our sense of community'. 'Our goal will be to reverse this trend. Mainstream government means making decisions in the interests of the whole community, decisions which have the effect of uniting, not dividing the nation.'

He would make politics cleaner, more open. The budget numbers would be updated during an election campaign, the speaker of the House of Representatives would have 'greater independence', and the auditor-general would be 'completely independent'.

'Honesty is being swamped by cynical election campaigns based on fear, or the big scare, or the massive lie,' he said. 'I would rather promise half of what people might want and honour 100 per cent of it than commit myself to everything and deliver only half of it.'

In this speech, as in every public appearance of Howard Mark II, more time was devoted to assuring voters that there was no real policy contest with Keating. On native title, for example, he said that the 'Mabo decision was a milestone in Aboriginal affairs'.

The most pointed of the four headland speeches was the last, on national identity, on 13 December 1995:

> The current prime minister must be one of the few leaders from any era, anywhere in the world, who appears to have so little respect for his own country's history that he is attempting to rewrite it. Put bluntly, Mr Keating has been engaged in an attempted heist of Australian nationalism. It is not my intention to

replace his attempted heist with a heist of my own ... It is not the role of any political leader to politicise patriotism.

Howard's homespun persona made sense against Keating in the mid-1990s in the way that it never could have in the 1980s because the nation had grown tired of deregulation. The 1980s were a time of economic crisis, but there remained a sense of cocky optimism, which aided Bob Hawke and Keating. They were doers, while Howard Mark I was seen as a whinger.

The fact that Howard was still standing, despite all that he had said and done, and all that had been said about him and done to him, forced voters to look at him in a new way. They had underestimated him, which made him seem more substantial the second time around.

The public didn't expect that much from Howard. They didn't really like him in the mid 1990s (the respect would come much later in his career), but that didn't matter for now because many of them had come to loathe Keating. What voters didn't count on was how much like Keating he really was. Howard would betray them almost immediately after gaining their trust by inventing the idea of the disposable promise. He said after the election that he would keep only his 'core promises', as if the rest of them had been just a little joke between him and the population that they needed to tell each other so they could make Keating go away.

BUT WHO is John Howard, and what does he really stand for? The key to unlocking his beliefs can't be found in any one document, statement, or speech. There was no Placido Domingo moment when it all came together. He is not that sort of politician. But his wilderness years offer clues to the prime minister he would become.

For five years, between 1989 and 1994, he moonlighted as a newspaper columnist for Rupert Murdoch. It was a form of political therapy, a post-modern version of Winston Churchill's autobiography. But where Churchill spent his exile piecing together his version of the past, Howard dealt with the present and the future. Initially, he wrote for the national broadsheet, *The Australian*. His first piece was published on 2 June 1989, less than a month after he had been stripped of his job. He transferred to his hometown tabloid, *The Sunday Telegraph,* in February 1990. A decade later, a young Labor maverick called Mark Latham would seek similar outlets for his frustrations, *The Daily Telegraph* and *The Australian Financial Review*.

Howard's prose was dry. But it was often revealing. He had given up on the Liberal leadership, so his words did not carry the taint of ambition. He would never be this open again. At times, Howard ignored party policy to put up his own ideas, knowing that his colleagues couldn't hurt him any more than they already had. On one occasion, he even appeared to revel in the Queensland National Party's impending defeat to Wayne Goss's Labor in November 1989:

> The Nationals warrant a spell on the sidelines. Their organisation deserves a clean-out … My advice to the conscientious conservative voter of Queensland troubled by events of recent years but not wanting a Labor government, is to vote Liberal and hope like hell they win enough seats to be the major party of a coalition government.

Like all columnists, Howard was prone to repeating himself. There are only so many thoughts a writer can have. The Howard staples were family, trade unions, multiculturalism, and the monarchy. He wanted to protect the first and the last, and tear up the monopolies of the two in the middle.

Here is a top-10 snapshot of Howard as commentator. The quotes are arranged thematically. He would like to forget some passages, such as his desire for an independent public service and the importance of having the United Nations onside when dealing with Saddam Hussein. But others, like his thoughts on leadership, reveal the template for his prime ministership. I have left out the columns that followed his return in 1995 because they were, well, political.

On multiculturalism:
The emergence of lobby groups, often speciously claiming the capacity to deliver large blocs of votes to this or that political party, is precisely the reason ethnic affairs in Australia has become so politicised in recent years ... If such groups did not exist, or more particularly, if political parties did not seriously respond to their attempts to auction off support, then it is far more likely that a bipartisan approach on immigration and post-arrival policies for immigrants can be re-established. [29 September 1991]

On reconciliation:
There is a guilt industry surrounding Aboriginal issues. It is strong, intolerant and if allowed to go on, likely to do great harm to relations between Aboriginal and other Australians ... Few Australians are much interested in symbolic contrition for the misdeeds, both actual and perceived, of earlier generations. [17 January 1993]

On Gulf War I:
Tacit Soviet acquiescence in the allied action against Iraq made possible the sweeping UN endorsement of Operation Desert Storm. In the old days, the Soviets would have used their security council veto and other nations would have sat on the fence; and the perception of unanimous world outrage against Saddam Hussein would not have been so stark. [3 March 1991]

On economic management:
Thirty years ago, the great challenge for democratically elected leaders in the Western world was not economic management. Sir Robert Menzies won elections in Australia on foreign affairs and defence issues. The great divide in Australia at that time was not about fiscal, monetary and wages policy. Since the early 1970s, all that has changed. [14 March 1994]

On industrial relations reform:
True enterprise bargaining won't happen in Australia until individual employees and their employers have the unfettered right, if they so choose, to enter their own employment contracts without the prior approval of a union, an employer organisation or an industrial tribunal. [1 March 1992]

On motherhood:
At a time when there will be a painful shortage of jobs, it makes sense to help wherever possible single-income families with dependent children to remain in that position. There is plenty of evidence that parents in two-income households with young children deeply regret the economic pressure which prevents them living on one income. [31 January 1993]

On the public service:
The relationship between ministers and public servants is a two-way street. Bureaucrats are meant to give fearless, professional advice and are normally expected to refrain from publicly criticising government policies or decisions ... The other side of the coin is that ministers are expected to carry the heat and burden of public debate and criticism of what, after all, are their decisions. They cannot expect bureaucrats to refrain from public criticism of their decisions and then feel free to shift the blame to, or publicly attack, bureaucrats when things go wrong. [8 July 1990]

On the coalition:
I favour a full nation-wide amalgamation of the Liberal and National parties. Such a merger would save the scarce resources now available to the two parties. [15 August 1993]

On leadership:
The art of political leadership in a democracy is a blend of confronting the electorate with the need for change, and the desirability of heading in a particular direction with a willingness to

accept the overwhelming weight of public feeling constantly expressed over a period of time. [27 September 1992]

On Bob Hawke and Paul Keating:

From its own vantage point, the Labor Party made the right decision to get rid of Hawke in December 1991. I find it hard to believe that Hawke could have won in March 1993. But this does not gainsay the fact that Labor's success in the 1980s owed much to Hawke's personal popularity and his capacity effectively to delegate responsibility within his own government. If there had been no Keating in the 1980s, Labor could still have won. If there had been no Hawke, I do not believe that this would have been so. [14 August 1994]

Castlenomics

SO, HOW MUCH did you make on your place? This is an invitation to skite that no other nation can relate to, because no other economy places so many of its eggs in the one basket. Two out of every three dollars of household wealth in Australia are tied up in bricks and mortar.

Offer a leader the choice between lower unemployment and a booming housing market, and the cynic who understands history will pick a recession with capital gain ahead of a recovery with flat or falling property prices. Gough Whitlam and Malcolm Fraser are the only two prime ministers since records began in 1960 to fight elections immediately after presiding over a capital loss for homeowning voters. Both were punished with massive defeats. The other common thread between the 1975 and 1983 polls is, of course, recession. Yet as Robert Menzies showed in 1961 and Paul Keating reaffirmed in 1993, not all recessions lead to a change in government. What binds 1961 and 1993 is that housing wealth still improved in the election year, after allowing for inflation. Menzies saw it rise by 4.6 per cent, and Keating by 3.8 per cent. By contrast, the real value of the nation's housing stock dropped by 3.8 per cent under Whitlam in 1975, and by 3.5 per cent under Fraser in 1983.

Housing wealth is not normally included in the media's rollcall of statistics because it comes out too long after the event to matter to the daily news cycle. But most people have a fair idea of what their property is worth which, in turn, affects the two biggest decisions they make as consumers and voters: whether to spend or save, and whether the prime minister deserves a kick up the backside.

When interest rates soared in the late 1980s, voters could console themselves with the thought that the real value of their bricks and mortar was climbing faster. As treasurer between 1983 and 1991, Keating achieved a return after inflation of 8.4 per cent a year for the nation's homeowners. But the party stopped when he became prime minister. Between 1991 and 1996, the real value of the nation's dwellings rose by only half that amount, at 3.8 per cent a year. It might have been enough at the 1993 election; but, by 1996, families were becoming a little impatient for the next property boom.

By the mid-1990s, the political parties began noticing that voters would cry poor almost by reflex, even when their material circumstances said otherwise. One of the most successful pollsters of the era, who did not want to be identified for this anecdote, was puzzled by the results of research he had undertaken for a private bus company during Keating's final term. Two middle-class neighbourhoods had been given extra services, and the operator wanted to see if they were happy with their new timetables. The first group was pleased, but the second complained that they were 'worse off'. After some head-scratching, the pollster realised why the latter group felt cheated. They had only received three additional trips a week; the first neighbourhood got five.

As treasurer, Keating tried to wean the nation off the property teat because bricks and mortar won't help pay off the foreign debt. His 1985 tax reforms had introduced a capital gains tax, a fringe benefits tax, the lowering of the top personal tax rate from 60c to 49c in the dollar, and the removal of the double taxation of shares. When combined with his earlier decision to scrap negative gearing, the process by which property investors soak the public purse to cover the interest bill on their mortgages, Keating's new tax regime turned the housing market on its head.

'In a capital-scarce country one must ration the capital carefully,' Keating told parliament in October 1985. 'Therefore, the capital must go to the most productive areas of the economy rather than into over-investment in real estate, or any other non-productive area of the economy, as has been the case over the years.' Negative gearing, he said, was 'one of the most blatantly abused tax shelters in the system.' It was 'an outrageous rort'.

His policies worked in the way that he planned. Investment in productive assets soared, and the share of national wealth going to dwellings fell from 50.6 per cent in 1985 to 46.8 per cent two years later. Property didn't lose its value; it just took a smaller slice of a larger cake — the smallest, in fact, in 12 years. But Keating didn't count on the power of the housing lobby to spin this readjustment into a national catastrophe. It is easy to forget how many vested interests Keating took on in the 1980s. The restaurant trade, for example, warned that it would be wiped out by Keating's closure of the tax break for business lunches. They were wrong because Australians were beginning to acquire a taste for eating out. Employment in restaurants increased each year after 1985. But the housing lobby was a different proposition. It tapped into the greed of two-thirds of the nation's households, the one-third that owned their home outright, and the other third that were paying off their mortgages.

In 1987, Keating relented and reintroduced negative gearing, but held onto the capital gains tax. Here's where I suspect Keating began to lose control of his destiny. The policy reversal on negative gearing helped to unleash the property boom of the late 1980s, which contributed to the severity of his recession. By 1993, dwellings took up a record 57.3 per cent of household investment — a rise of more than 10 percentage points on the 1987 result. With all that extra money sunk into quarter-acre blocks, it is little wonder that voters became grumpy when prime minister Keating couldn't show them the sort of profits they had taken for granted when he had been treasurer in the 1980s.

As galling as it is for Keating, the public associates him with record mortgage rates, and John Howard with record property prices. Between 1996 and 2004, the average real capital gain delivered by Howard was 17 per cent a year, which was four times better than Keating's final effort as the nation's real estate agent.

CHAPTER TEN

The End of the Beginning

DID Paul Keating underestimate John Howard? The answer should be obvious. Some of Keating's closest followers are convinced that he did, that he took too long to appreciate how good Howard would be the second time around. But surely Keating wouldn't concede it for the record? We are in the middle of the second interview, at about the seventh hour of more than ten hours' worth of conversations. Keating has just agreed that he 'probably' overdid his cold-shoulder treatment of the press gallery after the 1993 election. He switches the topic to Howard, which gives me the opening to ask the question.

> The press gallery dragged up the white-picket-fence reactionary and tried to say he was really up to beating me.
> *Question*: Do you think you underestimated him?

Keating is animated, but not upset. He must have thought about this phase of his prime ministership a thousand times. The first thought that pops into his mind is the time he lost in 1995 defending Carmen Lawrence from the Western Australian royal commission that Richard Court's coalition government had set up; time he should have devoted to attacking Howard:

> I spent most of 1995. You've got to remember, I beat Howard in 1987; it wasn't Hawke, it was me. Hawke certainly helped that he

was the prime minister; but I dogged him, as you know, in that campaign and blew his tax package to pieces. I've got the front page from the Melbourne *Sun*, 'Howard: my sums wrong'. I'd beaten Howard once, and Howard knows to this day, no matter what else he thinks out in Australia, he knows that I think he is a sub-form of politics, and I had to go through three opposition leaders in three years: Hewson in '93, and finally I'd knocked him over; Downer in '94, and I knocked him over; and in '95, six months of it, I'd spent on Carmen Lawrence in the parliament. Within only a two-month period I'd Howard in such a state … his nerves were already gone, you know. I said he had no policies and no structure, and it was all summed up in a cartoon in the Melbourne *Herald Sun*: it had a little fellow standing on Ayres Rock, it was Howard, with glasses, and there's a dog running away with a newspaper in its mouth, and it says, 'The dingo has taken my policies'. So I had him in real trouble. What the Liberals admit to in the book *The Victory* was they had no policies until January 1996. Had I had a four-year parliament, I would have thrown him in a corner like a rag doll, but I just didn't get the time to do it.

Keating barely draws breath as his mind hurtles back seven years earlier to the constitutional referendum of 1988, in which the public rejected, amongst other things, a four-year term for parliament. As it happened, 1988 was also the year in which Keating forced Bob Hawke to declare a timetable for the handover of the prime ministership. The thing that annoyed Keating almost as much as losing to Howard was that Hawke had denied him the leadership when he felt he could do most with it, before the recession. It is an elongated 'what if', and an insight into Keating's multi-layered thought process:

When [attorney-general] Lionel Bowen got Gough [Whitlam] involved in the four-year referendum debate, adding freedom of religion and local government, we lost the four-year referendum. The four-year referendum meant I lost the fourth year of dealing with Howard ... The end result was I didn't have enough time to catch up with him ... He needed to say he was me to win, and had I had 12 more months, I would have shown he was not me, free of the Lawrence matter.

Keating was being candid, yet he didn't answer yes or no. He believes to this day that he had Howard's measure, and that he still has Howard spooked in some small way. Against this, there is the view of those close to Keating who worry that obsession and denial fused into bitterness long ago, and that he will never get over losing to Howard. It is possible that both perspectives carry an element of truth. Two weeks earlier, in our first chat, Keating wanted to make it clear that he wasn't whinging about his fate:

I think that in the business of political entrepreneurship, which was the business I was in, 13 years of perpetual opportunity to rebuild, reshape, remake a middle-sized OECD economy, doesn't come too many people's way. I can't run out and say, 'Well, I was cheated'. I was in parliament for 27 years, exactly half of it I was either treasurer or prime minister. I'm quite happy about it. But the one thing that the '83–'96 years had, the one characteristic which went right through it, was urgency. That's the one thing that is not in either political party, conscientiousness and urgency.

Many on Howard's side today believe there is a simpler explanation: that anyone could have beaten Keating in 1996. Well, almost anyone. Alexander Downer was unelectable; they were sure of that, even though Downer would wonder years later whether he, too, could have won. It took time for the Liberals to get used to the idea that Howard was the most logical candidate to replace Downer as leader. By rights, the handover should have occurred after 'the things that batter' gaffe, in September 1994. But the Liberals dithered, and gave Keating the chance he didn't take to call an early election with Downer as his opponent.

Keating never really underestimated Howard; it was the

electorate he took for granted. He assumed their memory of Howard was the same as his, and that this would override their urge to be rid of him.

The final year of Keating, and the first year of Howard Mark II, 1995, was soaked in paradox. It would be the best policy year of Keating's prime ministership; a return to his Treasury form of the early to mid-1980s. In April, he signed the competition policy agreement with the states. In May, he turned the $4.5 billion of tax cuts he still owed voters into superannuation.

The super tax cuts proved so popular that Howard promptly aped them, as he would do with most of the policies Keating announced that year. Howard said he would devote the same amount of funds to 'superannuation or like savings vehicles' so the banks would also have a shot at competing for the honey pot. People would be 'no worse off', or 'short-changed by a Howard government', he assured voters.

Howard held back the detail of his savings policy until the 1996 election campaign. The document carried the title *Super for All*. On the opening page were two columns comparing the Labor and coalition promises. The idea was to show how little difference there was between Howard and Keating. 'The coalition will meet the government's co-contribution commitment.' On page six of the policy document, Howard explained that he meant every last dollar of the $4.5 billion payment: 'The coalition will inherit both Labor's proposal and the expectation that has gone with it. We will deliver the full benefit of the proposed contribution but will do so in a manner that is both efficient and equitable.'

The trick political question of the decade is who, ultimately, dishonoured the super tax cuts? Keating would jump to mind, because he didn't get around to placing the policy into legislation before the election was called. But it wasn't him. The first part of the answer will have to would until the second budget of the Howard government, in 1997, when this bipartisan promise had to be delivered.

THE 1996 CAMPAIGN was unique because it pitted the two politicians who had told, between them, the generation's biggest whoppers. They had been treasurers for the past two recessions, and each had cancelled tax cuts after an election victory. Let's score their mistakes, to give debit where it's due. Howard's recession in 1982–83 was the greater of two evils because it served no purpose. Under Howard, inflation and unemployment rose, in tandem, to double digits. Keating's recession in 1990–91 had higher unemployment for longer, but it destroyed inflation.

On tax cuts, Howard can plead guilty to the lesser charge of being in the wrong place at the wrong time because it was his prime minister, Malcolm Fraser, who issued the order to cancel the fist-full of dollars after the 1977 campaign. Keating had no one to blame but himself for finding the budget cupboard bare after the 1993 election. Yet Howard had told an equivalent fib ten years earlier, when he refused to pass on to voters the advice he had been given in the dying days of the Fraser government in March 1983. The secretary of the Treasury, John Stone, later to become a National Party senator, told Howard that the starting point for the deficit in 1983–84 would be $9.6 billion (or just under $40 billion today), which would be more than double what voters had been advised in the budget the previous August. Howard picked a number about halfway between the two, $6 billion, and revealed it during the election campaign. He admitted afterwards that the figure had been his, not his department's. In other words, it was a guess. 'I think that somebody who has been treasurer for five years is entitled in the course of a press conference to give some order of magnitude based on one's own personal estimates of the type of variation of the deficit,' he said after the 1983 election. Yet Keating's error in 1993 was worse, because he had the example of Howard a decade earlier to caution him, and no meddling prime minister like Malcolm Fraser to overrule him.

Where Keating and Howard sold the nation short, together, in 1996 was in agreeing that the budget had been restored to surplus when each had good reason to suspect that the opposite was true.

This is some of the touchiest ground in the Keating and Howard narratives because neither will ever accept responsibility for what followed. The politics of intolerance that Pauline Hanson was allowed to practise in the second half of the 1990s drew part of its energy from the public's disgust at the back-to-back breaches of trust from the governments of Keating and Howard after the 1993 and 1996 elections.

Keating denies he left the budget with a gaping hole in 1996. He brushes off the question. 'Oh no, no, no, no, no, no, no, nah. That's what the natural stabilisers do, and I think this is the right way to run policy.' He means by this that the budget corrects itself when the economy recovers. But that wasn't what he told voters at the time, when he said the budget was in surplus and the economy had never been in better shape.

Howard did, indeed, suspect that the budget was in trouble. 'I guess I wasn't completely surprised that there was a deficit.' A smile traces his face, then he laughs, recalling the shock when he was told that the starting point for the 1996–97 budget would be a deficit of almost $8 billion. 'I must say I was a little surprised at the size of it. It was huge. I was shown the figure on the day after the election.' He couldn't believe his luck, and his misfortune. He could nail Keating as a bad economic manager, the charge Keating had always made against him. But the size of the deficit meant he had commitments that did not add up — from the $4.5 billion savings policy he would inherent from Keating, to a micro promise to maintain funding in real terms for the government broadcaster, the ABC.

The mutual fiscal trauma can be sourced back to the first two weeks of May 1995 when Howard, and then Keating, signed contracts with the public that they could never fulfil. On 2 May, Howard said there would 'never ever' be a GST. The declaration meant the coalition would have to go to the election wearing a revenue straightjacket. There would be no new taxes or increases to existing taxes, Howard promised. On 9 May, Keating's government released its final budget with surpluses as far as the eye could see:

$718 million in 1995–96; $3.4 billion in 1996–97; $4.5 billion the following year; and $7.4 billion in 1998–99. What made the talk of surplus hard to believe was that the result for the past financial year, 1994–95, had been a *deficit* of $12.2 billion.

The last budget before an election is the one that flirts with fate, because governments seeking another term offer voters more than is prudent, and oppositions wishing to break a losing streak always try to out-bid them. Because Howard was keen to match every commitment that Keating made (so that Keating, and not coalition policies, could be the election issue), the 1996 campaign had an in-built bias towards profligacy. But because both men knew, implicitly, that the budget couldn't support another tax-cuts auction like 1993, they did the next best thing by promising smaller, targeted handouts. Yet even they didn't add up in the end.

In 1995, the budget was expressed as revenue plus the proceeds of asset sales minus spending. It is not the calculation used today, which removes privatisation from the equation. Keating said there was a surplus on both counts: the headline measure and what it now referred to as the underlying measure. While no figures were published for the latter before the 1996 election, Keating and Howard were operating on the assumption that there would be an underlying surplus in both 1996–97 and 1997–98.

There is no suggestion that Treasury cooked the books. But it was clear two months later, when the election was underway in February 1996, that if the department had been asked to provide a further update it would have predicted an underlying deficit for 1996–97. The treasurer, Ralph Willis, wasn't going to do this; and even if he had wanted to, Keating wouldn't let him. But Keating wasn't thinking straight. The revelation of a deficit would have suited him more than his opponent because it would have forced Howard to nominate spending cuts to pay for his programs. Keating never did get to ping Howard for having a secret agenda. The revelation of a deficit might have been the only card he had left to play.

Howard straddled the fence. He demanded that Keating 'throw

open the books'. But he also agreed with Keating's claim that all was well. 'There's a difference between the deterioration in this year's budget and whether or not the projected outcome for next year had deteriorated,' Howard said. He had to be kidding, surely? The respected private forecaster Access Economics, which had done the sums for *Fightback!* in 1991, released a report before the election that predicted an underlying deficit of $8 billion for 1996–97. Both sides had been warned.

And yet Howard sought to make honesty an election issue: Keating's deceit versus his decency. He wasn't deliberately lying in the way a sociopath would, just as Keating didn't set out to deceive in 1993. Experience had taught them both that budget figures bounce around. There was no point in panicking at the first revision, when the next estimate could easily turn a minus into a plus. Also, ego told them they had survived these sorts of scares before.

The consolation this time around (for me, at least) was that we in the press gallery did our job. We didn't repeat the blunder of 1993 when we failed to ask the simple question: Are these tax cuts affordable? The hole in the budget was public knowledge in 1996, even if it hadn't been made public, because the media greeted each policy announcement made during the campaign with raised eyebrows. By the final week, Howard sensed a voter backlash was brewing, and decided to drop one of his planned handouts to encourage private savings for fear it would not be believed. The irony is that he didn't need to promise so much to win. He was always going to win because the public had marked Keating for execution from the moment Howard returned to the leadership at the start of 1995—provided the Liberal Party remained united behind him, which it did.

THE 1996 ELECTION took both men by surprise. It was the most lopsided result in a generation. Labor's vote after the distribution of preferences collapsed by 5 per cent to 46.4 per cent, which was its worst result since the Whitlam routs of 1975 and 1977. Strangely, Keating's primary vote was almost identical to Bob Hawke's in 1990 — 38.8 per cent compared with 39.4 per cent. But Hawke had gobbled up the second preferences of the Australian Democrats in 1990. In 1996, Keating had no escape clause.

The coalition's primary vote rose by 2.9 per cent to 46.9 per cent; its two-party vote soared by 5 per cent to 53.6 per cent. Howard's landslide was the mirror-image of Hawke's toppling of Malcolm Fraser in 1983 when Labor claimed 53.2 per cent of the two-party vote. Nothing that was said, or done, in the campaign really mattered to the result because voters had made up their minds. There was a trace of bewilderment in Keating's voice as he chatted with journalists at the end of the night. 'I mean, when the brick veneers in the Blue Mountains vote Liberal, I mean, what are they thinking?'

On the Friday night before the election, Howard bumped into *The Australian's* then editor-in-chief, Paul Kelly, at a cafe in Hunters Hill, in Howard's electorate of Bennelong. Kelly showed Howard the final Newspoll, which had the coalition poised for a monumental victory with a primary vote of 48 per cent against Labor's 40.5 per cent. Howard told Kelly that it matched the coalition's research, which had been consistent all year. 'I made the comment to him it was basically the same as it had been about a month after I came back to the leadership, that we went ahead, and we never fell behind,' Howard says. 'I think we were behind on one occasion but that was probably a bit of a rogue poll.'

He had received a strong hint in the first week of June 1995 when Keating released his blueprint for a republic. For Keating, the issue had no real downside. A clear majority of voters favoured an Australian head of state, and the Liberal party room was split:

When Keating made his big statement, how he was going to have a referendum on this, that and the other, it got huge coverage and the gallery supported it. I made my reply and was universally rubbished by the gallery. I remember going to a sit-down lunch with all the *(Sydney Morning) Herald* people in Sydney, and I think

by a majority of 12–1 they all attacked me, my Neanderthal
position and all of this. The press was appalling. And in the next
Newspoll, there wasn't a flicker.

Before Keating's speech, Newspoll had the primary vote at 47–40
in the coalition's favour; after it, the score was 48–40. For Howard,
the message was that Keating had allowed himself to be diverted by
causes that would not switch votes:

> People thought, okay. Liberal republicans said, 'So what, it's not a
> first-order issue for us.' But his tactics that year, I mean, how he
> messed around with Carmen. He should have got rid of Carmen
> Lawrence. Surely he now recognises that?

Envy Lines

SO TOXIC was the feeling within the Liberal Party against Paul Keating before the 1996 election that a television ad was prepared to attack him for being wealthy. His two multi-million-dollar properties were shown in sequence and then, presumably for the sake of balance, the camera switched to Laurie Brereton's holiday house. The closing shot was of Bob Hawke's pad by the harbour. Vivaldi played in the background as if to remind voters that Keating was also into classical music. The mood piece concluded with a sarcastic voice-over that said: 'Labor claims this election is all about protecting workers. What are they protecting?' In her book *The Victory*, author Pamela Williams says that plans to air the ad were shelved after it was screen-tested with voters. 'People went crazy,' Liberal pollster Mark Textor told the party's federal director Andrew Robb. 'It actually drove them to defend Keating.' Perhaps the electorate couldn't see what was wrong with someone owning two properties.

The politics of upward envy is often confused with the politics of backlash. Australians rebelled against deregulation for much of the 1990s, but that didn't make them born-again socialists. Voters didn't mind Keating making money, so long as they could make some, too. The Labor supporters who defected to John Howard in 1996, and stuck with him in 1998, weren't the so-called battlers. They were middle-income and higher-income earners in Sydney and Brisbane.

Before we look at what the Howard years have meant, we have to delete some popular misconceptions about the battlers. Think of the 150 electorates in the federal parliament as three zones of 50 seats each: higher-income, middle-income, and bottom. The battlers reside predominately in the bottom-50 seats on the electoral income-ladder. Generally speaking, the battler electorates are in country towns and the bush, where the voters are older and earning less than the norm. I call them WW seats, for white and on welfare.

While the idea that Howard's battlers were once Labor voters is commonly held on both sides of politics, the truth is these people have been in the coalition camp going back as far as Robert Menzies. The Liberal and National Parties held the majority of the battler electorates throughout the 1980s, despite the rivalry between Howard and Peacock. They even had the majority of the bottom-50 electorates in 1993, despite *Fightback!*.

Labor's 1993 election win was built on the middle and top of the income-ladder, as were its victories in the 1980s. In 1993, John Hewson scared working families into sticking with Keating, despite the recession. You may read, and hear, in the media about 'battling families'. The term appears to be used interchangeably with 'working families'. But two-parent families sit, predominately, on the middle and top rungs of the electoral income-ladder, because both parents are more likely than not to be working.

You won't find many of these job-rich households in the WW seats. But politicians treat working families as if they were battlers because that's how these couples see themselves. Their gripe is the cost of living. The two-income families complain that mum has been forced to take a job to help pay off the mortgage. But these people are time-poor, not income-poor.

The two-income family became the dominant grouping in the 1990s — not the majority, because there is no such thing when talking about the broad spectrum of family types, but the most prevalent. In 1986, both parents working was the reality for only 29.5 per cent of all young families with at least one child aged five years or under. In 2001, the two-income model had risen to 34.5 per cent. Over the same period, the single-income family had fallen from 39.5 per cent to 27.5 per cent.

Howard identified more with the single-income family, which he had featured on the cover of the *Future Directions* manifesto of 1988. On becoming prime minister in 1996, he sought to send more money their way than Keating had, so they could keep the mother at home if they wished. But many of the single-income families that Howard helped out happened to be Labor sympathisers in the inner cities of Sydney and Melbourne. Dad was a high-income professional and mum was at home. The Liberals would later give these women the moniker of 'doctors' wives', a putdown meant to signify that they were rich enough to have the luxury of embracing the Keating social agenda.

In an economy where most families have both parents working, and those that can afford to have mum at home are higher-income earners, the true battling families are those without any job to speak of. This is deregulation's underclass, the families with dependent children where there is no breadwinner role-model. What is not widely appreciated is that the nation's 357,000 jobless families outnumber the 356,000 working families that fit the bill as the new mainstream, in which dad has a full-time position and mum works part-time. It is only when all job-rich families are included in the same table that they swamp the jobless families: 1.96 million versus 357,000.

Unlike working families, which come in many configurations, the majority of jobless families are easily identifiable: they are Australian-born single mothers. But politicians have no interest in these battlers because there aren't enough of them in marginal seats to matter.

The head-to-head that concerns the main parties is the one I mentioned in Snapshot #2: the entrepreneurs versus the trade unionists. Men who work for themselves, or who are nearing the age of retirement, have greater pull in the handout stakes than the women who are raising what may become Australia's first permanent underclass. At the 2004 election, Howard introduced the so-called mature age tax offset, an incentive designed to keep older workers in the labour force. Following the election, single mothers were told they would have their benefits reduced if they didn't find jobs. One voter is treated with kid gloves; the other has an accusing finger pointed at them.

Politically speaking, older men without work are prone to xenophobia and misogyny. The irony is that they needed a woman to articulate their hang-ups. Pauline Hanson had four grievances that resonated with the men of the WW seats: black welfare, Asian immigration, globalisation, and the Family Court. These men deserved the attention of the political class, because they were genuine victims of deregulation. But their success in claiming the mantle of economic casualty had the effect of crowding out black men and women, refugees, and white single mothers from the discussion.

Blue-collar men escaped the downward envy of the 1990s because they had previously occupied the centre of the income ladder. Their anger came as a shock to the system, but the system took heed of it. For Aboriginal Australians, refugees, and white single mothers, their position at the bottom was assumed to be their own fault because they had been there before deregulation.

IN 1996, Howard BEAT Keating on each rung of the electoral income-ladder — bottom, middle, and top. It is understandable that both sides of politics would notice the blue collars who voted for the coalition. But the bottom explained the extent, not the substance, of Howard's victory. The more important defectors were middle-class families.

Keating left Labor virtually empty in the bottom after dropping ten seats: nine to the coalition and the tenth, Oxley, south of Brisbane, to the independent, Hanson. Yet Keating did worse in the middle, where he ceded 13 seats. He surrendered another nine seats at the top.

The other way to appreciate Howard's triumph is to think in terms of football. The rugby league states of NSW and Queensland accounted for 22 of the 31 seats he picked up from Keating.

Howard's 12 NSW gains were mainly at the top and bottom, which makes sense because this is the nation's most divided state by income. The ten he collected from Queensland were skewed to the middle and the top.

Queensland became the nation's swing-state in the 1990s. Five of the past six federal elections were decided there. Queensland backed the loser just once, in 1993, when Keating claimed a majority of the vote in NSW and Victoria.

Before the 1990s, Australia could source its essence as lying somewhere between Sydney and Melbourne, a mix of brashness and reserve. The two cities held each other in check. The rise of Brisbane has shifted the balance of power in Australia, and time-warped the national debate. Brisbane is a white-immigrant city, which runs counter to the multicultural identikit of Sydney and Melbourne. It has the lowest overseas-born population of the mainland capitals, apart from Darwin. About one in three people in Sydney, Perth, and Melbourne are immigrants. In Brisbane, the figure is closer to one in five. The politics of backlash began here, because the nation's most parochial voters finally found a voice — first through Hanson, then Howard.

CHAPTER ELEVEN

Guns and Budgets

ASKED what John Howard has achieved as prime minister, Paul Keating says, without hesitation: 'Guns. I'll give him guns'. For a second, there is warmth in Keating's voice. The compliment is genuine; but as he searches for another, he screws up his face, then sighs. 'I'd like to give him more, but …'

When asked about Keating's contribution, Howard answers in the economic realm, and in the plural form, as in Hawke and Keating: 'The two big things they did, really big things, in my judgment, were, obviously, financial deregulation and tariff reform. I thought tariff reform was their most courageous thing, given their constituency. But bear in mind, those reforms had our support.'

The sound of grudging applause is amusing, and instructive. Keating praises Howard for an act of heroism barely two months into his term, then dismisses the next nine years. Howard credits Keating for his vision as treasurer, but not as prime minister. Strip aside the rivalry, and each answer confirms that real leadership involves poking your own side in the eye. It's not enough to gather a majority of voters on a difficult issue. Genuine change, in the national interest, comes about only when a government forces its rusted-on supporters to give something up — as the coalition did on guns, and Labor did on protection.

The puzzle of Howard is located in the contrast between his handing of everyday matters and moments of crisis. He is accident-prone when the pressure is off. But when confronted with tragedy, he transforms into a nation-rousing statesman. Port Arthur, a popular tourist spot near Hobart, set the tone on 28 April 1996 when Martin Bryant killed 35 people and wounded 18 others with a military-style weapon. It was by far Australia's worst mass-murder, and was front-page news around the world. The nation was united in its grief. Then, just as quickly, it divided after Howard detailed his plan to ban all automatic and semi-automatic weapons.

The shooters' organisations applied pressure, as they had done in the late 1980s, when they convinced the NSW and Victorian Labor governments to abandon gun-law reforms. In Sydney, 35,000 marched against Howard; in Melbourne, there were twice as many again on the streets.

Farmers and sporting shooters didn't want to surrender their pump-action shotguns and high-powered rifles to Canberra, and they resented the idea that city folk saw them as freaks. But some fringe elements rose to the caricature by warning of 'blood in the streets' if Howard had his way.

On 16 June, Howard went to Sale, in Victoria's east, to explain his policies to gun owners. He was advised to wear a bullet-proof vest. 'I did it just once. I'm sorry I did,' he tells me.

The National Party leader, and deputy prime minister, Tim Fischer, worried that the bush would split on this issue. But he also took a stand on principle, and supported his prime minister. His message to farmers was 'Give up some of your guns or lose the lot.' At his property in southern NSW, police stood guard after telephone threats were made to his wife, Judy.

It was a sad, bad time. There was no sense of proportion to the backlash. At Sale, one of the speakers suggested that law-abiding gun owners were being treated the same way that Hitler had treated the Jews. Not for the first time in his term, the overkill of his opponents would help Howard galvanise the nation behind him.

For the new prime minister, this was a gut call. It is a little-understood part of his make-up, but Howard has never been all the way with the USA. In particular, he abhors its gun culture. Gun-law reform had been one of his goals in his opening headland speech a year earlier. 'Every effort should be made to limit the carrying of guns in Australia,' he said. 'I have no doubt that the horrific homicide level in the United States is directly related to the plentiful supply of guns. How else does one explain the simple fact that in the United States the murder rate is ten per 100,000, against one per 100,000 in England and Wales and two in Australia.'

I had that quote in mind when I asked him nine years after Port Arthur if there were aspects of American society that he was determined we never follow:

> Because of my unapologetic friendship with [President] Bush and the closeness I've had with him, there is a tendency to see me as sort of loving all things American, I don't, actually. I'm an Anglophile, I am also an Americanphile, but I am an Australian nationalist above all. There are a lot of things about American society that I don't like. I don't like the insensitivity of their social welfare system, and I have always, therefore, supported a minimum wage, even though some of the people to the right of me on industrial relations don't. And guns is something I have always opposed. I think the murder rate in America is a product of their gun culture.

In the early days of the guns debate, Howard was in Sydney for a rugby test between Australia and South Africa. Walking into the stadium, he wondered if the fans would take him on, as football supporters are wont to when a politician enters their domain:

> Rugby crowds in Sydney are made up of a fair percentage of country people. But I was greatly encouraged by the response. People came up to me and said, 'Don't back down on guns'. People would stop you in the street. I remember two women in particular. They said, 'We can't stand your policies on anything else, we will never vote for you, but you are doing the right thing on guns.' The public felt that this was an opportunity to do something quite decisive.

Uniform gun-controls were passed in the federal and state parliaments by winter. Hundreds of thousands of weapons were handed in, and taxpayers forked out $500 million to compensate the shooters, dealers, and collectors for their losses. The most tangible sign of the policy's success was the sharp drop in the number of gun-related homicides that followed. In the five years before Port Arthur, 387 people were murdered with firearms. In the five years after, from 1997 to 2001, the number dropped by a third to 290. The total number of gun-related deaths fell by 56 per cent over the same period, from 2781 to 1781.

AS HE DONNED the flack jacket to face gun owners in Sale, Howard was bemused by the suggestion from some of the speakers at the event that his crackdown was prompted by opinion polling and the advice of staff. The opposite was true, he said; this was his own call, based on his instincts and his 'understanding of the feeling of the mainstream of the Australian community'. Howard told the mob that they had every right, if they wished, to punish him at the ballot box. 'If I am wrong, and you are right, then the democratic processes of the Australian community will vindicate you and condemn me,' he said.

The claim that Howard was poll-driven, even on something like guns, would become a persistent refrain from both right and left. It was one of the two accusations that tugged against his legitimacy from the outset; the other being his propensity to bend the truth when it didn't suit him, or when he felt he didn't need to hear it. He brought some of the grief on himself because he had sought an explicit mandate for honesty, then promptly broke his word by drawing a distinction between 'core' and 'non-core' promises. By late-May 1996, Howard had decided the hole in the budget was too big to accommodate all he had offered the electorate. The trick was to figure out which policies were considered non-negotiable by the public — that is, what he couldn't get away with. Once a white list had been drawn up, the government could zero-in on those commitments it could safely abandon without shedding too much political skin. To the outsider, this might appear to be a callous exercise, a confirmation of the conspiracy theorists at Sale who said Howard believed only in what he read in an opinion poll. But Howard had Labor's 1993 budget to remind him of what could go wrong. He was determined not to repeat Keating's mistake of ignoring public opinion.

Initially, the coalition thought it could manage without ditching promises. It imagined that Labor had left behind more than enough fat to trim on the spending side of the budget. The Treasury advised that a real deficit of $7.6 billion was looming for the coming financial year, 1996–97, not counting any of the coalition's election commitments. Keating had insisted there would be a real surplus in that year. For 1997–98, the underlying deficit would begin at $7.3 billion. When these numbers were made public ten days after the coalition's election victory, on 12 March, Peter Costello said that all promises would be honoured. The government would return the budget to balance by 1997–98 by 'taking measures to reduce the budget deficit by $4 billion in '96–7 and a further $4 billion in '97–8'. Read his lips: this $8 billion total would come through spending cuts and other efficiencies, not higher taxes. 'We will achieve this objective within the framework of meeting our election commitments including the commitment not to increase taxes.'

The hole widened by another $1 billion when Treasury delivered the next set of forecasts two months later, in May. But this was not the trigger for reneging on promises; it was the realisation that the coalition couldn't find the savings it thought were there. Keating could have afforded himself a private chuckle at this point because it meant that Howard now saw what he had realised in 1993, that the real problem in the budget was the revenue base. Low inflation meant that taxes were not flowing quickly enough into public coffers to support the level of public spending which voters considered non-negotiable.

There are two tests for the 1996 budget, the ethical and the economic. Obviously, Howard failed the first because he had told voters during the election that no circumstances would warrant the breaking of promises. He had been asked in the final week of the campaign, during his televised address to the National Press Club in Canberra, what would happen if 'you win the election and then you discover you are faced with a serious budget deficit':

> *Question*: Under what circumstances will you see it as necessary to cancel some of the many spending promises you have made to the electorate in the interests of ... fiscal responsibility?
> *Howard*: Well, the commitments that we've made in relation to reduced taxation and the other commitments we've made in our election policies, they will be delivered in full.

Explaining the broken promises the day after the budget was released, Howard hinted that he had made a very careful political calculation about which policies to keep and which he could afford to drop. He was relying on the public's short political attention span to get him through:

> When the Australian people voted for us, they had in mind the private health insurance rebate, the family tax initiative, the small business relief, the maintenance of Medicare and all those things. We have delivered on all of those in full. I have no doubt that on a scale out of ten in terms of keeping commitments, last night's Costello budget rates a 7 or 8 out of ten.

Later he clarified his view that, on economic responsibility, the mark was higher, at '9.9 out of ten'.

Enough time has passed to confirm that Howard did not need to be so ruthless with his promises because the budget was in better shape than Treasury had thought. The twist is that this partly redeems Keating because he did not leave a hole anywhere near as large as was asserted by the coalition. Sorting out this argument will give us a more honest picture of whose economic policies cemented the nation's longest decade—Howard's or Keating's, or a combination of both.

To unpack the numbers, here's how the budget unfolded behind closed doors. Costello began with a savings goal of $8 billion by 1997–98, then pushed that up to $9 billion when Treasury finalised its forecasts. To put these numbers in context, the 'gross expenditure savings' in *Fightback!* were valued at $9.7 billion by 1995–96. Costello achieved barely half his target: only $5.2 billion in cuts were deemed feasible. There was a grab-bag of changes to the tax side of the equation that had already been flagged, dealing mainly with avoidance and rorting. These measures added another $1.5 billion to the two-year deficit-reduction program, yet Costello was still $2 billion short of his stated goal of balancing the books by 1997–98. Reluctantly, the government agreed to look at raising taxes, in direct breach of its commitment to voters. This is where the polling came in handy.

At one point, the $1.3 billion diesel-fuel rebate scheme, which farmers and miners were rorting to claim a tax break for driving their cars 'off road', was to be abolished. Privately, Costello referred to the scheme as 'business welfare'. The plan was floated in the media, but the protests from the National Party convinced the treasurer to drop it.

Eventually, Howard and Costello settled on a new tax on the superannuation of higher-income earners, which was to raise $500 million a year. This brought the total revenue measures to $2 billion, to go with the $5.2 billion in spending cuts by 1997–98. This left the deficit at $1.5 billion. On the night of the budget, Costello said the books would be balanced a year later than he had hoped, in 1998–99 — which, conveniently, would coincide with the next election.

Of course, this didn't bail out Keating on the night. He had told voters the budget would be in surplus two years sooner, in 1996–97, and without the cutbacks the coalition had just announced. But something strange happened afterwards. The budget behaved as Keating had predicted, by swinging dramatically into the black. The surplus for 1998–99 was $4.3 billion, not the $1 billion that Costello said it would be. The following year it surged to $13.1 billion. These numbers would have been higher still if the Howard government hadn't spent some of the proceeds along the way.

Where Keating loses this debate on points is that the coalition's extremism of 1996 served a purpose that was not anticipated at the time, just as his own over-shooting on interest rates had vanquished inflation at the start of the decade. If Costello had not slashed spending and sneaked up taxes, Australia may well have been sucked into the Asian financial meltdown the following year. There would have been no prosperity — only the certainty that Howard would have lost the next election; and, perhaps, Kim Beazley the one after that. Of course, the reforms of treasurer Keating played a big part in sparing Australia from Asia's economic crisis, which Howard acknowledges. But the plaudits must be shared with Howard and Costello. Without the hardball of the 1996 budget to point to, the government would have found it much harder to convince financial markets to lay off Australia when it mattered in 1997–98.

One final thought on Keating's fiscal legacy: the Treasury that had served him with unflinching loyalty in the 1980s effectively double-crossed him in the 1990s by misunderstanding what a low-inflation recovery would mean for the budget's bottom line. Treasury confessed in 2005 that its forecasting record was weaker under Keating in the first half of the 1990s than it was for the Howard government from 1996 onwards. '[There were] significantly smaller errors over the more recent years, 1995–96 to 2003–04, than over the earlier years,' the department wrote of its guesstimates for GDP. Even this admission understates the nature of the unintended bias. The forecasting error-rate for Keating was twice what it was for Howard. Treasury also got inflation wrong each year between 1989–90 and 1999–2000. Again, the mistakes were larger on Keating's watch than on Howard's. Or, as the department put it in jargon, 'the size of the overestimate fell on average through the decade'.

THE DETAIL of the 1996 budget was less flattering for Howard. Some of the broken promises had already been announced to get the bad news out of the way early. For instance, the states had their funding slashed in June; the ABC was told in July that its budget would be reduced; and in early August the universities were advised that they, too, would have their grants cut, university students would face higher fees, and business would lose tax concessions for research and development. Each group had been assured, in writing, during the election, that their funding would be maintained. What each had in common, apart from betrayal, was the status of being a soft target. The coalition did not fear losing votes here.

Politics, and a dollop of ideology, also drove the largest spending-cut of all, the stripping of $1 billion from 'labour market programs'. These were the carrots that Keating had unveiled in his 1994 jobs white paper. The coalition removed them, leaving only the stick of mutual obligation, which was sharpened two years later into work-for-the-dole. Job assistance was deregulated to allow charities and private operators to bid for the reduced bundle of money. The theory was that these organisations were better at helping the unemployed find work than a government department could be.

Even so, there are some trends that are too big for any government to arrest. When Howard took office, there were 500,000 people on the disability-support pension. In Keating's recession, this payment had become a halfway house between the dole and the age pension for many of those too old to be re-employed but too young to retire. The coalition's changes to job assistance did little to help this group. Eight years on, their ranks had risen to 700,000.

Where this budget changed the nation was in the fine print, in its approach to education policy. We in the media missed it at the time because we were distracted, understandably, with the broken promises. But it was a decision that Howard thinks helped him win two elections, in 2001 and 2004:

> Prior to us winning office in '96, you couldn't get federal money for
> a new school in an area that was serviced by a government and/or a
> Catholic parish. And it really meant if you wanted to start a school

in one of those suburbs that was outside the government or Catholic system, then you couldn't get federal money for it, so we altered that.

One of the cross-currents of the 1990s was the population shifts that hollowed-out the middle-ring suburbs of the capital cities. Young families moved to quarter-acre blocks in the outer suburbs, while young singles headed to apartments in the inner city. It is an iron law of bricks and mortar that housing estates can be erected years earlier than the schools and hospitals that service them. The 1996 budget allowed federal funds to flow into the outer suburbs to help open private schools ahead of the state system.

Labor, Howard says, missed the rise of the low-fee-paying private schools. In 2001 and 2004, the opposition wanted to strip elite private schools of federal funds. The hit-list approach aggravated young families who, while they might not have used the schools in question, wanted the opportunity to do so in the future:

> Labor don't understand outer-metropolitan Australia. I don't think they ever picked the aspirationals, and the symbol of that was their [schools funding policy]. To many on the Labor side an independent school is Xavier or Scotch or Riverview, and then there are the government schools. They don't understand just how many there are in between; they don't understand that the growth area is in the $3000, $4000, $5000 low-fee schools, many of which came straight after the changes we made in '96.

The contradiction in the coalition's first budget is that it gave with one hand to private schools while taking from universities with the other. More than $1 billion in savings came from higher education. The universities had their grants reduced, and students had to pay more for the privilege of studying. It meant that Australia was reducing its investment in tertiary education while the rest of the world was increasing theirs.

When Keating left office, private schools received $1.8 billion from the federal government, while funding for higher education was more than double that amount at $4.5 billion. A further $800 million went to technical colleges. Ten years on, in the financial year 2005–06, a visitor from outer space could have been forgiven for thinking that the Howard government actively dislikes universities. Funding for private schools had trebled to $5.5 billion, and was now ahead of higher education, which had crept up at less the inflation rate to $5.2 billion. Technical colleges had also doubled to $1.6 billion. Howard let slip after the 2004 election that he thought some parents would be better off encouraging their children to go to tech, not uni, as if the future of the nation lay with more handymen.

Howard's policy goal was choice, and it has informed every decision from the first days of his government. Families would be given the means to select private schools over public schools. The same principle applied to health care. The budget implemented the coalition's election promise for a tax rebate to those families and singles that had private health insurance. Higher-income earners who refused to take out health cover would face a 1 per cent levy, a policy first pursued in *Fightback!*. These measures would redefine the role of government. Taxes would be collected, not to fund public services, but to facilitate a switch in demand to the private sector.

Keating's privatisation policy, which had caused Labor so much heartburn in the early 1990s, merely removed government from businesses it had no need to be in, such as banking and air travel. Howard was doing something infinitely more radical. He was transforming the federal government into an advocate for private schools and hospitals, in direct competition with the state governments, who had drawn the short constitutional straw of having responsibility for public schools and hospitals.

What Howard understood better than the post-Keating Labor Party was that there were more votes in helping parents defect to the private systems than in repairing the public systems. Labor responded by taking money off the private sector, most notably the elite schools. What it should have done, instead, was call Howard's bluff by leaving the private funding as it was, but offer substantially more to the public sphere. But these distinctions would not be clear until some years later. In August 1996, Labor felt it was again electable because Howard had dishonoured some of his election commitments.

LOOKING BACK, it seems amazing that Howard could get so tongue-tied. He said he would keep his 'core' promises, which became one of the decade's great clangers. What he meant, of course, was that he would break his 'non-core' promises. But he never used the latter phrase.

The 'core' promise first crept into his speeches and press interviews at the end of May, at the height of the guns debate. Here is an example of his rhetoric at the time, in all its contorted glory, from a radio interview on 5 July 1996:

> I think we can go a long a way toward getting the budget into balance over the next couple of years and we will certainly be trying very hard. But we won't be pushing that at the expense of keeping the core commitments that we made to the public in areas like Medicare and family taxation.

The 'core' promise became Howard's 'L A W'. It reduced him to Keating's level. Howard's standing with voters crashed accordingly, from a peak in early May when 67 per cent were satisfied with the job he was doing, to just 48 per cent in early August.

He now admits that the 'core' promise formulation was not one of his better moments. The term was clumsy, and it didn't make the point he had intended: in difficult times, governments must choose. He demonstrates what he really wanted to say by comparing two issues that had been on his agenda for nine years, but could not be contemplated until the Senate fell into his lap on 1 July 2005:

> It was the wrong terminology. All I was trying to do was to indi-cate that there were some commitments of the government that are

more important than others, which is surely an unexceptional thing to say. I mean, can anybody seriously say that industrial relations reform isn't more important to this government than changing the cross-media laws? So if we do IR, and we do other things, and we don't change the cross-media laws for a whole combination of reasons, it doesn't mean that we had set out to dishonour it. It's just that I give greater importance to the first lot.

As it turned out, we were able to implement the main elements of our campaign. We had to do certain things that we hadn't flagged that we were going to do, simply because we had to do it, like the superannuation surcharge, and some of the changes in the employment area, and some of the changes in the education area.

THINGS HAPPENED quickly in Howard's first year in charge of the nation. The day before the budget was released, protesters gathered near the public entrance at Parliament House to hear speeches, make a bit of a noise, and bang on the glass doors. No harm was intended, it seemed. This was the trade union movement, the environmental lobby, and assorted other causes letting off steam. But the protest became a scuffle, then a riot. The glass doors cracked, and the mob moved inside, smashing up the souvenir shop that sits immediately to the left of the public entrance. A few of us in the press gallery headed down to check out the scene, and we couldn't believe the violence. Nor could some of the former Keating government advisers who we recognised in the swarm. They appeared torn between joining the wrestle on the frontline and covering their faces when the television cameras pointed their way. Luckily, it didn't occur to any of the Labor staffers familiar with the layout of the building to redirect the crowd to run around the side of the building, to the unguarded Senate car park. From there, the riot could easily have become an invasion.

For Howard, the riot was the best possible publicity ahead of the budget. His opponents had over-played their hand, again. The following morning, 20 August, the day of the budget, the prime minister received the news that made, then almost broke, his first term. Mal Colston had been an unknown Labor senator for 20 years until he fell out with his colleagues over the spoils of opposition. He wanted to be the deputy president of the Senate, but when they refused he spat the dummy and moved to the cross-benches to become an independent. With that defection, Howard no longer needed to deal with the Australian Democrats to get his legislation through the Senate. The balance of power was now in the hands of Colston and Tasmanian senator Brian Harradine. Oh, and the government granted Colston his wish to be the deputy president of the Senate.

Yin and yang seemed to go into overdrive. The budget sailed through the Senate, as did the privatisation of the first third of Telstra later in the year. Both events seemed unlikely before Colston switched sides. But Howard's successes were short-lived. In between, in early October, he had to sack the first of seven government frontbenchers for breaching his ministerial code of conduct. Within a matter of days the bloodletting was forgotten as the government recorded a swing to it in a by-election for the former Labor seat of Lindsay, in Sydney's west.

'I think I had a good year in '96,' Howard says. 'We got a lot of the IR stuff through, we had guns, we had a very good budget, which was very well received.'

But there were four earthquakes rumbling by December, which would turn 1997 and most of 1998 into a nightmare for Howard, and the nation. Pauline Hanson had declared her jihad on Australian Aboriginals and Asian immigration. Labor was preparing to out Howard's new political friend, Colston, as a serial rorter of taxpayer expenses. The High Court had just handed down its Wik native title judgment. And an unholy trinity of business, the welfare lobby, and Victorian Liberal premier Jeff Kennett was urging the prime minister to introduce the tax he had said would 'never ever' be coalition policy again: the GST.

'Please Explain'

MY FAVOURITE Pauline Hanson moments involve arguments over meat pies and Malaysian prime minister Mahathir bin Mohamad in December 1996.

In her maiden year in federal parliament, Hanson asked John Howard four questions. It was the last in this quartet, on the evils of foreign investment, that contains one of deregulation's more witty lessons. She wanted to know what the prime minister was going to do about all those Australian brand names like pie-maker Herbert Adams that were falling into overseas hands. Herbert Adams was part of the food group that Australian multinational Pacific Dunlop sold to a US-based potato producer, Simplot, in 1995. Under the deal, the Americans also wound up with our apple pies, Nanna's, and the pastry pouch of gravy and gristle that is de rigueur at a game of Aussie Rules, Four 'n' Twenty pies.

Hanson challenged Howard on his pastryiotism on 10 December 1996: 'What is the government going to do to promote Australian ownership of our Australian companies?' Howard replied with the boilerplate defence of foreign investment, that it increases our prosperity, though he did add that he looked forward to 'the day when this nation no longer has to rely as heavily as it currently does on the savings of foreigners in order to sustain its high living standard'.

That day came in July 2003, when a Victorian-based company, Patties Bakeries, bought back the oven, taking Four 'n' Twenty and the other icons off Simplot's hands. But the factory had to be destroyed to save us from the yolk of Yankee imperialism. Patties closed the Melbourne plant where Simplot made the footy pies, and transferred the operation to its headquarters in Bairnsdale, about three hours east of the big smoke. The score: 290 jobs lost in Melbourne versus 100 gained in Bairnsdale. Steve Bracks' Victorian Labor government played an unwitting role in the transaction, having given Patties a taxpayer handout the previous October to underwrite the expansion at Bairnsdale. So much for the canard that protection saves jobs.

Hanson's tiff with Mahathir came nine days earlier, on 1 December 1996. He had called her 'a little bit moronic'. She replied that he ruled a 'racist country'. The pots and kettles were clanging and shrieking throughout the region.

She had a point: 'Now, until Mahathir cleans up his own backyard and starts treating the Chinese-Indian Malays as first-class citizens and stops the military from forcing East Malaysians, the indigenous natives, off their tribal lands, then, and only then, I might have some respect for what he has to say.'

Hanson's record at elections was mixed. She won in the seat of Oxley in 1996 as an independent candidate. Howard had dumped her from the Liberal Party a fortnight before polling day because she told the local paper, *The Courier-Mail*, that governments were responsible for racism because they were 'looking after Aborigines too much'. But her sacking came too late to change the ballot papers, which still recorded her as a Liberal, for what that was worth.

Hanson seized fame after her first speech to parliament on 10 September 1996 for saying the sorts of things that some politicians had said before, against Aboriginal Australians and against Asian immigration. What made her different was her gender and her voice. Howard sensed her appeal was due, in part, to her personality, and refused to take her on.

'Here was this slightly inarticulate woman, struggling in a very Australian accent to get her point across,' he says. 'It had enormous appeal.'

But she could never work the system to her advantage. Hanson failed at her next four election attempts between 1998 and 2004, thrice in the federal parliament, and once in the NSW state parliament. In between, her One Nation Party went within a seat of winning the balance of power in the Queensland state parliament at its debut in 1998, then imploded.

Hanson was a brand. People could project on to her what they really thought about themselves. If she was a racist, that made you tolerant. If she was speaking out for ordinary Australians, that made you better than the elites.

She said a lot about Australia north of the Murray River. Almost 1 million people voted for her party at the 1998 federal election, and two-thirds lived in Queensland and NSW. Hanson also proved that her home state is cursed with an erratic court system after it wrongly jailed her for electoral fraud in 2003. Her conviction was quashed on appeal.

Accidental celebrity like hers had only one place to go after politics and the martyrdom of false imprisonment. That was reality television, where she was a very popular contestant in the first series of 'Dancing with the Stars'; she made it all the way to the final, thanks to the audience vote.

PAUL KEATING puts Hanson at the 'soft end of the spectrum', with 'Hitler at the extreme end', and France's Jean-Marie Le Pen 'in the middle':

I wouldn't have tolerated Hansonism for one second. I would have had no truck with them at all; not that I'm saying that Kim Beazley did. But you've got to cut the cloth to suit yourself. The idea that we would be more rigorous, that the Labor Party would seem to be more rigorous about proper migration than the Liberal Party under a prime minister like this, is, of course, nonsense. You can never win the argument, the same argument, on his turf. But whether you want to win it or not, there is the central point, what are these distinctions between the civic and the human community, that's the key point.

Howard's attitude to Hanson irked a lot on his own side of politics, Victorian premier Jeff Kennett among them. I'll leave it to Howard and Kennett to explain their contrasting responses to her.

Howard says the One Nation vote was too big to be merely an expression of prejudice: 'I thought it was quite wrong to just attack her as being an extremist or a Nazi. There aren't a million Nazis in Australia, but almost a million people voted for her.'

He says he wanted to deny Hanson oxygen, without insulting the public:

I think the Labor Party and the commentariat misread my handling of Hanson. I understood why Hanson had support, and it wasn't so much the redneck stuff, it wasn't racist. She did make some totally unacceptable statements, totally, and quite wrong. What she said about Aborigines, what she said about us being flooded with Asians, it was wrong, it was inflammatory. But I was strongly of the view that the more she was attacked, the more she would become a person who attracted sympathy and support. You really had to hold your nerve and let her blow herself out. A lot of people in my own party disagreed with me, but I think they were wrong and I think I was right. I think I was vindicated by events.

The state in which One Nation had the least traction was Kennett's Victoria. He takes credit for that:

From the word go, while I respected her right to say what she did, I believed she was profoundly wrong, profoundly divisive. From the moment she — well not from the moment she said it, because it wasn't picked up by the media till about ten days later — but from the moment the media started running it, I objected profoundly to what she was saying. We went on the front foot, well before anyone else, particularly at the federal level. I think it was that quick response that stopped Hansonism getting a real foothold here, not that a lot of people didn't agree with her, because I think there is a huge amount of racism below the surface in Australia, unfortunately.

I ask Kennett for his thoughts on Howard's approach:

He handled it differently. I don't think I'm being, in any way, anything else but being honest when I say that each of us have our own different experiences and our own passions.

Suddenly, the Kennett stream of consciousness slows to a trickle. Now he is picking his words carefully, pausing between each. He doesn't talk like this often:

I don't think John has ever been as close to non-English-speaking Australian communities as I feel I am close to them. That's not to say he doesn't realise the importance of them, etc, etc. I'm not as close to cricket as he is. No two people are the same; that's not a criticism, that's just stating a fact.

Kennett suspects that Howard's gut instinct was to first see how the public would react to Hanson before he committed himself:

He does that on a few things. Sometimes he creates it, sometimes he responds to it. Now that's fine, that's the way he operates, so it's not a criticism. I'm a lot more passionate and a lot more emotional. John is a lot more considered, he is a much better politician, he's still in office and I'm not.

As for Hansonism, Kennett says: 'I think Australia is over it, absolutely over it and, as you say, she's now appearing on reality TV.'

CHAPTER TWELVE

Unmaking the Keating Society

THE LESSON John Howard learned in his worst year as prime minister, 1997, was when to stop listening to vested interests so he could start talking to the electorate. He had assumed he would know where to draw the line between consultation and decision, between hearing people out and making up his mind. After all, he had had almost 22 years of experience in parliament before he took over the country, and eight of those had been in government. But, if the truth be known, Howard was a little intimidated by power in his first term. He agonised over issues longer than he needed to. He nominates his approach to the native-title debate as the low point:

> I think I made a big mistake in '97 with my handling of Wik. I remember thinking at the time that I've got to talk to everybody and reach an understanding. It was a mistake. I should have talked to people, quickly made up my mind what I was going to do, say, 'This is our policy', and go out and win support for it. We ended up antagonising both sides, and the government lost a sense of direction.

The tension at the heart of Howard's first term was the absence of a positive agenda. The early wins on guns, the budget, industrial relations, and the part-privatisation of Telstra concealed the weakness in his campaign strategy against Paul Keating. It was a plan to win an election, not to run the country. By minimising the differences between them, Howard had denied himself a mandate of his own, and created a vacuum that seemed to compel bad news to fill it. Wik was the flashpoint.

In December 1996, the High Court found that native title could co-exist with pastoral leases. Howard said the court had gone too far. It had given Aboriginal Australians more than they expected. He wanted to bring 'the pendulum back to the middle — back from the absurd point it reached after the Wik decision'.

When Howard met with the premiers early in the New Year, they told him he should respond by extinguishing native title. He said he couldn't, because the High Court would strike down such legislation as unconstitutional, and they'd all be back where they started.

Howard was caught in a pincer of expectation and antagonism. The right wanted him to wipe out native title, and thought him weak for saying no. The left assumed he wanted to punish Aboriginal Australians, and didn't want to believe him when he said he was seeking the middle ground.

Howard couldn't find the language to break the impasse because he was trying to fight two battles at once: the issue at hand, and the legacy of his predecessor. Native title had been Keating's baby, and Howard was left holding it.

Cabinet spent five months on the matter before it came up with a ten-point plan. That should have been an early clue that selling this policy would be a nightmare. Ten changes to something people didn't understand in the first place? Why, voters thought, was Howard wasting his, and their, time on a Keating obsession?

It took Howard only a few minutes to undo all the work he had put into a compromise when he addressed a reconciliation conference in Melbourne in May 1997. It was the prime minister at his least dignified. He came to defend his ten-point plan, but was at cross-purposes with the audience. As Howard's temper rose, people jeered, stood up, and turned their backs. It wasn't the words themselves; read in isolation, they do not appear so provocative. It was his lectern-thumping tone. 'I made a mistake,' Howard told me later. 'I got angry because people were interjecting on Wik. But I still shouldn't have reacted like that; it was a mistake.'

Four months on, in September 1997, he took a prop with him to the ABC television studios for an interview with the '7.30 Report'. This was another miscalculation because it inflamed both camps.

'Let me just show you a view of it,' Howard said. 'This shows 78 per cent of the land mass of Australia coloured brown on this map. Now, the Labor Party and the Democrats are effectively saying that the Aboriginal people of Australia should have the potential right of veto over further development of 78 per cent of the land mass of Australia.'

Howard had begun 1997 with 50 per cent of voters satisfied with the job he was doing and only 36 per cent dissatisfied. But by May he had slipped into the territory previously occupied by Keating, in which more people said they were against him than for him. He would not have a plus sign in front of his personal standing for another year-and-a-half, until after he had won the October 1998 election.

The free-fall in Howard's approval rating threw out a conflicting signal about how Australians felt about themselves at this point. Howard was convinced that one of the reasons he had beaten Keating so handsomely in 1996 was that people were fed up with Labor's 'zealous multiculturalism'. He made the case early in his term, before Pauline Hanson had begun to find her voice in the race debate, so it can't be said that he was reacting to her when he said the following:

> Now, of course, some of it [the coalition victory] was due to the weariness of the former government. But a great deal more was due to the fact that we communicated as a group of people that understood the mainstream aspirations of the Australian people, [that we] were prepared to put behind this country some of the suffocating social censorship and political correctness which has been another very bad legacy of the former government. It will once again be possible to debate sensitive issues in this country

without being accused of being a racist, or an extremist or a bigot. I think it is immensely important for the quality of public debate that that be the case.

By Howard's reckoning, Keating had suppressed sensible discussion on matters such as Aboriginal affairs and the level of the immigration intake by calling his opponents racists. What he really meant was that he, Howard, had been silenced in opposition. This required a rewriting of history because the politicians who hurt him most on race in the late 1980s had been those on his own side who attacked his position on Asian immigration. Yet in lifting the 'pall of political correctness', as he described it, Howard had, unknowingly I suspect, unleashed the dogs of intolerance upon himself. The argument switched from what you couldn't say under Keating to how much people could get away with under Howard.

As prime minister, Keating could dominate the race debate at the politician-to-politician level, because he was running a positive agenda on native title. Attacking him proved to be a fraught exercise, as John Hewson found when he described the passage of the Mabo legislation as a 'day of shame' and instead came across as a crank. But Keating could not influence the argument that was running at the margins of the community; if anything, he was fuelling it. Howard thought he was releasing a safety value. But he lost control of both the official debate and the one below the line in the real world because he had no way of moderating the extremism to the right of him.

The timing of the Wik judgment did not help. It came just three months after Hanson's maiden speech to parliament. This gave her a continuing controversy to put her name to, and a constituency to galvanise: the farmers who now feared that Australian Aboriginals would take over their land. Howard was running a mixed message because he opposed the High Court on Wik, but supported the concept of native title. Hanson and the conservative premiers of Queensland and Western Australia had the simpler argument: abolish native title.

The media again had no interest in balanced reporting, but this time there were two reinforcing biases at play. Those who were outraged by the debate inflamed it by ridiculing Hanson and Howard. Those who were titillated went looking for the next outrageous quote.

'You have got to say the media was appalling in the way in which it conducted itself,' Jeff Kennett says of the reaction to Hanson. 'It was a woman saying it, different gender, and bingo. If the media are appalled at what happened, they have got to accept a lot of the responsibility for it.' I agree.

IN HIS FIRST headland speech as opposition leader in June 1995, Howard said he was happy with the thrust of Keating's native-title legislation:

> For my part, I found no quarrel with the High Court decision. It seemed entirely appropriate to the circumstances of the Mer people in the Murray Island. That is not to say that every ingredient of the *Native Title Act* was a justifiable legislative response to the Mabo decision. However, the High Court of Australia has now spoken the final word on the constitutionality of the *Native Title Act*. It will not be repealed by a future coalition government.

Two years later, in September 1997, on the night he produced his browned-out map to scare voters about the potential for native-title claims over 78 per cent of Australia, Howard said that the legislation he had inherited from Keating was 'a mess'. When he finally secured his Wik amendments in the Senate almost a year later, in July 1998, after Tasmanian Independent Brian Harradine 'blinked' to avoid a race-based election, Howard said: 'The Keating act was fatally flawed to begin with.' He was changing his position with hindsight.

For Keating, the Wik amendments were a personal blow. They curtailed native-title rights over existing pastoral leases, and only revived them when the pastoral lease expired. The states were also given the right to set up their own systems to administer pastoral leases.

This is one of the topics that revives the head-kicker in Keating. He has just finished showing me a year's worth of his personal files, taking me through the cabinet debates of 1993, and all the consultations with indigenous groups and with industry. He is like a proud father showing off his daughter's wedding album. Then he turns his thoughts to Wik, and lets fly:

> To gratuitously seek to wipe out the underlying title was a shocking thing to do [and] the culprit was Howard. If it wasn't for the conscience of some people in the Labor parties in the states, a lot more would be wound back.

Keating says Howard handed power to the states because he didn't want to compensate Aboriginal Australians for their loss.

> So the sneaky way was to give the powers to the states then extol the virtues of some kind of settlement for pastoral-lease holders, which the equivalent of was to give them freehold title, as if they didn't have enough. So the Aboriginal people who had been there for the millennia have their rights wiped out and the squatters get a freehold.

Jeff Kennett says Keating has less reason to be upset than he might realise. 'Paul probably says it was appalling, and that's fine; you are entitled to your opinion,' Kennett tells me. 'But did it destroy what was set up? No, it didn't destroy [native-title rights], and that's the test.'

With Keating gone, Howard wanted to claim native title as his own, which meant the position in the centre, between the extremes of what he saw as unfettered rights for Aboriginal Australians to obstruct economic activity and the desire of primary industries to be rid of native title entirely. But where Keating's Mabo legislation was greeted with cheers and hugs in the chamber and an all-night celebration in Gareth Evans's office, the passage of Howard's Wik legislation in July 1988 felt like being released from hospital after a car accident. 'It allows the Australian community to move onto to other issues,' Howard said of the deal.

Harradine told the Senate he had agreed to compromise because the alternative was a race-based election. 'Put yourself back to three weeks ago,' he said. 'We were heading headlong into a divisive double-dissolution election which would have torn the fabric of our society and set race relations back 40 or 50 years.'

The context Harradine referred to was the Queensland state election a month earlier, in June 1998. It was the first election contested by Hanson's One Nation Party. The coalition government of Rob Borbidge viewed her candidates as a lesser evil than the Labor opposition, so the Nationals and Liberals swapped preferences with One Nation. Howard watched on, knowing that what followed would inform his own election tactic. What happened was one of the decade's whoosh moments. The Queensland coalition lost power to Peter Beattie's Labor. One Nation claimed 11 seats in the 88-member parliament, and pulled in a primary vote of 22.7 per cent. Labor calculated that 7 per cent of One Nation's support came off its own base vote, and another 14 per cent from the coalition. There was no need for Howard to analyse the result. Hanson was a political wrecking-ball. He promptly dropped any plans he might have had to preference One Nation ahead of Labor at the upcoming federal election.

If the federal election had been held then, with Wik unresolved, and One Nation on the rampage, Howard would have lost, making him the first one-term prime minister since Labor's James Scullin was wiped out at the December 1931 election by the Great Depression. I suspect the Queensland state election marks the moment when the Labor Party truly lost the plot. Kim Beazley's opposition misread the One Nation vote as a magic-carpet ride back to power. They assumed that these battlers, former lifelong National Party voters, would come to Beazley in the same way that they had to Beattie, via One Nation's second preferences.

Howard had other ideas, of course. He took a plane, then a car, to the heart of Hanson country, north-west of Brisbane, to conduct an old-fashioned town hall meeting. The idea was to let people vent their frustrations at him so he could prove to them that their prime minister was willing to hear them out. Keating had been there in spirit five years earlier, when he spent an hour-and-a-quarter in a Sydney radio studio fielding angry callers from the NSW and Queensland bush on native title. Howard wanted to do it in person, and chose the Wondai RSL for the session of political primal scream therapy.

'I deliberately picked that area to go and listen to what people had to say,' Howard says. 'It was a noisy, scratchy, untidy evening, but it was worth doing because I was seen as engaging with people and trying to listen to them.'

The federal electorate that covers Wondai is Wide Bay, which is named after the bay that Captain Cook sighted on 18 May 1770. Wide Bay sits second-last on the electoral income-ladder, the 149th-poorest seat in the nation out of 150. Two-thirds of its families said they earned less than $1000 a week at the 2001 census. Only 29 per cent of voters had tertiary qualifications, which is less than half the rate for the nation's most-educated federal electorate, Sydney, which covers the inner city. Wide Bay had been a safe National Party seat, but One Nation now made it line-ball.

The questions to Howard from the floor of the Wondai RSL jumbled race with economic rationalism. One person echoed the 'I'm not a racist, but' sentiment that Keating faced five years earlier:

I am not against Aboriginal people, I have got some good Aboriginal friends. What I am looking to is Australia to be stable throughout everything without wasting money where it could probably be, you know. I'm not saying 'no more Mabo claims', I'm saying to halt the Mabo claims to put the money in better places, maybe for low-percentage loans for farmers or something like that.

Howard's answer is too long to requote in full, but his opening thought gives a good idea of the difference between him and Keating in dealing with this side of the Australian mosaic. Where Keating argued, Howard was more deferential:

> Well, sir, I think that was a very, very strong speech in favour of our native title legislation, with one or two exceptions. If you are saying to me that there is an enormous amount of confusion, if there are significant disincentives to investment in parts of Australia and there is concern about the present native title mess, you are absolutely right. I agree with you completely.

Another speaker claimed country folk represented the real stolen generation:

> If you care to take a little look around this room and look at me and the people my age, you're looking at the parents of the stolen generation. Stolen from the land, stolen from regional Australia. We were stolen by the ideology of yours and previous governments, the ideology of political correctness, economic rationalism. I think most people would call it irrationalism.

Howard replied:

> Well, I don't quite know where to start with that one. But could I start with political correctness because, I mean one of the reasons why I get heavily bucketed by some sections of the Canberra media is that I've been very critical of political correctness ... I share much of the anger in rural Australia about political correctness.

He moved on to economic rationalism with a neat turn of phrase: 'You asked me about economic rationalism. I'm an economic realist.'

Howard had, of course, been an economic rationalist earlier in the 1990s. He had told an audience in Peter Costello's electorate of Higgins, in Melbourne's inner-east wealth belt in October 1991, that economic rationalism 'has never really been tried in Australia — if the Liberal Party fails to understand this, it will do our nation a great disservice'.

Keating had disowned economic rationalism before Howard, in time for the 1993 election, but then he lost the mob on national identity in 1996. Howard thought he had the model right when he beat Keating with economic realism and social conservatism. But now the voters were turning against him. To deregulation's outsiders, Keating and Howard were interchangeable. These people understood intuitively that the Keating–Howard economy didn't have a job for them. It was politics and politicians that they didn't like. And there were enough voters who felt this way in Queensland alone to unseat the Howard government.

But something didn't seem to add up. Why did Queensland, and to a lesser extent NSW, embrace Hansonism, but not Victoria, which had been the state that took the heaviest fall in the recession? The simple explanation is that Victoria, the home of multiculturalism, was offended by Hanson's anti-black, anti-Asian platform. By contrast, Queensland had the lowest immigrant population of the mainland states, and so it didn't see the offence in her utterances. Yet this can't be the reason because the polling showed that Hanson's supporters weren't motivated primarily by race, even if she was. The Liberal and Labor Party research agreed on this score: globalisation, not multiculturalism, drove the backlash.

What troubled the Hansonites was their sense of powerlessness beyond the tariff wall. They looked for scapegoats, and seized whatever was in the headlines at the time. If it was native title, they'd repeat the slogan to pollsters that blacks were more equal than whites. If the topic was taxation reform, they'd complain that the rich were getting tax cuts while they, the poor, were copping the GST. After Wik had passed through the Senate, the main parties noted a redeeming drop in voter antagonism towards Aboriginal Australians. At the next Queensland state election, in 2001, Hanson's supporters switched their attention to more bread-and-butter concerns such as petrol prices.

But there is another immigrant angle to help explain why Queenslanders were the voters most attracted to Hanson. Queensland is a people magnet for interstate migrants. The state's capital Brisbane collects about 1800 more Sydneysiders and Melburnians each year than it sends the other way. The demographic tide began moving a generation earlier, when the Queensland National Party government of Joh Bjelke-Petersen abolished death duties on 1 January 1977. Although the other states followed his lead, they couldn't stop their taxpayers from heading to the Gold Coast for a better life. By the 1990s, no one thought much about the numbers, only that they were running Queensland's way. Between 1992 and 2004, the sunshine state increased it share of the nation's economy by almost two percentage points, from 15.5 per cent to 17.3 per cent, at the expense of Victoria and NSW.

But who exactly was defecting to Queensland? While the people flows were adding to the state's population and its wealth, the state was still behaving as if it were a loser from economic reform. Perhaps a generation of interstate migrants had triggered a form of white racism in Queenslanders, who were envious of all those cashed-up southerners. A more likely explanation is that interstate migration has been diluting Queensland of its diversity. Drilling into the most recent data, I found that Sydney and Melbourne have been engaged in a massive double-cross of the sunshine state. They are shedding their early retirees, and their less-skilled workers, in exchange for Queensland's best and brightest. Brisbane collects 2000 more retirees and low-skilled workers from Sydney and Melbourne each year than it loses. But it forfeits about 200 more young professional workers a year to the nation's two largest cities than it gains. So Brisbane's net interstate migration of 1800 is effectively at its own expense, because the global worker has moved south.

One Nation voters were predominately older men, in their forties and fifties, without work and on welfare. They lived along the Queensland coastline, but that did not necessarily make them locals. Some were economic refugees from the southern states, including multicultural Victoria. The deputy prime minister and

National Party leader Tim Fischer gave me this assessment of why Hansonism gained traction in the late 1990s:

> There was real poverty, and adding to it real bush poverty, and adding to it another group of poverty. A lot of people had moved to the hobby farm blocks, etc around South-East Queensland especially, and on the outer margins of Melbourne and Sydney. They had their tweed shirts, and they suddenly found they had to find 400 bucks to cart water to their place because they were in drought. They just found it progressively tougher and harder, and the little mini Shangri-La that they thought they got with their ten acres of land had become a nightmare financially and every other which way, you know public transport. So they became very angry and they became even more angry because a lot of them had guns.

In opposition and in government through the 1990s, the line that Fischer would hear repeatedly from the people he met outside the nation's capital cities was 'there is no such thing as a level playing field'. It was regional Australia telling the politicians that they were mugs for deregulating Australia's industries when the rest of the world wouldn't return the compliment by opening their markets to us. Hanson tapped this feeling with her economic nationalism, Fischer says.

HOWARD WAS both innocent victim and instigator of the race debates of the second half of the 1990s. He mistook his personal story, the controversy over his comments on Asian immigration in 1988, as the national experience. He felt that politically correct forces on the left were telling ordinary Australians that they weren't allowed a different view on multiculturalism or reconciliation. I have always held some sympathy for Howard's critique of 1980s-style multiculturalism. The problem begins with the term. Multiculturalism is an oxymoron. It is meant to describe Australia as it is, an open society that does immigration better than any other nation. But multiculturalism as a political exercise was inherently absurd because the only voices the media were prepared to amplify in the 1980s were those of the ethnic groups that they were already familiar with, from southern Europe. In the real world, Generation W — the Australian-born children of non-English immigrants — have little interest in ethnic politicians. They don't need representatives from their parents' community to speak up for them because they have already made a bigger connection, as members of the nation's mainstream. The parents of Generation W worry that their Australian-born children are too Australian.

Howard thought that ethnic politicians were encouraging separatism. But the ethnic politician who mobilised enough voters to test the nation's social cohesion was Hanson. Her white outcasts had less in common with mainstream Australia than Generation W.

Hanson annoyed the coalition on two levels. She was luring the coalition's battler voters to One Nation at the same time as she was driving the Liberal Party's capital-city constituency directly to Labor. This was the lesson of the Queensland state election, and the lesson of the Wik negotiations. The conventional wisdom holds that Howard won the race debate in the late 1990s. I'd argue the opposite, that it hurt him and he knew it. He had authority in his first year, primarily because of gun-law reform. He lost the respect of the electorate in the following two years because the national dialogue had become toxic on his watch.

HOWARD WANTED to rise above it all, but he couldn't because there were simply too many distractions. Chief among them was the painful realisation that many of his ministers weren't that smart. Between 12 October 1996 and 25 September 1997, Howard would lose five ministers and two parliamentary secretaries for breaching his code of conduct, by holding shares which conflicted with their public duties, to making false claims for taxpayer-funded travel expenses. The scandals developed a momentum of their own. Each sacking, each resignation, sent the media into a guessing frenzy over who the next victim would be. The coalition had led Labor by 49 per cent to 37 per cent in March. By November 1997, it trailed by 37 per cent to 45 per cent.

The first beneficiary of the travel-rorts row was Hanson's One Nation Party, which by chance had just been launched in March. The coalition vote fell from 49 to 40 per cent in a month, and all of it went over to the One Nation column. But Labor didn't pass the coalition on the primary vote until October, when the public were fascinated by its new recruit, the defecting leader of the Australian Democrats, Cheryl Kernot, who happened to share with Hanson a Queensland pedigree.

At its most basic level, Howard's *annus horribilis* of 1997 was about the nation's swing-state, Queensland. Hanson challenged him from the right and, briefly, Kernot did the same from the centre. But Howard had the sense to change his message to establish a better connection with the voters here. He thought he had it in 1996, when Queensland delivered him the landslide against Keating. But he now understood that their support for him had been a rejection of Keating, nothing more. To earn their backing in his own right, Howard would have to find a way to tell them a story that they could relate to. It was only then that he could begin to change the nation.

The misconception about Howard's first term is that the emergence of Hanson somehow vindicated his own critique of Keating's social agenda. It didn't, because he lost control of the Australian conversation. Howard's first term was, by his own admission, not a great one. The blunder that Kim Beazley's opposition made was to assume that this was all there was to Howard. They didn't credit him with the smarts to remake himself, to learn on the job.

Labor's error was to look in the wrong spot for victory. They wanted Hanson to unseat Howard via the bottom-50 seats on the electoral income-ladder. This seemed like a good idea at the time, but it involved Labor seeking office on terms that had never worked for it before. The Labor governments of Gough Whitlam, and of

Bob Hawke and Paul Keating, had switched coalition votes in the middle and the top, not the bottom. The coalition always held a majority of seats in the bottom, as we've seen, even when Labor was in power.

The implications of the change in tactics was not apparent then because not many people would have had access to the necessary income analysis. I certainly couldn't attempt to make sense of the story until much later, in 2002, when I had been out of the press gallery for three years, and the 2001 census had been released. But Howard did when it counted because his party's polling was more sophisticated than Labor's. It showed him where the coalition was truly vulnerable, and that was in the middle and top. This was where *Fightback!* had floundered in 1993.

Labor wanted to tell a social story to the top, and an economic story to the middle and the bottom. In a nutshell, it thought well-off Liberal voters craved Keating's triple R agenda of reconciliation, republic and engagement with the Asian region, while the battlers at the bottom wanted pre-Keating protectionism. But Howard had already figured out on his return to the opposition leadership in 1995 that Liberal republicans would never desert him on national identity, so long as he offered them a better bet on economic management. In the second half of the 1990s, that meant tax cuts. It was the bottom that wanted to hear the social story because, as they didn't work to begin with, no amount of cash could improve their circumstances. These distinctions matter because they hold the key to Howard's belated comeback in the second half of 1998 after the multiple agonies of Wik, travel rorts, and Hansonism.

BY THE WAY, what did happen to Wik in the end? The Wik and Wik Way people spent another four years before the courts after their High Court victory. In October 2000, the Federal Court gave them native title over just 6136 sq km of the 17,700 sq km they had originally claimed, which covered 'mainly Aboriginal areas'. This is one way to count how much Howard had wound back native title.

But common sense kicked in afterwards. The Wik and Wik Way people, the pastoralists, and others began negotiating an extension. Another four years on, in October 2004, an agreement was signed to double the native title rights and interests to 12,530 sq km. In the same month, the nation's biggest cattle producer, the Australian Agricultural Company, signed a memorandum of understanding with the Waluwarra/Georgina people over the 1.2 million hectare Headingly Station, south-west of Mount Isa in western Queensland. Finally, after a decade of politically inspired fear and loathing, the people were getting on with the job of reconciliation. The word from regional Australia was that native title did not cause an economic catastrophe. Properties did not lose their value. 'Tree clearing, for instance, is a far bigger worry,' Kerry Herron, the chairman of valuers Herron Todd White told *The Australian* in October 2004. Native title, he said, was 'a non-event'. Another 'Seinfeld' moment.

Hip Pockets and Hypocrites

IF JOURNALISTS AND POLITICIANS could swap eaves-dropping rights on each other's work behind closed doors, we'd want to be flies on the wall at a cabinet meeting. There we could see all the egos of a government seated around a table. We could take mental notes on the bullies and the crawlers, the bullied and the crawled to. We'd see who has the prime minister's ear, and who makes his eyelids heavy. Tim Fischer once told me the restless, and recurring, thought he had when he was caught in a long cabinet meeting was that the room had no windows.

If I were a politician with a bent for anthropology, I'd want to check out the budget lock-up. Once a year, journalists are taken out of the comfort zones of their offices and herded into the cavernous committees rooms in Parliament House. Theoretically, we have six hours of mass confinement in which to scrutinise the budget papers before the treasurer gives his speech to the nation at 7.30 pm — time to prepare our reports and commentary for that evening's current affairs programs and tomorrow's newspapers. Election tax packages also involve lock-ups, although they tend to run for an hour or so.

The lock-up is a festival of the absurd, and it begins with a deferential hush as we read the treasurer's budget speech, and thumb through the main budget paper. Then comes the murmur. This is the bit I'd want to hear if I were a politician. By the half-hour mark, every journalist will have done the mental arithmetic on what the budget means for them. In 18 years of lock-ups, I have

230

heard highly paid reporters banter about the tax cuts that were coming to them just twice, in 1998 and 2005. They liked the GST package in 1998. And they loved the generosity of the 2005 budget, which was underwritten by the booming Chinese economy. As a rough guide, these were the documents that gave average earners a tax cut worth less than $10 a week and the typical highly paid journalist about $60–$80 a week.

Placing a dollar sign next to a voter is supposed to come naturally to politicians. Each side should know who their target is, what they earn, and how they will respond to a bribe. Labor's greatest gift to John Howard as prime minister was to think of the nation as poorer than it really was. In the five years between the two GST elections, 1993 and 1998, Labor forgot what it took to win. Kim Beazley aimed his handouts at a spot on the income ladder that no upwardly mobile worker, let alone a press gallery journalist, could relate to. He thought he was talking to real Australians, but I believe he underestimated how fast incomes were rising.

I remember vividly the discussions with Labor advisers who thought Howard was committing political suicide by skewing the tax cuts in his GST package to people like us in the political class. Howard's income-tax cuts delivered 52 per cent of the cash to the top 20 per cent of the taxpayers who were earning more than $50,000 a year. When Beazley's tax package was released a fortnight after Howard's, Labor gave only 20 per cent of the benefits to the top 20 per cent of earners, so the remaining 80 per cent was spread to the 80 per cent of taxpayers earning less than $50,000.

Labor's package failed the examination of the press gallery lock-up. A colleague stabbed at the tables with his finger and complained that he was being offered only $5 a week. 'I can't believe it; they've really stuffed it up. There's *nothing* here for the middle class.' Later that day, a well-known pontificator, who would have been earning twice what I was, told me that Labor had created a new 'poverty trap for the middle class'. I thought they were being precious at the time, but they were on to something. Voters imagined themselves earning these incomes one day, and didn't want Labor telling them there would be no reward for getting there. Howard said later that Beazley was treating people on $50,000 as 'rich'.

Yet there was a conflict between what we reported in the late 1990s and how we reacted behind closed doors when both sides showed us the money in their tax packages. Howard got a bad run in the media in 1997 and throughout 1998 largely because he deserved it. But when he switched the conversation to the kitchen table with the GST, we were slow to grasp why he was now on firmer ground.

The race card or a wad of cash? What happens when a prime minister flirts with a double-dissolution election on native title and announces in virtually the same breath that the 'never ever' GST will become coalition policy again? The collective wisdom in the press gallery was that Howard would lose both ways. The Hansonites and middle Australia would shun him because of the GST, and the blue-rinse set would turn on him because he had snuggled up to One Nation, if not in 1998, then certainly at the 2001 election, after they had confronted the new tax system in the raw. But the collective subconscious of the press gallery had already made its call. When presented with a tax cut, the personal becomes the political. Howard was on a winner because Beazley didn't know how to play the politics of prosperity.

Paul Keating understands this, and it makes him fume today that Labor abandoned his model when Howard became prime minister. By that, Keating means, of course, the policies associated with his economic self. Labor clung to his social agenda.

He throws me a curve ball when I ask him where he thinks Labor went wrong in its fight with Howard. He suggests that Labor was never really the party of meritocracy. Perhaps it just got lucky with Bob Hawke and him between 1983 and 1996, he wonders. Labor has been an agent of change three times in the nation's history: during World War Two with John Curtin, briefly in the early 1970s with Gough Whitlam, and then Hawke and himself. Apart from that, nothing. He gives me his take on Labor's history, from the party's modest beginnings, the crack-up with Billy Hughes over conscription during World War One, and the one-term disaster of James Scullin during the Great Depression, before Curtin rallied the nation in World War Two. But the Curtin years were the aberration. Labor promptly turned socialist after the war, and turned off a generation:

> The Chifley years simply squandered the Curtin inheritance. Chifley was trying to nationalise banks, trying to build a command-and-control structure, which the country didn't need. I regarded Chifley as a very modest performer and so his government was defeated accordingly. What have we got then, we've got the Labor Party in the '50s and '60s rent by division but also rent by division over ways and means. Then we take the Whitlam government, which had clarity about the need for an assertion of our national character but a complete confusion between ways and means, between economic outcomes and economic objectives. So if you look through the 83 years until Hawke and I come to office, there is no ability on the part of the federal Labor Party to put anything in place like the '83 to '96 years, no technical ability, no grasp of the major economic issues in a systemic kind of way.
>
> You might have had Curtin's manful measuring-up to the challenge of the war, and his ability to move people around in respect of things like conscription. But take that out of it, and the Labor Party from 1900 to 1983 is a pretty modest beast.

Since 1996, Keating says, Labor has turned its back on upward mobility:

> And you may say, well, will we see the likes of the '83 to '96 government again? Well, maybe, maybe not. Institutionally you could have no confidence that the Labor Party could now breed it. In fact, it probably never bred it; it was more good luck than good management.

I mention that politics is the last closed shop in the economy, and he replies that the Liberal Party is more connected to the real world than Labor:

> It's the political equivalent of the Sydney taxi industry, that's what it is. You know, little groups of owners, you know, with part-time drivers in their pockets. The Liberals have actually showed more promise in understanding the need to open it up than the Labor Party does.

I'm interested in how Keating would have handled Howard. He gives me an anecdote about the 2004 election. While Mark Latham was finalising his tax and welfare changes, Keating called to urge him to cut the top personal rate of tax from 47 cents in the dollar to 39 cents. Don't worry about what the Labor pollsters say, it would drive Howard mad, Keating told him. But Latham had already baulked at this option earlier in the year and wasn't in a mood to revisit it. He wound up offering a tax cut of about $8 a week to those on less than $52,000 a year, whom the coalition had denied a tax cut in the 2004 budget. In other words, Latham had taken the same approach in 2004 that Beazley had lost with in 1998. No need to guess how Latham's tax tables went down in the press gallery lock-up.

Keating didn't have anything more to do with Latham, though he did ring just before polling day to wish him luck. Latham replied that he expected to struggle, but he was happy that he got to run his argument in the campaign about 'easing the squeeze' on families.

Keating shakes his head: 'I said "Listen, mate, you know what the squeeze on families is in Sydney, how they move up from a two-bedroom apartment to a terrace house, how they trade in their Commodore for an Audi, that's the squeeze on families". He says: "You're joking".'

Later that evening, Keating hosted a small election party that became a wake once it was clear that Labor had lost for the fourth time to Howard. A woman in her early thirties who works for one of Keating's friends approached him for advice. She and her partner had a small two-bedroom apartment in inner Sydney, and wanted to ask the former treasurer and prime minister whether they should upgrade to a $1.2 million terrace. 'Will we be safe to buy if we enter into a fixed loan?' Keating recalls her saying.

'These are voters for Labor, and they are crying into their beers about losing, and the next question is, how do we move up? This is the squeeze on families.'

CHAPTER THIRTEEN

The 'Government Salvation Tax'

I CAN'T REVEAL what he said, because the speech was off the record. Actually, I've forgotten the precise phrase, and didn't have the sense to write it down at the time. But it was the only occasion, I suspect, that John Howard had ever delivered a vowel-perfect impersonation of a colleague before a room-full of journalists.

It was 5 December 1997, and Howard was the guest of honour at the annual press gallery dinner, where seven years earlier Paul Keating had told us he was the Placido Domingo of Australian politics. Howard was taking us through the history of the GST when he touched on one of the humiliations he had suffered as treasurer at the hands of Malcolm Fraser.

He put on his best patrician accent and repeated the words that Fraser used to kill Howard's plans for a consumption tax in 1981. Something about unintended consequences and inflation. The mimic was good-natured. It was, in fact, so close to Fraser's voice that it drew chuckles from some of us in the audience. Most, though, were only half-listening. The GST is not a topic to arouse journalists on a Friday night.

Howard and the GST were joined at the hips. They grew up together in politics. In 1975, a year after Howard arrived in parliament, the Asprey inquiry into the taxation system first recommended a consumption tax to Gough Whitlam's Labor government. Whitlam ignored the idea, and there it lay buried until treasurer Howard resurrected it five years later. He had convinced

Fraser to leave the door ajar at the 1980 election, neither ruling in nor ruling out a broad-based tax on consumption. But Fraser lost interest the following year, and relations between the two men became irretrievably poisoned. Fraser didn't bother telling Howard that his GST was dead. Howard learned of the veto from political journalist Michelle Grattan, who had been tipped off by Fraser's office. Yet Howard took his plan to cabinet anyway, knowing it would be rejected by Fraser.

Keating used to bait Howard about that one, telling him he had been rolled. When Keating suffered his own prime ministerial rebuff on the GST from Bob Hawke in 1985, Howard returned the sledge. Keating replied:

> I am not like the leader of the opposition [Howard]. I did not slither out of the cabinet room like a mangy maggot and then go and leak a story to the press about how I was beaten by Malcolm Fraser. I fought it out in the country and in front of the public under the cameras of the tax summit. I do not mind taking the loss … The fact is that I tried and the former treasurer did not.

As opposition leader, Howard tried again in 1987. He drew up plans for massive income-tax cuts and an 8 per cent retail tax. But the retail tax never saw the light of day because Joh Bjelke-Petersen scuttled it as part of his doomed plan to come to Canberra. Keating rubbed Howard's nose in it again after the tax cuts he took to the July 1987 election were found to contain a double-counting error.

These would have been just some of the thoughts that were flashing through Howard's mind as he was laid low with pneumonia in July 1997. 'I spent a lot of time thinking in hospital,' he says. 'I had alluded to tax reform in an interview before I got crook. I had three weeks off. I was in hospital for a week and I had two weeks' convalescence. I was off for virtually a month, and when I came back I decided we had to do the GST.'

The interview he was referring to had come two months earlier, in May, at the end of another crazy week in parliament that seemed to be part of the natural rhythm of 1997. Peter Costello had just released the government's second budget. Its centrepiece was a modest rebate of 15 per cent on the tax people paid on the interest they earned on their savings or the contributions they made to superannuation. No one would recall this policy today, but it is the answer to the trick political question of the 1990s that I posed in chapter 10: who dishonoured Keating's super tax cuts?

The budget papers said the measure would deliver $2 billion a year by 2000–01. Translation: it would be less than half the L A W promise of $4.5 billion, which Howard had told voters in 1996 he would deliver 'in full'. Difficult as the new policy might have been to explain, it was still a handout, and the government should have won some kudos for it, right? Wrong. The day after the budget was unveiled, Howard inexplicably attacked the savings rebate. 'I will not be claiming it,' Howard told parliament after Labor questioned him on its fairness. Costello was furious.

The first rule in politics when you muck up is to change the topic, fast. On the Sunday, four days after he ridiculed his government's savings rebate, Howard put the GST back on the table. But he left himself room to manoeuvre:

> I am conscious of what we said before the last election and I'm not going to walk away from that commitment, and it remains rock solid. But, looking forward, you have to acknowledge that the Australian taxation system is less than perfect and I don't know how anybody could argue otherwise.

Of course, Howard had said a GST would 'never ever' be policy again and that he would not increase taxes or introduce new ones in his first term. Much as he might have wanted to keep those promises, the conservative side of politics had been hounding him for almost a year to revive the GST as a matter of national interest. The pressure originated with the business lobbies immediately after the election. By October 1996, Victorian premier Jeff Kennett had joined the clamour.

There was an element of belittlement going on; Howard was, in effect, being told how to govern. Kennett said 'there should be a broad-based tax' and called on Howard to show 'leadership'. He also warned that the economy was heading for another recession. Howard was not happy. 'I think Jeff ought to take a holiday,' he said of the recession warning. As for tax reform, he said: 'It's always easy, of course, to debate the other bloke's agenda. I'm responsible for my agenda [and] the federal Liberal Party agenda this term does not include any contemplation of a GST.' In November 1996, Costello described the GST as having 'been invested with some snake-oil qualities—it has some certain advantages, but you wouldn't want to over-claim it'. In January 1997, Howard backed up his treasurer, warning that 'people get this false idea that it is the economic elixir of Australia'.

The denials seemed genuine, but there was a sense that something was being cooked up. Immediately after the 1996 election, the business group closest to the government, the Australian Chamber of Commerce and Industry, had convinced the peak welfare group, the Australian Council of Social Service, to join the campaign for tax reform. Howard watched the debate with interest even as he tried to douse it. But he didn't start thinking seriously about the GST until the winter of 1997, when he caught pneumonia on a visit to the United States. As his health recovered, he weighed up the pros and cons of a GST election. On 5 August, at the start of the final week of his three weeks off work, the High Court helped him make up his mind by striking down $5 billion worth of state and territory taxes on tobacco, alcohol, and petrol. The federal government introduced temporary surcharges on top of its own excises to cover the shortfall, but the patch-up job was not sustainable in the longer term.

Howard could have been forgiven for thinking the High Court owed him this break after the rough hand it had dealt him on native title. The judgment allowed Howard to claim that the existing indirect tax system was broken, and that a GST was the obvious solution. He also had $5 billion worth of leverage with which to bring the states and territories into the GST debate.

240 THE LONGEST DECADE

The one unarguable benefit of a GST is that it beats the half-baked system that had been allowed to evolve after the World War Two, where the Commonwealth taxed some goods, but not others, and the states and territories taxed some services, but not others. Keating's defeat of John Hewson's 15 per cent GST in 1993 did not prevent the federal wholesale sales tax from rising after the election, or state and territory governments from seeking new ways to tax services, such as the NSW government's hotel-bed tax. A GST offered an end to the silly games, for all levels of government. Yet efficiency is the reason least cited for cleaning up the indirect tax system. Politicians needed voters to think there was something more involved in the deal — the means to reduce personal taxes.

When the Liberal Party tested voter attitudes in 1997 and compared them to the polling done for *Fightback!* six years earlier, it detected a subtle change. Although the electorate remained hostile, it now felt a GST was 'inevitable'. Howard can thank Keating for this. Voters still remembered the 'betrayal' of the 1993 budget. But a GST still represented a monumental gamble. Some of Howard's cabinet colleagues thought he was crazy.

The tax package that Howard took to the 1998 election differed in four important respects from the original *Fightback!* plan.

First, the GST was set at 10 per cent, not 15 per cent, which meant fewer existing taxes would be abolished. The federal wholesale sales tax was to be removed, as were nine smaller state taxes, including those on bank transactions. But the states got to keep their payroll taxes, and Canberra held on to the petrol excise — consumption taxes that Hewson had wanted to abolish in *Fightback!*. Howard would give the $27.2 billion in GST revenue to the states, so he could tell voters that the rate would be frozen at 10 per cent because no increase could occur without the agreement of all the states.

Second, the personal income-tax cuts on offer were about half as generous as Hewson's original formula had been.

The third contrast was on spending cuts. Howard didn't repeat the *Fightback!* mathematics of using expenditure savings to fund the bulk of the personal tax cuts.

Finally, Howard made sure he gave back more than he took with the GST. He offered a new, expanded rebate for private health insurance, and extra family payments. He could do all this because the budget surplus would be big enough to cover all bases by the start date for the new tax system — 1 July 2000. That is, he had finally collected enough bracket creep to pay for tax cuts.

But there was a fiddle in the numbers. The tax cuts were put at $13 billion in 2000–01, yet $2 billion of that total came from cancelling the savings rebate from the 1997 budget. Yes, the $2 billion that honoured less than half the $4.5 billion L A W promise was now being recycled for the GST campaign. Howard saw no point in persisting with the savings rebate after he had undermined it.

Of the $11 billion in actual tax cuts, almost half — $4.8 billion — was paid for by dipping into the surplus. This is the bracket-creep component, the return of money already owing to taxpayers. Another $3.2 billion came from the tobacco excise that the Commonwealth was collecting on behalf of the states and territories after the High Court judgment. The government liked this money so much that it kept it. The remaining $3 billion in funding for the income-tax cuts was soaked from business. After all the fiddles, the real value of the tax cuts was about half what the government said it was. But voters hadn't received a tax cut since the first round of the L A W ones in November 1993, so there was a sense of expectation in the electorate.

Howard released the tax package on 13 August 1998. Kim Beazley replied on 27 August, with a $5.5 billion tax cut (half the value of Howard's), and no GST.

Howard's tax cuts were tilted towards single-income families ahead of dual-income families, and higher-income singles ahead of the lower-paid. Beazley reversed Howard's priorities. But in seeking to be even-handed, Beazley ceded much of the middle and all of the top to Howard.

Beazley allowed Howard to outbid him for the wallets of too many swinging voters. Howard had the larger offer for single-income families above $45,000, dual-income families above $50,000, and for single people above $35,000. Keating, by contrast, had bettered Hewson across these sensitive points on the income ladder in 1993.

There was mushiness to the 1998 election. Beazley presented himself as a cuddly father figure, or friendly uncle. Voters liked that side of him. But they couldn't get a fix on where he stood beyond his opposition to the GST. Howard accused Beazley of lacking the 'ticker' to lead the nation. The prime minister, by contrast, presented himself as a doer. But what he was doing was reducing public policy to a single issue that had already been debated to death. The electorate responded by damning the main parties with their lowest combined primary vote in history. Between then, they collected just 79.6 per cent of the first ballots. One Nation claimed 8.4 per cent of the primary vote for the right, and the Australian Democrats and Greens took another 7.7 per cent between them for the left, with the remainder spread amongst independents and other minor parties.

At 6.40 pm on election night, Howard was advised to prepare a concession speech. The Liberal Party federal director, Lynton Crosby, had just completed an exit poll of voters: it predicted a Labor victory, by 53 per cent to 47 per cent. Howard laughs about it now, but it is a reminder of how close he had come to being a one-term prime minister:

> I think I administered the last rites in the green room at Kirribilli.
> It was exactly the same figure as it had been in the final Newspoll.
> One Nation did us huge damage.

Crosby's numbers were out by 2 points. Labor won the popular vote after the distribution of preferences, by 51 per cent to 49 per cent. The swing against the government was 4.6 per cent. On face value, it was a re-run of the last GST election of 1993, in which Keating prevailed with 51.4 per cent of the two-party vote.

Howard was saved because he had something to sell. He also had the power of incumbency and Beazley's modest ambitions to push him over the line. Labor didn't expect to win going into the campaign; but when it saw the wave was breaking its way, it realised it had forgotten to bring its surfboard. The opposition had war-gamed for an honourable defeat, not victory, so it didn't have the resources in place to capture some of the government seats that appeared on the radar late in the campaign. Going into the election, Howard had a 30-seat buffer. He dropped 18, a disaster by any objective measure. But the real failure was Labor's. It had lost a winnable election.

Beazley's 18 gains were distributed as follows: six seats from the bottom of the electoral income-ladder, seven from the middle, and only five from the top. He restored Labor's traditional majority in the middle of the ladder—26 out of 50. But the coalition retained the majorities at the top and bottom, and a majority of seats in every state except Victoria and Tasmania. NSW and Queensland were again decisive, as they had been in 1996.

Howard won because of deregulation, not in spite of it, because he made a better pitch to the top and the middle than Hewson had done in 1993. And he also fended off Hanson at the bottom. Labor didn't see it at the time, but it would have captured more seats if it had dared to compete with Howard for the middle-income and higher-income Liberal voters, and the upwardly mobile former Hawke–Keating voters. The proof is in the 12 seats that saved Howard, in which the combined swing to Labor was just 1.2 per cent, or a third less than the national swing of 4.6 per cent. These near-miss electorates comprised five top, five middle, and only two bottom seats. But Beazley aimed too low. He was looking for the Hansonites to give him power. By doing this, he confused the nation's political and social debates by seeing deregulation's cup as half empty instead of steadily filling.

The argument on national identity became nonsensical after the 1998 election. The Howard huggers saw his victory as vindicating the prime minister's conservative social values. The Keating fan club was inclined to agree. But that required both sides to pretend that the decisive seats at the top of the electoral income-ladder, where the so-called elites resided, stuck with Howard in 1998, and again in 2001, because they approved of the monarchy, abhorred the symbolism of reconciliation, and were ambivalent about engagement with Asia. In reality, these people simply voted for the man they trusted with their money. When they were given the chance to pass judgement on Keating's social agenda at the November 1999 republic referendum, they voted yes. But they were in the minority then. The republic lost 45.1 per cent to 54.9 per cent, because Howard managed to split the republican vote.

Look at the argument the other way around. Would Howard have won in 1998 if he had supported Keating's triple R program and still introduced a GST? The answer is yes, because there were never enough vulnerable seats at the bottom for Labor to steal. What really troubled Howard at the bottom was the idea of One Nation winning seats in its own right. With the Hansonites off his back, he could tack back to the centre of the political spectrum. Howard says the GST saved him:

> I think the GST was a net plus in terms of the reputation of the government, that's my view. A lot of people don't agree with that; they think we would have done better in '98 if we didn't have a GST. I'm not sure about that. We always do better when we are advocating something because we are seen to be standing for something.

He also says his opponents drew false comfort from Hanson's near double-digit primary vote in 1998. 'The electorate was volatile,' he concedes. But that did not mean the public had returned to Labor:

> Labor completely misread the 1998 election, the size of the One Nation vote. One Nation made that rather odd decision to prefer-ence against all sitting members; and because, with a big majority, we, by definition, had more sitting members, Labor did unexpect-edly well out of that. But it didn't mean that that was really half the

Labor vote they'd lost in '96 returning, and I think Beazley fundamentally misunderstood that. And that affected him from '98 right through to 2001. He thought he was halfway there. His primary stayed virtually static. One Nation took 7 per cent off our pile and handed half of that to Labor. In 2001, half of those One Nation votes came back to us, and then in 2004, in mathematical terms we [got the rest].

They still haven't gone through any of the policy reappraisals that we went through after we lost in 1983. That industrial relations debate that went on through the Liberal Party in the 1980s, that was very difficult. But it had to be had, and it fundamentally reshaped the post-Fraser Liberal Party.

Keating makes roughly the same point, though he doesn't give any credit to Howard for picking the mood better than Beazley. In Keating's view, Labor had forgotten how to win, which allowed Howard to win by default. 'Howard nearly lost in '98; you see, they didn't like him by '98,' Keating sighs. 'But they'd lost our middle-ground vote by now.'

THE RELIEF of winning the 1998 election created a false sense of security in the government. The GST was assumed to be as good as passed. Howard thought he understood Tasmanian independent senator Brian Harradine. They had dealt on Telstra in 1996 and on native title before the 1998 election. The GST, Howard reasoned, would be no different. But Harradine wasn't comfortable. He asked for, and got, five months allocated for four separate Senate committees to scrutinise the fine print of the legislation. Here he could test the government's claim that everyone would be a winner from tax reform.

The Senate's GST inquiries were a goldmine for nit-picking journalism. In the end, I think we all lost the plot—politicians, the press, and vested interests alike. The point of the exercise, from the government's perspective, was to give Harradine a sense of control.

But it became a gripe show that pitted voter against voter, lobby against lobby. The government was asking Harradine to name a price, to nominate the groups he thought should receive more compensation for the GST, so that the new tax could be passed before 1 July 1999, before the Australian Democrats assumed the balance of power in the Senate. Howard had a figure in mind, an extra $1 billion in handouts for pensioners and the like. He always liked to talk to the electorate in billion-dollar headlines. But Harradine didn't want to negotiate until the Senate committees had completed their reports.

Meanwhile, fellow independent Mal Colston, whose vote Howard was prepared to accept again, was in negotiations with the Director of Public Prosecutions. Stricken with the stomach cancer that would eventually kill him, Colston told the DPP he was not fit to stand trial on fraud charges. The DPP insisted that Colston have an independent medical assessment. Colston wrote to the prime minister and the attorney-general Daryl Williams on 29 April 1999 to accuse a member of the DPP's staff, the Labor Party, and some in the media of conspiring against him. The letter was dropped in the press boxes. While the names were blacked out, it was obvious that mine was one of them — there was no one else in the press gallery with a six-letter Christian name and an 11-letter surname. The DPP had wanted the trial to start in June, but held back while the question over Colston's health was cleared up. Colston played hardball. His office leaked his own medical records, which warned he could be dead by the middle of the year.

The question for Howard was whether he had, in fact, understood the lesson of 1997, when his government was first tarred by its association with Colston. A GST delivered on this man's casting vote would have been compromised. Colston's position was politically untenable. If he were too sick for court, as he would prove to be in the end, did anyone seriously expect him to make a considered judgment on the most complex piece of tax legislation in the nation's history? By the end of April 1999, Labor was back in front in the polls, by 43 per cent to 41 per cent, on the back of the government's GST shenanigans.

On 14 May 1999, Harradine put an end to the charade when he said the GST was 'inherently regressive' and he could not pass it in any form. Howard was gobsmacked. The obvious question now was, would he talk to the Democrats, who supported a GST but without food in the tax base? 'No, no, no, we are not going to exempt food,' he said. 'The case for changing food is less now than it was 24 hours ago because we have significantly increased the compensation. I am more interested in keeping faith with the Australian people than in keeping faith with other parties.' He threatened a double-dissolution election. He couldn't be serious?

If the essence of the Howard years could be bottled, the label would say: 'In time of crisis, swallow pride immediately.' Harradine killed Howard's GST on a Friday. By the following Tuesday, Howard accepted the need to remove food from the GST to save his leadership. History would be tempted to view this moment as a neon-light epiphany. But the truth is more mundane, though probably more illuminating. Howard works best in a crisis because it is only when he is confronted with his political mortality that he has to think as the electorate does, free of ideology. Howard the policy purist believed a GST without food was not worth the effort. Howard the politician saw no GST as the greater evil because the public would ask, rightly, what was the point of having him in charge of the nation if he couldn't get his program through the Senate.

The government had dismissed the Democrats, telling them they were irrelevant to the tax debate. Howard had said he wouldn't talk to them. So how did he and Democrats leader Meg Lees manage to strike an agreement within a fortnight of Harradine's bombshell?

Howard met Lees eight times between 20 May and 27 May 1999. The first three rounds revealed Howard's modus operandi for polite negotiation. He allowed Lees and the Democrats' treasury spokesman, Andrew Murray, to take the floor so they could talk until they had gotten everything off their chests. This point of the discussion resembled a tutorial. On the government side of the table sat Howard, Costello, and their chiefs of staff. Howard wanted to show Lees and Murray and their two advisers that the government was willing to gulp huge quantities of humble pie on the GST.

The Democrats talked and talked. They dominated the first meeting on the Thursday, then the next two on the Friday and the following Monday. On the Tuesday, everyone got a little tense. Howard accepted that food would come out of the GST, but he didn't want Lees to dictate how it would be paid for. She wanted the tax cuts trimmed across the board. Howard was only prepared to sacrifice those voters on more than $50,000, even though he told them at the last election that they were not 'rich'. Wednesday found both Howard and Lees downcast. Lees had the Democrats' deputy leader, Natasha Stott Despoja, snapping at her heels. Stott Despoja had publicly warned Lees that it was 'difficult to make this tax fairer'. She didn't realise then how close she had come to scuttling the deal with that comment. Another public attack, Lees feared, and the Democrats would have rebelled, but Stott Despoja bit her lip. Howard met Lees twice on the Wednesday before they returned to the main negotiations with Costello and Murray. They sealed their pact the following evening.

They held a joint press conference on the Friday, 28 May 1999, to announce the new tax system Mark II. Howard said he had achieved '85 or 90 per cent' of his original package. And that was the point. There could be no Howard, he realised, without the GST.

Food had been tax-free under the old tax system. Keeping it out of the GST net would blow a $3.9 billion hole in the new tax system. To pay for this, Howard stripped $1.3 billion from the promised personal-tax cuts and allowed the states to keep $2.6 billion in taxes that were to be abolished by the GST.

The Howard-Lees income tax scales now delivered hip-pocket outcomes similar to those that voters had rejected in Labor's election platform. The prime minister said the tax cuts for the four out of five workers earning less than $50,000 had been preserved. 'It will represent a massive injection into middle Australia,' he said. 'It will reward the hardworking backbone of the Australian nation which represents those families in particular.'

This quote is worth fact-checking because it will help resolve the riddle of whether the GST was, indeed, worth the effort. When he launched his election tax-package in August 1998, Howard gave himself one very simple hip-pocket test: 'The top marginal rate paid by 81 per cent of taxpayers will be 30c in the dollar or less,' he said. 'You can almost call it the "bracket creep abolition provision" of the tax plan.' In other words, the top two rates would apply to no more than 19 per cent of voters.

Problem was, the promise was broken on the day the new tax system started. By 1 July 2000, there were a touch over 20 per cent of taxpayers on the 42c and 47c bands. By 2002–03, that figure had risen to 26.1 per cent. About 200,000 voters had been catapulted by bracket creep to the very top rate of 47c. These upwardly mobile workers would be itching to dump Howard — but Labor wouldn't offer them an alternative. Howard needed three more rounds of tax cuts between 2003 and 2005 before he could achieve his goal of having four out of five workers paying no more than 30c in the dollar. Each new instalment would be paid for out of the previous year's bracket creep, so taxpayers were really just treading water. Even then, Howard had only dealt with the bracket creep at the top of the income ladder. The total tax bill for workers in the middle rose each year under the new tax system.

IMPLEMENTING THE GST proved to be the hardest job of all. The Reserve Bank had begun lifting interest rates again in November 1999, ending a five-year honeymoon for borrowers after the rate hikes that effectively killed off Paul Keating's government. Each move up pushed down support for Howard and his government. Against this backdrop, the 1 July 2000 start date for the GST became a moment for a national teeth-gnashing. Would the sky fall in? It seems so silly looking back, because the day of the switch from the old to the new tax system was never going to amount to much. Fresh food was GST-free, so the first trip to the supermarket would be benign. It was the tax cuts that poured in pay packets over the course of the first week that drew more comment from voters. But three fuses had been lit, which would all go off by the end of the year. The paperwork associated with the new tax system had turned 2 million Australians into tax collectors for the government, petrol prices began creeping higher because of the GST, and the property market was behaving erratically.

The fear that house prices would rise by 10 per cent after 1 July triggered an irrational cycle of selling and renovating. A year's worth of activity was compressed into the first six months of 2000, and a buyers' strike followed in the second half of the year. To avoid the 10 per cent GST, home buyers had, in their panic, increased the cost of building materials by 20 per cent. The Reserve Bank had no idea this would happen, and was still lifting interest rates in August 2000 when the property market had already turned turtle. So severe was the slump that it shrunk the national economy by 0.6 per cent in the final three months of the year. But this minus number for GDP would not be released until the following March, when it would wreak political havoc.

The government's vote collapsed in early 2001 because voters felt ripped off. They didn't like the forms they had to fill in every three months under the new tax system, and they loathed the idea that petrol prices were about to pass $1 a litre for the first time. From the contemporary perspective, when the nightmares of bird flu, global warming, and terror smother the media, they seem like petty grievances. But this happened to be Howard's most miserable moment of all in politics because voters seemed to have made up their minds that he was a penny-pincher. He was now again as unpopular as prime minister Keating had been immediately after the L A W tax cuts were dishonoured.

Enter Howard the compromiser. On 22 February 2001, he simplified the business activity statement. On 1 March, he caved in to the motoring lobby by reducing petrol excise by about $1 billion a year. On 7 March, the GDP number for the December quarter was released, and the newspaper headlines said the economy was officially on the brink of recession. Howard reached again into his bag of goodies and pulled out a gift for young homebuyers. The first home-owner grant that was meant to sweeten the GST was doubled to $14,000. Peter Costello was becoming exceedingly annoyed with Howard, and something seemed to snap inside the treasurer when the beer drinkers got their turn at the handout queue on 3 April. Costello threw what insiders said was a 'spectacular sulk' by refusing to announce the reduction in excise for draught beer. It was left to Howard's office to inform the public of the detail, even though this was the treasurer's policy jurisdiction.

Costello's mood would darken further on 8 May 2001 with the leaking of a memo that the Liberal Party president, Shane Stone, had written to Howard three months earlier, which laid the blame for the GST nightmare at the treasurer's feet. Stone gave Howard a checklist of groups that had been alienated by his 'mean', 'tricky' and 'dysfunctional' government. 'Perhaps the most telling and recurring comments centred on the view that we had gone out of our way to "get" the very people who put us there,' Stone told Howard. 'The self-funded retirees, the small business sector, self-employed professionals, farmers—middle Australia.'

What remained of the surplus was given to the elderly in the 22 May budget. A $300 cheque was sent to the nation's 2.2 million pensioners and part-pensioners, while self-funded retirees were allowed to earn twice as much tax-free private income than before.

Costello guaranteed that the budget would still be in surplus, and he and Howard repeated the promise later in the year during the 2001 election. But voters had been misled. In three crazy months between February and May, Howard had taken a healthy surplus of $6 billion from 2000–01 and turned it into a $1 billion deficit for 2001–02. Not even Paul Keating had done this badly as treasurer when a surplus of $6.6 billion in 1989–90 almost vanished the following year. But treasurer Keating had had an excuse then: the economy was tumbling into recession. Prime Minister Howard had emptied the cookie jar for strictly political reasons, and denied himself the option of continuing reform of the personal-tax scales. Yet Howard deserves some applause. His GST handouts acted as an unintended buffer against the world recession that would come in the second half of the year. Australia grew as the US went backwards, which was the first time in our history that we didn't catch a cold when the world's largest economy sneezed.

'I know I was criticised in 2001 for trying to spend a bit of money on certain things,' Howard says:

> The electorate felt, rightly or wrongly, they felt they had been diddled on the petrol excise thing; it was just the way it came out. I was determined to fix it, and if I hadn't have fixed it, we might have paid quite dearly for that. And, just for the record, we were recovering before the *Tampa* came across the horizon. Labor should have won that by-election in Aston [in July]. If Labor had won in Aston, it would have been a lot harder. I think Aston exposed Beazley's policy paucity and his real weakness. He was still coasting.

AMONG THE many powers attributed to the GST on its passage through the Senate was that it would bring an end to financial bickering between Canberra and the states, and extract $1 billion a year from tax cheats. It did none of the above.

Labor had warned that the GST would ignite inflation, which it didn't; lead to recession, which it almost did in the second half of 2000; and help it surf into office, which never happened. Of all the straws that Labor clutched at, the revival of inflation happened to be the least realistic. The Keating–Howard economy had settled into a low-inflation groove by 2000. The technology boom was driving prices down; as was import competition; as were the steady stream of lower-paid, but highly skilled women moving from university or maternity into the workforce. Keating couldn't get the GST up in 1985 because Bob Hawke knew voters wouldn't wear the price increases that would follow for life's necessities. It was the same reason Malcolm Fraser gave to Howard in 1981. Australia was ready for the GST in 2000 because workers and employers had been taught, by now, that they had couldn't pass on the cost to someone else. They would just live with it. They would learn to enjoy this cut-throat environment, in a way, because inflation had sneaked off to another location, from goods and services to assets such as property.

The GST proved to be more successful in an area neither side of politics could have guessed. It became a nice little earner — even without food in the tax base. The GST collected about $1 billion more each year than was forecast. It has made the states appear wealthier than they could have dreamed, and that Howard had probably intended. On its fifth anniversary, on 1 July 2005, the Commonwealth and the states were still playing 'pass the parcel'. Neither were game to record the tax in their budget papers. The federal government said the GST was a state tax; the states said it belonged to Canberra. 'I don't think the GST's failed,' Howard said in March 2005. 'I think the use of the GST [by] the states has failed.' The GST was officially an orphan.

Snapshot #13

The Rise of the McMansion

REMEMBER the wog mansion? It used to be a put-down when I was growing up in Melbourne in the 1970s. Popular culture didn't know what to make of the faux Roman or Hellenic columns, the water features, and the giant olive tins in the backyard that were recycled as pots for the tomatoes. There was no grass to be seen, of course. We wogs equated cement with civilisation. Inside, there was the beige carpet and the plastic runners our mothers rolled over the top to preserve the pile in its full acrylic glory. The monumentalism fitted with the numbers. Italian-born and Greek-born Australians have home-ownerships rates of about 90 per cent, compared to 70 per cent for the Australian-born population.

Today, the wog mansion has an Anglo imitator, the McMansion. It has the same configuration as its ethnic predecessor — four bedrooms, two garages, and a pool room. Only it is more antiseptic. A television sits in every room, which means regular trips to Ikea to buy a TV stand for each. But no one questions the tastes of the families who move into McMansions — 'Kath & Kim' notwithstanding — because they decide elections.

The more substantive differences between the wog mansion and the McMansion is in the mortgage. If new Australians couldn't buy their houses outright with cash, they'd do the next-best thing and acquire the freehold title within a couple of years. But that was another time. The McMansion rose at the end of the 1990s, when Australians came to view debt in the same way that the corporate spivs had in the 1980s—as a birthright.

Now, have you forgotten the current account deficit? It was the sword of Damocles that hung over the first dozen years of deregulation, from the floating of the dollar in December 1983 to the debt truck that John Howard used as a prop against Paul Keating in the run-up to the March 1996 election. Every month, the gap between what we sold the rest of the world and what we wanted to buy from it would run to a billion dollars or more. Every month, another billion dollars would have to be borrowed from overseas to cover the gap. Howard and Keating divided on economic policy precisely where the McMansion met the current account deficit at the end of the 1990s—the bank manager's office.

Let's take the time capsule back to the moral panic of the Keating years to see how the McMansion and the current account deficit became entwined under Howard, and why it helps explain the reactions to the *Tampa* and Iraq. In May 1986, when treasurer Keating warned that we were in danger of becoming a banana republic, the interest bill on the foreign debt was chewing up 14.5 per cent of export income. It peaked at a mind-boggling 20 per cent of export income in the September quarter of 1990. Add another 6 or so per cent for the dividends we paid foreigners on the assets they owned here, and Australia had crossed what historian Geoffrey Blainey warned was the debt danger-zone, when one dollar in every four of exports was being sent straight back overseas. Australia had only passed the 25 per cent mark twice before, in the 1890s and 1920s. 'Each time we were toppled and the human hardship was on a large scale,' Blainey said during the March 1990 federal election campaign, in a speech designed to spook. Echoing the numbers game then underway, Blainey said: 'We are now so accustomed to these monthly rises that we applaud when the rise in overseas debt is less than we expected.'

Blainey was wrong; the world did not foreclose on the Australian economy. But Howard Mark II played the debt card for all it was worth at the 1996 election. The foreign debt was the biggest number he could get his hands on. Five minutes of economic sunshine was the better line because it captured the times. But the foreign debt ran into the hundreds of billions and, if you divided it by the Australian population, you could make every man, women, and child think that Keating had sold us all to the slave traders of international capital. At his election campaign-launch, Howard said:

> When Labor came to power Australia owed the rest of the world about $23,000 million. We now owe the rest of the world $180,000 million. Nothing, my friends, symbolises absolutely completely and comprehensively more than that disgraceful figure the total failure of Labor's economic management over the last 13 years.

It was hyperbole, because Australia's capacity to repay that $180 billion had improved dramatically, thanks to the lower world interest rates and the surge in exports due to the restructuring of the economy. Prime minister Keating had left office in 1996 with the foreign debt burden at just 11.3 per cent of export income. The figure kept improving under Prime Minister Howard. By 2003, it had fallen to 7.8 per cent, which happened to be lower than the 8.4 per cent level he had left it as treasurer 20 years earlier, even though the net debt was now heading past $400 billion. We could end the history lesson here and declare victory for the Keating–Howard economy. But to do that, we'd be ignoring the elephant stomping up and down the corridor: household debt.

As corporate Australia learned to repair its balance sheet in the 1990s, the mantle of reckless borrower was being passed to middle Australia. Families and singles, boomers, and Gen Xers greeted the doubling of house prices and the halving of nominal interest rates as the excuse to double the size of their mortgages, or to max out their credit cards. The household debt burden was rising as the foreign debt burden was coming down. The graphs crossed in mid-2003, when households found themselves more exposed on their mortgages and credit cards than the economy was on its overseas borrowings. This was a first for the open economy, and a warning that we had taken our mania for bricks and mortar to new type of debt danger-zone.

Under treasurer Keating, the interest bill on household debt had peaked at 8.4 per cent of disposable income at the end of the 1980s, which was less than half the foreign debt burden at the time. The mortgage accounted for 5 per cent, and consumer credit the other 3.4 per cent. Keating meant for this to happen because he had jacked up the official interest rate to 17 per cent to kill the boom.

Under Prime Minister Howard, the household debt burden broke 9 per cent for the first time in history in the September quarter of 2003, and it reached 10 per cent by the time of the 2004 election, comprising 7.9 per cent for the home loan and 2.1 per cent to repay the credit card bill. Yet official interest rates were just 5.25 per cent at the time — so the punters had only themselves, and both sides of politics, to blame.

The trouble began with the new tax system. Immediately after the GST was passed in June 1999, Howard turned his mind to reform of the business tax system. He wanted to include an income-tax sweetener in the package to promote his ideal of a share-owning democracy. In September, the government announced that it would halve the rate of capital gains in exchange for the removal of existing concessions. This was supposed to trigger a share-trading frenzy, which would give Australian technology companies a better chance of attracting feisty foreign investors. There was also an element of payback involved. Howard had opposed the capital gains tax when treasurer Keating introduced it in 1985, and campaigned in 1987 for its abolition. The former tax commissioner Trevor Boucher accused Howard of 'fiscal vandalism' that would entice tax avoiders 'like bees to a honey pot'. But Labor passed the legislation because this time it didn't want to get between the upwardly mobile voters and another customised tax cut.

The Australian character is not that hard to read. Give a voter a choice between a parcel of shares and a block of land, and they will take the property over the stress of having to read the market results in the financial pages of the newspaper each day. Howard believed a lower capital gains tax would build an enterprise nation. What it achieved, instead, was the rise of the McMansion and its inner-city sister, the apartment tower.

The number that confirmed this was the current account deficit. There have been six blow-outs since 1979: one under Malcolm Fraser; three that can be sheeted home to the Hawke–Keating governments; and two with Howard's prime ministership on them. Let's call the final pairing Howard's Episodes I and II. Each carried the same order of magnitude, a jump in the deficit of 3 per cent of GDP.

Episode I ran from 1997 to 1999, and it followed the script of the previous four cycles, in which the boom in imports, funded by overseas borrowings, had a productive purpose. Three dollars in every four went into factories, office blocks, and equipment for business. The balance, 24.1 per cent, wound up in housing.

Episode II, between late 2001 and 2004, broke the mould. More than half, 56.7 per cent, of the increase in the current account deficit was devoted to erecting McMansions and apartment towers. This confirmed yet another record for Howard's mortgage nation, the first blowout in the current account deficit that belonged to ordinary Australians. The real-economy transaction went something like this: Australians stopped saving, so the banks had to look overseas for the funds to lend to home-buyers.

Need another clue? In the last full financial year of the old capital gains tax regime, 1998–99, the Australian Taxation Office was $700 million in the black in its dealings with property investors. In the first full year of the new rules, 2000–01, when the introduction of the GST was warping demand, total rental deductions exceeded rental income by $700 million. A blip, perhaps? No, the shortfall was $600 million in 2001–02, then $1.2 billion the following year, then $2.4 billion in 2003–04. Mark that as another first. Even at the height of the late-1980s property boom, Keating's tax system could still find more landlords making profits than were declaring losses after deducting the cost of the loan and other expenses.

THE MCMANSION is the defining structure of the Howard years. The suburban castle with four or more bedrooms accounts for 60 per cent of the 1.2 million houses and apartments erected between 1994–95 and 2003–04. There are now 200,000 more McMansions than the total number of houses and apartments with one or two bedrooms: 2.1 million versus 1.9 million. Only the three-bedroom house is more popular with 3.8 million dwellings, but its share of the cake is shrinking.

'Kath & Kim' scripted their McMansion as a pit stop between circuits of retail therapy at the Fountain Lakes shopping mall. The political class assumed the McMansion was the story of young families moving to the outer suburbs and shedding their former loyalty to the Labor Party. It turns out that both caricatures were right. Families with one or two children were responsible for 48 per cent of the McMansions built under Howard. But another 42 per cent went to childless households, and the template for this baby-boomer McMansion is Kath and Kel at home alone with their gadgets and gym equipment.

Here's the rub. The home-ownership rate remained stable under Howard despite, or, probably, because of the boom in McMansions. What changed was the mix between those who owned their home outright and those who had a mortgage. In Keating's final year, 41.8 per cent of households had freehold title, while 29.6 were borrowers. By 2003–04, the tables had turned: 34.9 per cent owned their homes outright, while 35.1 per cent had mortgages. By dipping into their equity to build and to renovate larger houses, the young families and the baby boomers, together, drove up general house prices to the point were it took two incomes to qualify for a mortgage.

The typical household of the Howard era spent more than it earned, because it learned to use bricks and mortar as a line of credit. And it spent much of its time in front of the television watching programs about property. The most popular local series in 2003, the year we went to war in Iraq, was a contest between four couples to spruce up a derelict apartment building in Sydney's peroxide heart of Bondi. Each pairing was given a flat to renovate, a tight budget, and a ticket to B-list fame in exchange for their privacy. The plotline of 'The Block' was the cycle of argument-cuddle-argument that partners engage in when they peel back the wallpaper and rip out the carpet. The cameras recorded every tantrum, every tender moment, and a truck-load of tedium in between, and the highlights were telecast on the Nine Network on Tuesdays and Sundays for three months..

More than three million people tuned in for the final episode in August 2003 when the four finished products were sold at auction. As each apartment went on the market, the price rose, from too much to way too much. The first fetched $655,000; the second, $670,000; the third, $747,000; and the winner, $751,000. If a regular Sydney couple wanted to buy one of the two-bedroom units, they would have needed a combined salary of almost four times average earnings to qualify for the mortgage

The audience for the finale was the largest since the 2000 Sydney Olympics. One way of looking at it, perhaps, was that Australians had finally regained their sense of humour after the terror attacks on the United States on 11 September 2001 and the first of the Bali bombings on 12 October 2002. But something more basic was at play here; the nation was turning inward.

'The Block' was the most successful in a stampede of shows devoted to the cult of bricks and mortar. Others included Seven's 'Auction Squad' and Nine's 'Renovation Rescue', names that left nothing to the imagination. No other government could claim a TV guide like it, not even the former Labor regime at the height of the late 1980s property boom. The TV industry didn't see real estate as a viable format until after Howard had sanctioned the boom with his cut to the capital gains tax in September 1999.

CHAPTER FOURTEEN

Howard as Warrior

PIN-POINTING THE FORTNIGHT when John Howard commenced his second honeymoon as prime minister is easy. It's the meaning of this late career-surge that is contentious because it acts as ballast for both the Howard huggers and Howard haters. One side sees the *Tampa* as the moment when a true Australian fulfilled his potential as a strong leader and exposed the moral bankruptcy of the left's world view. The other sees an evil genius, a manipulator of the community's irrational fears, who confirmed his own and the public's moral bankruptcy. Forgive me if I disagree with both sides.

On 27 August 2001, Howard announced that 433 asylum-seekers rescued at sea by the Norwegian freighter the *MV Tampa* would not be allowed to land on Australian soil. The boat people were fleeing the Taliban regime in Afghanistan, but had come via Indonesia, and that's where Howard wanted them to return. The asylum-seekers told the captain of the *Tampa*, Arne Rinnan, to take them to their intended destination, Christmas Island, and the world suddenly seemed to go insane.

Immediately before the standoff, voters had Howard marked down for early retirement. Only 40 per cent were satisfied with the job he was doing, while 50 per cent were dissatisfied. The private polling of both sides had Labor on course for a narrow victory. Howard's approval rating had been below 50 per cent since early February 2000, an 18-month stretch of unpopularity that mirrored his earlier black spot between April 1997 and October 1998.

The *Tampa* flipped the tables. When the next Newspoll was taken, between 31 August and 2 September 2001, there were 50 per cent satisfied and only 40 per cent dissatisfied with the prime minister. He stayed at 50 per cent for another week, then jumped again after the 11 September terrorist attacks on New York, Washington, and Philadelphia. By late September, Howard was in super-hero territory, with 61 per cent satisfied and only 31 per cent dissatisfied — a respect-rate of two to one.

The public had returned him to where he had been with Port Arthur in 1996 and East Timor in 1999. Only this time, the good vibes would last, because there would be no Pauline Hanson, or native title, or GST, to distract voters. The *Tampa* became the moment when the electorate called a halt to its decade-long game of bashing the government.

Howard's revival in the second half of 2001 is tainted by the asylum-seeker issue. The question that will have historians arguing for years to come is whether he could have won in November 2001 without the *Tampa*. The related question for the public is whether its response to the *Tampa* was the era's defining expression of xenophobia.

I have a valuable clue to work with because in our first interview Howard revealed his basic calculation for electoral success: 'If you have got low- and middle-income families contented with you, and if you are getting an above-average portion of the over-55s, it is very hard to lose.' His analysis matches Labor Party polling I have been shown.

Today, one in three voters are aged over 55. The figure has been rising with each election as the population ages. In 2001, 31.3 per cent of those enrolled answered to the demographic nickname of 'grey voter'. In 2004, they had increased their share to 33.2 per cent of the electorate.

On any objective measure, the 2001 budget was excessively generous to the over-55s. So it is tempting to accept Howard's argument that he was on course for victory before the *Tampa* came. Assume for a moment there had been no boat people, but that Al

Qaeda had still struck on 11 September. It is hard to imagine why self-funded retirees would have switched to Beazley when Howard had just lavished them with a tax break.

But the *Tampa* did matter to those grey voters who were on the age pension, or the disability-support pension. It helped the Hansonites come back home to the coalition, because it transformed Howard from penny-pincher to patriot.

The 2001 election does not warrant the title of contest, because voters were in no mood to change to Kim Beazley at any stage in the campaign. The coalition's primary vote jumped by 3.6 per cent to 43.1 per cent, and Labor's fell by 2.3 per cent to 37.8 per cent. The coalition gained at the expense of One Nation, whose primary vote fell by almost half from 8.4 per cent to 4.3 per cent. Labor shed support to the Greens, whose vote almost doubled from 3 per cent to 5 per cent, although these ballots came back to Labor as second preferences. The coalition won the two-party vote by 51 per cent to 49 per cent, which reversed the 1998 election result. Labor lost two seats in total, and the coalition gained two to increase its majority from 12 to 16. The electoral income-ladder remained as it had been in 1998, with the coalition enjoying solid majorities in the top and bottom, and Labor the majority in the centre.

Race may have swung the Hansonite seats, but this was only half the story of the 2001 election. The upwardly mobile voters whom Labor had lost in 1998 remained lost in 2001 for strictly economic reasons. The vote-switcher for young families had nothing to do with the *Tampa*. They were more interested in the doubling of the first home-owner grant six months earlier.

Between 1992 and 1999, first-home borrowers accounted for about one in five of all home loans issued. The pre-GST spike reduced that figure to one in seven as the baby boomers crowded out the young families in the rush to beat the new tax system. They saw prices rising beyond their reach, and they blamed the GST.

By doubling the first-owner grant, Howard brought young families back to market at a critical stage in the electoral cycle. In Queensland, their ranks almost trebled from 12.9 per cent to 30 per cent of all borrowers between June 2000 and June 2001. In NSW, they jumped from 13.2 per cent to 21.3 per cent. Labor's polling showed that young families saw Howard as a sugar daddy in the second half of 2001.

At it most crude level, race influenced the vote of no more than 10 per cent of the electorate in 2001. The remaining 90 per cent were thinking as they always had, about the kitchen table, and they divided roughly 50–50 between coalition and Labor. Howard didn't need the *Tampa* to prove to the community that the economy had turned the corner. He would have won without it.

AS HE BOARDED the people-smuggler's boat with his mother and three brothers in late August 2001, Ali Alamein, then 15, imagined Australia was just like New York or London, with 'huge buildings, shops and shiny streets'. A week later, after his family became part of the human cargo that changed the course of federal politics, Ali thought Australia didn't want to know him. Three years on, as the 2004 election approached, he smiled as he recalled his third, and most lasting, impression of Australia from the vantage point of a country town in central Victoria.

Shepparton wasn't the metropolis he dreamed of, nor was it the redneck backwater he feared during his stint in detention on Nauru between September 2001 and 2002. 'I had this feeling that I wouldn't be accepted,' Ali told me. 'But after coming here and meeting all these people, all these kind people, all these beautiful people, it was very good. Of course, there were people who were a bit racist and treated us bad, but you know, there are bad people everywhere.'

The Alameins are a window into the nation's evolving view of asylum-seekers. Ali's mother, Sakina, became a star of the Rotary speakers' circuit. His older brother Hassan opened a labour-hire firm supplying refugee workers on temporary protection visas for the fruit-picking industries on both sides of the Murray River. As we spoke, Newspoll had just confirmed that public sympathy towards boat people had risen markedly. In August 2004, 61 per cent of voters said some or all asylum-seekers should be allowed to land in Australia. In late-October 2001, in the final days of the border-protection election, the majority was firmly the other way — 56 per cent of voters wanted all boats stopped. We asked a new question in 2004, whether voters agreed or disagreed with the actions the government had taken on the *Tampa* issue. Only 35 per cent said they did; 43 per cent said they did not.

This is part of the answer to the question of whether the *Tampa* brought out the dark side of the community. Initially, there seemed to be little sympathy for the asylum-seekers. But the longer the debate ran, the more the government had to lose as evidence of bungling piled on revelations of cruelty. There were no children thrown overboard, as Howard and his senior ministers had claimed during the 2001 election. There were virtually no Pakistanis on the boats pretending to be Afghanis and Iraqis, as the government had also claimed. By 2005, the Immigration Department was exposed as a rogue outfit. It had detained a mentally ill Australian citizen, Cornelia Rau, because it suspected her to be an illegal immigrant. It had deported another Australian citizen, Vivian Alvarez, to the Philippines.

Let's take the emotion out of this debate and allow the numbers to speak for themselves.

In 2001, Howard said the people who were intercepted by the Navy and shipped to Nauru and Manus Island would not be allowed to land on Australian soil. He also said Australia would take its fair share of those found to be genuine refugees, but suggested that other nations, especially Norway, should pitch in.

The *Tampa* and its human cargo of 433 made world headlines on 27 August. Four days later, Ali's boat, the *Aceng* (also known as *SIEV 1*), carrying 228, mainly Iraqi, asylum-seekers, sailed straight into the vortex. The Navy spotted the *Aceng* near Ashmore Reef on 1 September, just as the government was finalising the deal to end the confrontation with the *Tampa*. The Pacific Solution, as the Prime Minister dubbed it, began with these two groups of asylum-seekers, who were fleeing the Taliban and Saddam Hussein. The *HMAS Manoora* collected the *Tampa* boat people on 3 September, added the *Aceng* boat people to its load on 8 September, then set course for Nauru.

In the next four months a further eight boats, carrying 1000 or so people, were intercepted and the asylum-seekers transported to Nauru and Manus Island for detention and processing. Another four boats, carrying about 600 people, were turned back to Indonesia. On the second anniversary of the Pacific Solution, in September 2003, Howard claimed vindication for his hard line. 'The great bulk of them were not found to be legitimate refugees.'

He was wrong — 985 of the 1547 people assessed offshore proved to be genuine refugees. Another 77 were accepted on humanitarian grounds. The success rate was 68.6 per cent. Add to that the 131 *Tampa* Afghanis offered sanctuary by New Zealand before the *Manoora* docked in Nauru, and 71.1 per cent of the 'illegal imigrants' who Howard had shaken his fist at turned out to be human beings in need of protection.

But what of the rest? Some 420 Afghans from the *Tampa* and other boats had been convinced to return home in 2002 and 2003. The government paid each single person $2000, and families $10,000, as part of a resettlement package. Translators working for the Immigration Department told the Afghans they were better off going home because they would never get to Australia, that Australia did not want them. A handful of Afghans dug in their heels. Qurban Ali Changizi was 22 when he was taken to Nauru in early 2002 after two months on Christmas Island. He said no to the package because, as he explained to me later, 'I didn't think the money would save our lives.' Qurban waited four years, and endured repeated rejections of his claim, before he was finally accepted as a genuine refugee in October 2005 — and he had nothing but thanks for the government for giving him his 'freedom'. Of those who went back, he heard that at least one had died, and that many of the others had left Afghanistan again and were on the Pakistani and Iranian borders. If they had stayed with him on Nauru, chances are they would have pushed the success rate for asylum-seekers towards 80 per cent, or even higher.

But some refugees proved to be more Australian that others. The government was reluctant to accept those people who had been on the most controversial boats — the *Tampa*, and *SIEV 4*, the fourth so-called suspected illegal entry vessel. This is the tale of two sets of Afghans and two sets of Iraqis.

Of the 424 Afghans on board the *Tampa*, 244 were accepted as refugees, 179 returned to Afghanistan, and one died on Nauru. New Zealand took 209 of the 244. Australia gave sanctuary to just 29. Another five went to Sweden and two to Norway. So far, this is broadly consistent with Howard's claim that he would not let these people land on Australian soil, and that Australia would take its fair share of the refugees.

Another 493 Afghans were picked up from subsequent boats, but the government was more inclined to welcome them. Australia took 201 of the 252 post-*Tampa* Afghan refugees, while New Zealand received only 44, and Canada seven.

Perhaps this was just the luck of the draw. But the pattern repeated with the Iraqis. The people on *SIEV 4*, the children-overboard boat, went to Manus Island along with another, smaller group of Iraqis from another vessel. Their combined numbers were 343. The remaining 345 Iraqis, including Ali Alamein's family, were taken straight to Nauru. Guess how the successful refugees in these two blocs were distributed? Australia accepted only 44.1 per cent of the children overboard Iraqis processed on Manus Island, but 67.1 per cent of their brethren who went through Nauru. New Zealand, by contrast, took 55.2 per cent of the former, but 26.2 per cent of the latter.

This appears to be politics at its most calculating. The government wanted to minimise the number of witnesses from the *Tampa* and *SIEV 4* coming to Australia, where the public and the media could get to know them better that the slur of queue jumper, or child abuser. An aspect of this strategy was confirmed after the election. The Defence Department admitted it was instructed during the campaign by the minister, Peter Reith, that no flattering photos or film footage was to be taken of the asylum-seekers. 'We got some guidance ensuring there were no personalising or humanising images taken of SUNCs,' the director-general of Defence public affairs, Brian Humphries, told the Senate committee into the children-overboard affair. SUNC, by the way, was the jargon that Defence used to describe the asylum-seekers. SUNC meant 'suspected unlawful non-citizens'.

One quirky footnote is that Howard can't make the boast that he stopped all the boats from entering Australia. *SIEV 3*, carrying 65 people, snuck through the ring of steel sometime in mid-September 2001. Initially, these boat people were slotted to go to Nauru, but the government now concedes that 60 'were transferred to the onshore case-load'—code for the fact that their claims for refugee status were heard on Australia soil.

IT WAS 8 October 2001, and Wafa Al Madani's family was being torn apart by dictatorship in Iraq and democracy in Australia. Her father, Hamoud, and brother, Haydar, had only recently disappeared into Saddam Hussein's web of prisons and torture chambers. Now her mother, Nadeema, and another brother, Abdalla, were swimming for their lives off the coast of Christmas Island after the boat that falsely promised them freedom began sinking. As Wafa prepared to abandon the stricken vessel, a quick-thinking crew member from the *HMAS Adelaide* enlisted her to assist with the rescue mission. 'One of the staff from the Adelaide said, "Come here to help me with this child",' she says. With the young boy firmly in her arms, but her own mother and brother nowhere to be seen, Wafa jumped on to the life raft. Earlier that day, the prime minister told voters: 'I don't want in Australia people who would throw their own children into the sea.'

Wafa recalled a roller-coaster of emotions—the escape from Iraq, the mayhem on the Indian Ocean, a year in detention on Manus Island and, eventually, acceptance as a genuine refugee in

Shepparton, in Victoria — on a mild winter's afternoon in August 2004. The latest twist in the children-overboard affair is barely 24 hours old. Howard's campaign alibi — that no one told him the claims were untrue until after the 2001 election — appears to be in tatters. Former federal bureaucrat Mike Scrafton says he did inform Howard that no one in the Defence Department believed the story any more, three days before voters entered the polling booths. But the Al Madanis don't want to talk politics today. 'In Iraq, we don't say anything about the government,' Wafa jokes. Her story, told in halting English and through an interpreter, is a mix of pride, anguish, and bewilderment, but not of bitterness. The children-overboard slur still hurts, however. 'I don't have a child, but I was helping one,' the 27-year-old tells me. 'Even the animals don't do something like this to their children. We came here to save our children, to save ourselves, not to throw children in the water.'

She recounts how she sat on the life raft, searching the scores of panicked faces in the water for her mother and brother, when a voice called out: 'That is my son, that is my son.' It was the boy's father, waving furiously from a second life raft. For a moment she was happy. But once the boy had been returned to his father, her attention switched back to her mother and brother. 'There were so many people in the water, but then I saw them.' The pair were clutching a piece of wood and paddling towards Wafa's 'plastic boat', unaware that she was already safely on board.

What distinguished this group of 219, mainly Iraqi, asylum-seekers was the election. They were the first boatload to be intercepted during the campaign itself. A series of mis-understandings saw the government claim on 7 October that children had been thrown into the water. Photos of the rescue taken on the following day were misrepresented by Peter Reith as proof of the alleged incident.

What set *SIEV 4* apart from all other boats after the election was its strike rate. This boat carried more genuine refugees than the other ten. The precise figure is not available because the government says it is too difficult to do the sums on a per-boat basis.

But a reasonable guess can be made by digging beneath the Manus Island data. The 219 asylum-seekers were transferred to Manus Island in mid-October 2001. Another 140 Iraqis joined them in January 2002. Of this combined group, 96.5 per cent, or 331, were resettled by November 2005, although a handful were not deemed to be genuine refugees and, as mentioned earlier, most went to New Zealand, not Australia.

Look at that figure again: 96.5 per cent. *SIEV 4* proved to be carrying the largest proportion of genuine refugees. Yet Howard continued to cast doubt over the character of this boatload. In an interview with ABC's 'Compass' program broadcast during the 2004 election, he was asked: 'Have you thought of speaking to any of them or making a public statement acknowledging that that was a slur and it was wrong?' The prime minister replied: 'No, I have not because it [the claim] was made at the time in good faith and there was also an element of their general behaviour at the time which was not very responsible in relation to the care of their children.' He did not explain what behaviour he had in mind.

When we spoke again, in December 2005, as part of *The Australian's* book on the Howard era, the prime minister repeated that he had no regrets:

> They don't carry any visible signs of being demonised, to the extent that they have been accepted. I don't know that people know that they were on that particular boat. The demonising of them in a personal sense is a bit of an exaggeration. [This issue] figured far less prominently in the public's mind before the election than it did afterwards, because it became the great excuse why Labor lost the election. But if it had never arisen, I don't think there would have been any difference in the result, I don't think a vote would have shifted. People voted for our tough border-protection policy. They didn't vote for us because of children overboard.

He's right, of course, but it means the opposite point can equally be made: that the government didn't need to be so heavy-handed in its treatment of the asylum-seekers to win a federal election.

> *Question*: But it almost gives your critics an easy out.
> *Howard*: But the most powerful reply to that is that they irresponsibly sank the damn boat, which put their children in the water. I'm sorry, if I had have been told definitively, if I had been told that that story was completely wrong, I would have said so, but I wasn't and my last act before the election was to put that video in the public domain so that I wasn't accused of concealing it, because it was ambiguous. Watching that video, you couldn't tell whether people were being thrown in the water or not, it was just impossible. But after all, they did sink the boat.

The Navy's incident summary, published as part of the Senate inquiry into the controversy, had said there was a 'threat' to throw a child in the water. But this official report was contradicted by the crew of HMAS *Adelaide* who intercepted the *SIEV 4* and then rescued all of those aboard after the disabled vessel sank.

Navy gunner Laura Wittle revealed in August 2004 that the man concerned wanted to get his child on to a rescue boat. He was not threatening to throw his child in the water, she said. A photo of Ms Whittle rescuing a child as the *SIEV 4* was sinking on 8 October was used incorrectly by the government during the 2001 election campaign as evidence of children having been thrown into the water on 7 October. Ms Whittle said the crew of the *Adelaide* felt 'betrayed by the politicisation of the incident'.

So did they sink 'the damn boat', as Howard asserted? There is no firm evidence either way. I reported Howard's claim on 27 February 2006. *The Australian's* national security editor, Patrick Walters, followed up the story the next day, quoting Defence sources who said it was impossible to know why the boat sank. 'It's a subjective judgement. *SIEV 4*'s longevity as a platform was suspect,' one source said in Defence-speak. Crew members of the *Adelaide* had said that some people on the boat were trying to damage it.

Let's assume there was deliberate sabotage. The motive for destroying the engine is easier to comprehend than the claim that these people threw their children in the water. They disabled the boat to force the Navy to rescue them because they didn't want to be sent back to Indonesia — or, worse, to Iraq. In any case, it's hard to see why the actions of a few should be allowed to condemn the 96.5 per cent who were found to be genuine refugees.

ALI SAYS his fellow Iraqis had no idea what they had stepped into when they were rounded up by the *Manoora*. The *Tampa* boat people were out of sight, on another deck of the ship. When they reached Nauru on 19 September, Ali noticed a team of Afghan translators, but no Arabic translators. Then he saw the Afghans, who by now had been at sea for 23 days.

This was one very grumpy mass of humanity. Most of the Afghans and Iraqis were reluctant to move and had to be lured off the *Manoora* after the Navy spiked the food given to their children with chilli. Only 13 went without protest, and Ali's family were among them. They wanted freedom, they said; they didn't want trouble. Ali was just five when his family escaped from Iraq in 1991. They spent the next ten years in exile in Iran, but the authorities wouldn't let them work and in the end tried to push them back to Iraq. Ali's father, Ahmad, left Iran in July 1999 for Australia. He was detained for ten months at Port Hedland before receiving a temporary protection visa. Stung by the experience, Ahmad sent word back to his wife that the trip wasn't worth the risk, but Sakina was undaunted. 'I needed to come,' she says. 'My little boy, he needs his father. I have five sons, all need their father.' The eldest, Yasir, remained in Iran. The mother and four boys left Iran on 31 May 2001 and travelled legally until Indonesia, Ali says. When their three-month visas ran out, they set sail for Australia. The people-smugglers made $US14,000 from the venture.

The family spent 50 weeks in detention on Nauru, and slowly

assimilated the information of a world that seemed to have gone mad, including the events of 11 September 2001. 'For the first two months we had no idea what the hell was going on,' Ali says. 'After we comprehended what was going on with the political things, at that stage I thought, "Wow, they are doing everything wrong, they are playing with our lives, this is not the way to treat us." We thought the world has gone crazy, because we're human as well. At that time I thought it was not worth it.'

Life on Nauru was unbearable. 'No running water. If there was water, it was too hot to have a shower,' he says. They would place ice blocks on their stomachs or under their backs so they could sleep off some of the tedium. The ones who did best in these trying circumstances were those who could shut down their minds. 'Not knowing what your future is, the whole thing made you blind.' The family was rejected on the first round, but accepted on appeal. Ali was dizzy with joy. 'I wanted to fly; I was really happy it was all finishing.' When the *Aceng* numbers were tallied by the UN Human Rights Commission, more than 90 per cent were found to be genuine refugees like the Alameins.

English is Ali's second tongue. The Persian dialect he learned in Iran is his best language; the Arabic he remembers from his first five years in Iraq is his weakest. 'If I went to Iraq in three years [after his temporary protection visa expires in 2007], I'd be in my last year in uni, I will have almost established my life. I couldn't possibly at that stage go back to Iraq and learn a new language, a trade, to establish my life again.' Australia fits his open personality and his dry sense of humour. He has a battle wound to show for his time on Nauru, a nasty red blotch the size of two 50c coins on his right shin. It was a mosquito bite that became infected. 'I couldn't walk for a couple of days. I have no birthmarks; that's the only mark I've got, from Nauru,' he laughs. Asked if he heard that Nauru was supposed to be both bankrupt and slowly sinking into the Pacific Ocean, he flashed one last grin: 'I know, that's ironic. Nauru was part of Australia once. I think it will one day become part of Australia again.'

JOHN HOWARD changed the colour and culture of Australia's immigrant program from white and olive-skinned to yellow and black — that is, from European to a mish-mash of Asian, Kiwi, Middle Eastern, African, and Pacific Islander. It has to be said this bluntly for the fact to sink in. Ever since white settlement in 1788, Australia could count on the majority of its immigrants to come from Europe. When Paul Keating left office in 1996, the Anglo-Celtic-Continentals still comprised 56.7 per cent of our total overseas born. Howard ended the Euro streak in June 2004, when the figure fell to 49 per cent.

Who would have thought that Howard, of all prime ministers, would have broken the mould? Especially when he had used his first term in power to slash the immigration intake, and to shift the focus from family reunion to skills.

Howard ceased being an immigration-cutter after the 1998 election. On one level, he had no choice. As the economy moved to a higher growth trajectory, the government was compelled to look overseas to plug emerging gaps in the labour market. But there was also an element of conversion involved. Howard had become increasingly comfortable with the Chinese and Korean immigrants in his electorate of Bennelong, in Sydney's inner north. The Asian-born accounted for 13.7 per cent of the voters in 1996, and 18.4 per cent by the 2001 election. He found they shared his small business and family values.

Howard admits his attitudes have softened. He says Asian immigrants have embraced Australian culture more readily than some in the community had thought was possible in the 1980s. 'I think [their integration] has been quicker [than it was for the Greeks and Italians],' he told me in April 2002. 'I just don't hear people talking about it now, even as much as they did five years ago, and I have an electorate which is very Asian.'

Peter Nicholson summed up the new alliance in a cartoon for *The Australian*. The setting was a typical quarter-acre block overlooking the water. An Asian, dressed in a suit, is startled as he spots a wretched refugee family stumbling onto the shore below.

'Queue jumpers!' he yells. 'You're a real Aussie now, mate,' a grinning Howard tells him.

Labor never gave Howard the credit for changing his mind. They saw his border-protection policy as an extension of his anti-immigration persona of the 1980s. But Howard says his critics have him wrong. The electorate, he says, draws a distinction between the regular immigration program and 'illegal immigration'. He can be both open and closed on this issue, because that's the same way the public sees it.

By June 2005, Howard had completed his sixth consecutive financial year with a net immigration intake above 100,000. Bob Hawke's record in the 1980s, at the apotheosis of multiculturalism, had been five years in row. In other words, Prime Minister Howard had bettered the very numbers that Howard Mark I had previously criticised.

The top four new arrivals of the Howard era have been the New Zealanders (127,000), the Chinese (60,800), the South Africans (47,400) and the Indians (43,800). Ignore the Kiwis for a moment, because they would have come here regardless of who was in power in Canberra. We are the first place they think of when they want to chase a higher standard of living, or an easier life, or both. What that leaves is the discretionary component of the immigration program, namely the people that Australia bids for, in direct competition with the likes of the United States and Canada. Howard's first choice has been the Chinese.

Yet the Howard conversion does not mean Australia is home free as an open immigrant nation. Each new intake faces a degree of xenophobia that is beyond the control of politicians. The defining immigrant image of Howard's Australia may well be the mob violence on North Cronulla beach, in Sydney's Sunderland shire on 11 December 2005. It was, in essence, a turf war between young men, and about who had the right to chat up the local girls. This is a parochial pocket of the city, with a higher-than-average Australian-born population. It has the hallmarks of a Hansonite town, with the notable exception that this is a high-income suburb.

If the clash had involved rival surfer gangs, the media would have mostly ignored it. But this was race-related violence of a type Australia did not expect to see in the television age. It began as a community march to reclaim the beach after the race-related bashing the previous weekend of two life-savers. But it turned into a post-modern lynching. Young white men chanted 'fuck off Lebs' and 'fuck off wogs' as they kicked and punched anybody of 'Middle Eastern appearance' they could lay their hands on and feet into. The chant escalated to 'kill the Leb' when the pack chased a young Muslim girl, and then a police officer who was trying to defend her, into a kiosk. Lebanese–Australian youth retaliated over the following two nights, bashing innocent bystanders, and smashing cars and shop windows in the neighbouring beach-side suburbs of Brighton-le-Sands and Maroubra. No one was killed, but the nation's pride was wounded by the footage repeated around the globe. The only thing that left and right seemed to agree on was that Sydney was the most likely venue for such a confrontation.

As the debate raged, I went back to an April 2002 interview I had conducted with Howard on multiculturalism, to re-read an observation he had made about the Sunderland shire, south of the Georges River. We had been comparing Australia's immigration record with that of the US. I mentioned that we didn't have the ethnic ghettos of the US. Howard replied with a statistical snapshot of race and politics:

> That's right. I'm more familiar with Sydney than Melbourne. You have some suburbs that are more Anglo-Celtic than others. The Asian population is spread. There is a very heavy Asian population on the north shore [of Sydney] now, and right through in areas of my electorate. Not so mixed south of the Georges River, that seems to be a bit of an Anglo-Celtic enclave [he laughs at this point]. You go outside of the cities, I mean look at those electoral maps, you've got an electorate like Peter Slipper's [Fischer, in south-east Queensland]. It has got about 93 per cent either Australian or UK-born.

It was the cricket tragic in him speaking, the one who could recite the batting averages of his favourite players. It told me, more than any other quote, that Howard understands the difference between an ethnically diverse electorate and one with a predominately white constituency. He could be both an open immigrant prime minister and a defender of traditional Australia values because he understood how to talk to both sides of this debate.

As chance would have it, my second interview with Howard in 2005 came two days before the seaside violence. I had asked him if he thought Muslims would be absorbed as quickly into the Australian mainstream as the Asians had been:

> I think most of them, yes. But I do think there is this particular complication because there is a fragment which is utterly antagonistic to our kind of society, and that is a difficulty. You can't find any equivalent in Italian, or Greek, or Lebanese, or Chinese, or Baltic immigration to Australia. There is no equivalent of raving on about jihad; but that is the major problem, and I think some of the associated attitudes towards women [are] a problem. For all the conservatism towards women and so forth within some of the Mediterranean cultures with which you would be familiar, it's as nothing compared with some of the more extreme attitudes. The second one of those things is a broader problem, but, to be fair to them, it's an attitude that is changing with the younger ones.

In the Right Place at the Right Time

JOHN HOWARD seemed to acquire a Teflon coating after the *Tampa*. But the incongruity of the war on boat people was that Australia declared real wars against the regimes from which the asylum-seekers were fleeing. The context of the *Tampa* changed on 11 September 2001, as dread became the new currency of politics in the west. On the day before the terror attacks, the last day of innocence for post-modern America, Howard had his first meeting with US president George W. Bush in Washington:

> One of the things I have learnt is that things you don't think are priorities emerge from nowhere. I wouldn't have thought in the middle of 2001 that fighting terrorism would be the commanding issue of the rest of my prime ministership. I spoke to Bush, I had my very first meeting with him on the morning of the 10th of September, and we didn't talk about it. Nobody knew it was coming.

Actually, Bush's successor, Bill Clinton, feared it was coming. On the day Howard and Bush talked about other things, the former US president was in a private room at Melbourne's Crown Casino with Howard's former Liberal Party enemy, Andrew Peacock. Thirty hand-picked guests, who swore to keep their names secret, each wrote five-figure cheques to hear Clinton deliver an off-the-record speech and take more than two hours of questions. Peacock was the host of the function, an irony that would not have escaped him as Howard and Bush were preparing to get together on the other side of the equator.

Clinton felt it necessary to explain to the Melbourne gathering who Osama bin Laden was. On 10 September 2001, his surname did not carry the same power of recognition as a Hitler or a Stalin.

'The biggest security threat of the next 30 years, I think, is likely to be not countries going to war with each other or even lobbing missiles at each other,' Clinton said in his off-the-record speech, which was leaked to me a year after the event:

It is likely to come from non-national actions — from terrorists, narco-traffickers, organised criminals armed with sophisticated weapons. I'll give you just one example. You remember a couple of years go, one of the worst days of my life as president was when two American embassies were blown up in … Kenya and Tanzania. A lot of Americans were killed. More Africans were killed. They were killed by a terrorist organisation headed by Osama bin Laden, a Saudi exile living in Afghanistan, communicating with followers over the internet. They have exceedingly sophisticated weapons and are doing everything they can to get their hands on chemical and biological weapons.

On 11 September 2001, Clinton was holidaying in Port Douglas. Howard was still in Washington and grasped, immediately, that the world had changed. The US would strike back, and he knew that Australia would be a part of the operation.

The toppling of the Taliban in October 2001 was a popular cause. Two out of three voters (66 per cent) supported the deployment of Australian troops to Afghanistan. This was an engagement in the same league as the first Gulf War in 1991 (69 per cent in favour) and a little behind the intervention in East Timor in 1999 (77 per cent).

But the war in Iraq belonged to a new category. Support only rose above 50 per cent when the shooting started in March 2003, and peaked at 57 per cent when Saddam Hussein's statue was torn down in Baghdad the following month, in a stage-managed event for the television cameras. When the occupation proved to be more bloody than the invasion, the Australian public reverted to its original anti-war call. Twenty months on, in December 2004, 58 per cent of voters said it was not worth going to war in Iraq. It took Australians more than twice as long to turn against the Vietnam war, from 59 per cent who said it was right to get involved in July 1965 to the 55 per cent who wanted to bring the troops home in August 1969.

Very little of what the prime minister said to justify the war in Iraq has withstood the passage of time. The contradictions are apparent just by following the quotes:

People make the mistake that George Bush is just hankering after a war, he's not. He doesn't want a war any more than you and I do. [23 January 2003]

The Australian government knows that Iraq still has chemical and biological weapons and that Iraq wants to develop nuclear weapons. We share the view of many that, unless checked, Iraq could, even without outside help, develop nuclear weapons in about five years. [4 February 2003]

I couldn't justify on its own a military invasion of Iraq to change the regime. I've never advocated that. Much in all as I despise the regime. [13 March 2003]

I am pleased to report that the coalition's major combat operations in Iraq have been successfully concluded ... Now that the major combat phase is over and efforts in Iraq rightly turn to humanitarian assistance, we have begun to bring home our defence personnel ... It is our intention to ensure that the period of coalition control is kept to a minimum and that the responsibility for governing Iraq is taken up by an Interim Iraqi Authority as soon as practicable. [14 May 2003]

I obviously acknowledge that the stockpiles have not been found. The intelligence material in front of me presented a very strong circumstantial case that was convincing. It did not provide irrefutable proof. I didn't expect it to. Now we made an honest assessment, taking that into account. We also took into account the importance of the American alliance. That was a factor. [14 July 2004]

Question: Mr Howard, why did Australia knock back the request from the United Nations to provide some more security reinforcements in Iraq?
Howard: Because we believe the contribution we have made, so far, which has been in excess of most, is appropriate. We made a big contribution for our size at the sharp end. We said all along that having done that we would not participate in significant peacekeeping operations. [19 October 2004]

When the weapons of mass destruction were not found, the justification for the war switched to regime change and to fighting terrorism. Yet Howard pulled out most of the troops after President Bush declared, prematurely, an end to major combat on 1 May 2003. And when Iraq descended into chaos, Howard was willing to risk offending his ally by rebuffing repeated requests for more help. It was only after significant pressure from the Americans, and after both he and Bush had been re-elected at the end of 2004, that Howard was prepared to change his mind. When he announced the deployment of extra troops on 22 February 2005, he said Iraq was at 'a titling point'. He also expected voters to mark him down for the backflip. That they didn't reaffirmed Howard's unique status amongst the coalition of the willing in Iraq. Of the three members of the Anglo alliance — Bush, Great Britain's Tony Blair, and Howard, — only Australia's prime minister could point to a rising, not falling, approval rating. More often than not, the international media paid Howard the compliment of not mentioning his part in the war. In July 2004, *The Economist* magazine ran a cover story to defend the case for war despite the absence of WMD. The headline was 'Sincere deceivers, and the picture accompanying it was of Bush and Blair. Howard's face did not make the cover.

THERE WAS a faintly comical edge to our engagement in Iraq. We had a foot in each camp: as a member of the coalition of the willing *and* as Saddam Hussein's bag man. The Australian Wheat Board happened to be the largest supplier of kickbacks to Saddam's regime. The public revelations of the AWB's misdeeds in late 2005 and early 2006 tarnished Howard's 10th anniversary as prime minister.

The joke is the AWB was sprung by the coalition troops who had hoped to find WMD. After the fall of Baghdad in April 2003, hard evidence was uncovered that Iraq had used companies such as Australia's monopoly wheat exporter to side-step the international sanctions that were supposed to prevent it from re-arming. Saddam's henchmen persuaded the AWB and others to pay 'transport charges' and 'after-sales service' to front companies in places such as Jordan (which had no trucks and provided no after-sales service). The money was then funnelled back to Iraq, in breach of the UN rules. In another context, these transactions could have been dismissed as the price of doing business in the Middle East; a bribe that had to be made to secure a contract in a dodgy market. But Iraq was the one market in which this sort of behaviour was forbidden by international law.

Under the terms of the 1991 settlement to the first Gulf War, Iraq agreed to disarm. But the international sanctions to ensure it complied presented a conundrum for the UN: how would it keep Saddam in his box without starving the Iraqi people? Enter the oil-for-food program. It allowed Iraq to continue selling oil to the west. The oil revenue was paid into a special UN account, which food suppliers such as the AWB would then draw on as payment for what they exported to Iraq. Saddam wasn't meant to see a cent either way.

It turns out that the AWB provided around $300 million to Saddam via the back door, which represented some 14 per cent of the more than $2 billion in rorting identified by the UN between 1999 and 2003. The AWB had viewed the scam as no skin off its nose. The 'transport fees' and 'after sales service' that the Iraqis demanded, and received, came out of the UN account, not the AWB's bottom line.

This is a case study in the amorality of monopoly. It could apply to any business in any capitalist or command economy. But there is a disturbingly Australian trait revealed here. We like having it both ways. Voters respected Howard because our troops in Iraq were reputedly the best fighters, and because they also avoided significant casualties. Farmers also applauded Howard for the frantic efforts on the eve of the war to protect Australia's wheat sales to Iraq. We wanted both the kudos from the Americans for helping to oust Saddam as well as the commerce from Saddam before he fell. But most of all, voters didn't want to know the detail of the war, even though they disapproved of Australia's involvement in the first place.

An interesting footnote was that Howard used Saddam's rorting of the oil-for-food program as another justification for war in March 2003, even though the coalition troops had yet to find the final proof that such manipulation had occurred. On this front, at least, Howard got the reason for war right:

> The oil-for-food program has been immorally and shamefully rorted by Saddam Hussein, who has used the proceeds of it to acquire his weapons capacity and support it. It has to be said, and the Australian public should be reminded, that we had these economic sanctions because Iraq did not disarm … Worse still, having through his policies made those sanctions necessary, the Iraqi leader has compounded the sins inflicted upon his people by rorting the very oil-for-food program which was designed to, in some way, mitigate the impact of the economic sanctions. So he is doubly guilty of betraying his obligations to the Iraqi people. [27 March 2003]

To defend his government, Howard claimed it knew nothing of the AWB's activities, even though Australia was obliged under international law to ensure that the sanctions were adhered to. The oil-for-food program was supposed to be the means to avoid another war with Saddam. But Australian wheat-growers made the second Gulf War more inevitable by encouraging Saddam to dodge the sanctions. The Australian public, however, echoed the government's view of the matter: it didn't want to know about it.

CHAPTER FIFTEEN

A Quarry with a View

THIS IS WHAT SELF-ABSORPTION looks like up close. At the end of 2003, Newspoll asked voters what they'd like to see happen in the year ahead. Twenty propositions were put, from the trivial to the big questions of war and national identity. Only two issues went off the dial with more than 80 per cent of voters in favour. The top wish for 2004 was 'stamp duty relief for first home buyers' — 84 per cent said yes. The next best, one point behind, was 'legislation to improve conditions for factory-farmed chickens'.

Housing and battery hens were the unifying concerns of the mortgage nation. They rated above the United Nations taking charge of the peace in Iraq (74 per cent), an ID card to combat terrorism (60 per cent), another referendum for a republic (57 per cent), the release of all women and children from immigration detention-centres (54 per cent), and Shane Warne returning to the Test cricket team when his drug ban expired (53 per cent). The least popular idea, by the way, was the full privatisation of Telstra, which only 19 per cent of voters wanted.

But the temptation to sneer should be avoided at all cost, because apathy is not a feature unique to the longest decade. The same thing happened in the 1960s, when the nation last enjoyed 'full employment'. The 1960s are recalled as a decade of social turmoil. But voters paid less attention to the Vietnam War at the ballot box than is commonly thought. The coalition won two elections despite it, in 1966 and 1969. At the 1966 poll, Harold Holt recorded the biggest win in history, 56.9 per to 43.1 per cent, and it was read as an endorsement for the war. The campaign was, after all, about Vietnam. But pollsters found that voters were looking to their hip pockets, not South-East Asia. The Gallup Poll titled its report 'Vietnam was not an issue', and put the indifference this way: 'Against every two people who named conscription or Vietnam as one of the most important issues, there were five people who named hospitals and education, four people who named pensions, and three who named prices.' Those who did mention Vietnam were more likely to be for the war than against it.

Political research is a little more sophisticated today, but the message is basically the same. Petrol prices, interest rates, and Medicare are more important in good times and in bad than, say, the war in Iraq or our treatment of refugees. Even support for the environment, the ultimate expression of altruism, can be traced back to house prices. Labor pollsters Hawker Britton found in early 2004 that concerns for green issues were greater in those suburbs where property was more expensive. In other words, the ordinary Australian who favours protecting the environment can source his or her green values to the selfish calculation that more development in their neighbourhood equals less trees equals poorer views equals lower house prices. The 2004 election campaign found Labor leader Mark Latham lamenting to his diary that more people watched 'Australian Idol' than his leaders' debate with John Howard. But why was he so surprised? It has always been so.

AUSTRALIA IS A quarry with a view, a first world consumer and services economy, supported by a third world commodities base. This is neither a criticism nor a compliment. It is, simply, the break we have on the rest of the world. We are, also, too young to carry cultural baggage. Howard took some time to come to terms with this side of the Australian character; but, once he grasped it, he became a more effective leader.

Look back over the Howard era. The first phase between 1996

and 2001 was an arm-wrestle with Hansonism. It was no different in its tone to the Keating prime ministership that preceded it between 1991 and 1996, when the legacy of the recession haunted every decision, every debate. Take a non-partisan view of that ten-year stretch of Australian history and you'll see that Howard and Keating were confronted with a public that was dangerously engaged, because it felt cheated by the open economy. The blue-collar men who had lost their place in the grand scheme of things in the 1980s carried a grudge throughout most of the 1990s. It was only after 2001, when Australia had dodged a world recession, albeit a shallow one, that Howard finally achieved his goal of making us 'comfortable and relaxed'.

So which version of the mob is the true expression of the national soul — the one that screamed, or the one that went shopping? The answer, of course, is both. The real message here is that Australia got over its distaste of deregulation. It weathered the Hanson meteor shower.

'I don't think there is any doubt, and I sense it as I go around the country, that the optimism, the self-confidence, and everything has been stronger over the second five years of the almost ten years I have been prime minister than the first five,' Howard tells me:

> There are a number of reasons for that. One of them was our capacity to survive the Asian downturn [in 1997–98]; that was very significant psychologically. Most people, including us, thought that that would be hard, and the way in which we managed our way through that, I thought the Reserve Bank did a good job on that, holding its nerve on the currency; that was the Reserve Bank's finest hour in some respects. I remember thinking around the time of the 1998 election that we were going to face, and I think both Peter Costello and I warned, that we were going to suffer the effects of it.
>
> Getting agreement on the GST in 1999 was very important psychologically. It wasn't entirely what we had wanted, but if we had not been able to get an agreement on that, that would have

broken people's confidence in the capacity of government, the system, to deliver significant reform where the other side of politics was totally opposed to it.

This is Howard's take on when the open economy turned the corner. It shares the credit with the Hawke–Keating governments. If the economy Howard took on as prime minister in 1996 had been the same as the one he had left as treasurer in 1983, it would have been sucked into the Asian financial crisis. The 1990s would have been the 1970s revisited, when government changed hands four times in the nine years between 1972 and 1983 from coalition, to Labor, to coalition, to Labor.

Bob Hawke and Paul Keating gave the nation a shot at prosperity, and John Howard had the good luck, the persistence, and the leadership strength to be in charge for the payoff. There is no question he extended the boom. It was Howard who engineered the 2001 escape, albeit by crashing, then reviving, the property sector through the roller-coaster of the GST and the halving of the capital gains tax.

There is one thing about Australia I can't make up my mind on: the balance between open and closed, because I suspect the Australian people have yet to work out where they want government to draw the line. Robert Menzies was an economic conservative and a social-policy liberal, as were Gough Whitlam and Malcolm Fraser.

Hawke and Keating were the first to open the nation on both fronts, the economic and the social. They deregulated ahead of the western world in the 1980s, whilst also using government as an instrument of redistribution by targeting welfare to those who needed it and by promoting minorities through policies such as multiculturalism. Keating took this one step further on reconciliation and the republic, and seemed to have the nation in the palm of his hands when he won the 1993 election. But he blew up quicker than you can recite the letters 'L A W'.

Howard presents a conundrum, which applies equally to the

electorate. He followed Keating on the economy, and in fact saw the project to a conclusion of sorts with a surplus budget, the GST, increased power to the federal government, and further deregulation of the labour market. But Howard threw a switch that no leader had considered in more than a century of federation: muscular social conservatism. He kept the economy open, but closed the debate on the society because he wanted to reassert old Australian values.

He redefined government as a conduit for individualism. Taxes were raised to redistribute to the winners not losers of economic reform. Families, who tend to sit at the top of the income ladder, and are more likely to have a mortgage, received tax cuts at the expense of younger singles. But Howard also gave a voice to one group of reform's losers, the blue-collar men who Keating had ignored in the early 1990s after he had taken away their jobs. He understood before Keating did that Australia had been fractured by deregulation, and that a majority at the ballot had to be built, one voting bloc at a time.

Howard's success would appear to confirm his dual approach, liberal on the economy and conservative on the society. But the twist is that the more winners that deregulation creates, the more recruits there are for the Keating agenda. For instance, does anyone seriously expect the monarchy in Australia to survive the passing of Elizabeth II? The question of whether Australia can remain as Howard sees it will be one for the people to decide over the next decade, after he has departed the scene.

THERE HAVE been eight elections since deregulation began. Labor claimed the first four, from 1984 to 1993. Howard won the most recent quartet. The 2004 election was the first to be decided by the winners of the open economy. A mini-library of books were written about what didn't happen. All had Mark Latham as the protagonist — six were about him, and one was by him. This was thrice the number of books that were published on John Hewson in 1992, when an economics professor was being sold as a national saviour.

But the bigger story of 2004 was Howard's. He lost control of the national dialogue in the first half of the year as the media, and the electorate, instinctively opened its ears to a fresh voice. One of the constants of Howard's prime ministership has been the predictions of his early demise. He has appeared, at times, so unsure of himself that the media assumed him dead and buried. Latham made Howard look old at first. It happened so fast that it seemed preordained, and for the simplest of policy reasons. Labor had already drawn level with the coalition on 41 per cent in the polls when Latham hurled the grenade of parliamentary superannuation at Howard on 10 February 2004. He announced that, if elected, he would shut down the super schemes for federal MPs, judges, and the governor-general. 'These schemes are well outside the community standard in Australia and have become out-of-date,' Latham said. 'They offer superannuation benefits seven times more generous than the current contribution scheme available to the general public.' Latham added a personal touch, offering to reduce his own entitlement if he were promoted to the job of prime minister. Two days later, Howard folded. He did so even though he did not believe in what he was doing, and had resisted doing so for the previous eight years. But the public was on Latham's side, and Howard was prepared to give his opponent an early win so he could give himself the chance to switch the debate back onto issues that favoured the government.

At the height of his honeymoon in mid-March 2004, Latham had Labor apparently storming to power, with a primary vote lead of 46 per cent to 41 per cent, according to Newspoll. 'Curious, but not committed,' was how Labor's internal polling read the mood of the electorate. Howard's biographer, David Barnett, wrote in an otherwise laudatory piece in *The Australian* to celebrate his hero's 30th anniversary in politics on 18 May that Latham's early honeymoon was one of 'only three really bad moments' that Howard had endured in his career:

He was shaken in 1989 when he was dumped by his party as leader. He was shaken, soon after he became Prime Minister in 1996, when his wife became seriously ill. What has it all been for, he wondered. And he was shaken when Mark Latham became opposition leader after eight years of Latham's two carping predecessors and was immediately embraced by the media as the next prime minister, as if nothing good had come from the Coalition government.

But Howard felt he had to become someone else to beat Latham. He agreed with Latham on many policies, in the same way as he had with Keating in 1996, so the 2004 election had to be a question of character, not content. If the new Howard had met his former self of the 2001 election campaign, chances are they would have had a shouting match. On a bad day, the two Howards might have even come to blows. Latham briefly energised the upwardly mobile voters whom Labor had abandoned since 1996. Working women, in particular, took notice of the SNAG card Latham played with his agenda for reading to young children, and a new maternity payment to replace Howard's baby bonus. Here, in Howard's early response to Latham, was a hint of where the new centre was forming in Australian politics, a centre more feminine and cosmopolitan than either side was ready for.

The baby bonus was supposed to be Howard's trump card at the 2001 election. He unveiled it at his campaign launch, in the same speech in which he encapsulated the war on boat people with the slogan: 'We decide who comes to this country and the circumstances in which they come.' Mothers were offered a payment of $2500 a year for their first-born child. But they had to remain out of work for five years to receive the full $12,500 benefit. Problem was, he had pitched the policy to a woman who no longer existed. The baby bonus fell almost 50 per cent short of the spending target set for it at the 2001 election. It was half as popular as Howard had hoped for because women were twice as likely to go back to work as he had expected.

In April 2004, Latham offered a $3000 tax-free gift to all new mothers, working and stay-at-homes, to replace the baby bonus. A month later, in the May budget, the government announced a $3000 maternity payment which Peter Costello said would 'roll together the existing maternity allowance and the baby bonus into a new payment'. It was, in other words, a backdown.

In this transaction, an undeniable truth of the Keating–Howard economy had been confirmed. With deregulation, Keating and then Howard had unleashed social forces beyond their control. Mothers worked because they wanted to, and because they had to, — despite the fact that Keating, and then Howard, would have preferred for them to stay at home to raise young children.

The 1990s were the 1960s without the housewives and without savings. The world that Keating and Howard grew up in had been based on two conceits: that protection could keep all men employed, and that most women would stay at home to play mother to the children and to their men. When unemployment returned to 5 per cent at the end of 2004, I rechecked the data for the nation's previous golden era to see what zero unemployment really looked like in 1969, the year that Keating entered parliament. Back then, the Bureau of Statistics divided the workforce into three groups: men, married women, and 'other females'. Men had a full-time unemployment rate of less than 1 per cent; and for those seeking part-time work, the figure was zero. For 'other females', the results were 2.2 per cent and zero respectively. But the totals for married women concealed a mismatch between the rhetoric of the Menzies era and the aspirations of the then young baby boomers. The full-time unemployment rate was 1.8 per cent, but for married women seeking part-time work it was 8.6 per cent. Mothers were dying to get out of the kitchen, but the blue-collar economy had no way of satisfying their demands.

When the Keating–Howard economy was born with the floating of the dollar in December 1983, the employment cake was still divided along male lines. Full-time men held almost three out of every five jobs in the economy — 58.6 per cent. Full-time women had 24 per cent, while part-time women accounted for another 13.5 per cent. The balance of 3.9 per cent went to part-time men. This is another way of looking at the 60–40 society that I described in Snapshot #1. To be more precise, the employment cake was divided 60–35–5 between full-time men, all women, and part-time men.

As Howard approached the ballot box in October 2004, the nation was moving, inexorably, to a 45–45–10 split. Full-time men had only 47.2 per cent of the jobs. Full-time women were largely unchanged at 24.5 per cent, but their part-time sisters had almost doubled their share to 20.3 per cent, for a total of 44.8 per cent. Part-time men had also doubled their ranks, to 8 per cent. Despite a decade-and-a-half of growth beyond the tariff wall, the full-time male had lost 11 percentage points of the jobs cake — with 7 going to part-time women and 4 to part-time men.

Howard, at the age of 65, did not spring to mind as the man best suited to represent a two-income society. But Latham, paradoxically, had even less claim to it at the age of 43 because he frightened young families. The voters who expressed their preference for Howard in 2004 were mortgaged to their retractable clotheslines. They didn't trust Latham with their home loan, just as they didn't trust Kim Beazley in 2001 and 1998.

The coalition won eight seats from Labor in the mortgage belt, where the proportion of families paying off their home was higher than the national average of 26.5 per cent. No election has ever been as simple to analyse. What is forgotten, though, in the drama of Latham's resignation from parliament soon after the election, and the publication of his diaries, is that Labor actually won four seats off the coalition. But all were below the mortgage belt, where fewer voters than the national average had a vested interest in the interest-rate debate. This happened to be Keating country, in high-income electorates where voters rejected Howard on Iraq and the war on boat people. Ironically, Latham didn't chase their votes on these terms, because he agreed with Howard on asylum-seekers, although not Iraq.

On the electoral income-ladder, the coalition reduced Labor's majority in the middle rung with a net gain of two seats, and extended its own lead at the bottom by another three seats. The new parliament saw the coalition with 35 of the 50 bottom seats, 21 of the 50 in the middle, and 30 of the top 50.

The Latham package, his personae and policies, stopped coalition women from defecting to Labor, and also sent Labor women into the coalition camp. This was a double whammy that mirrored the 1993 election, when Hewson drove coalition women to Keating because of his assault on Medicare. Latham, like Hewson before him, wasn't helped by the media profile of his estranged first wife. In his diaries, Latham wrote of Gabrielle Gwyther: 'the first wife is campaigning for Howard'.

The election result flattered and vindicated Howard. The coalition's two-party vote rose 1.8 per cent to 52.7 per cent, and it won control of the Senate — which, Howard admits, no one expected. Unfettered power allowed Howard to morph from tentative reformer to revolutionary. By the end of 2005, he had the full sale of Telstra passed, the culmination of his life's passion to fully deregulate the industrial relations system put into legislation, and a dramatic hardening of the nation's counter-terrorism laws enacted. It is too early to assess the impact of the industrial relations changes. They could be wiped out by the next Labor government, as Howard had scrubbed the Keating agendas for reconciliation and the republic in the mid-1990s. Or they could deliver the next round of prosperity, as Keating's crunching of inflation had done in the early 1990s, but was not so apparent at the time.

The paradox is that Keating also received perverse validation from Howard's triumph over Latham in 2004. Perhaps now, Keating hoped, the penny would drop that Labor could not return to power without playing to its former strength in the middle and the top of the income ladder.

Yet Howard's victory came at an unnecessarily high price. To beat Latham, Howard felt that he had to bombard the electorate with handouts. He met Latham's challenge on working women with a budget family package worth $19.2 billion over five years. When the government learned that some families had received bribes they weren't entitled to, because of a departmental computer glitch, it chose to let the matter rest: no one had to give the money back. A further $14.7 billion in tax cuts over four years were awarded to those on more than $52,000 a year. The press gallery applauded the political genius, as it always does, because it remained fascinated by Howard's ability to recover from near-death experiences.

But Howard didn't stop there. During his election-campaign launch, he unveiled eight separate promises that were costed at about $1 billion each. Two lots were for grey voters, a further two for families with young children, and one each went to small business, doctors, schools, and water conservation. In four successful election campaigns, Howard delivered across-the-board personal tax cuts just once, at the GST poll of 1998. He preferred to dish out the bucks one voting bloc at a time, to make sure there were no surprises on polling day. He learned that the secret to winning was to run government as a frequent-flyer program, with rewards based on loyalty, not need.

When I ran my frequent-flyer line by Jeff Kennett, he launched a carefully worded critique on the Howard era:

It's awful. The principles that I thought we held dear are not the principles that are being followed today. When I was overseas last year [in 2004], I was in France, and I'd heard that we had given $3000 to encourage, well to reward, people for having a child. I almost died, I mean that was just to me so totally ridiculous and unacceptable. I almost went straight up to the little bar and had another bottle. But where's the big picture stuff?

'I think Jeff is missing the point, with great respect,' Howard replies:

That was part of a whole package of measures that were designed to put a greater emphasis on having children … Jeff might mix with people for whom $3000 doesn't mean anything, but to a battling family in western Sydney, $3000, when a child comes along, is a king's ransom. It means a great deal to a lot of working people who are having their first child. I don't think that's greed.

I'll leave the last thought on this particular argument to the electorate. While Howard was pouring all that money into middle-class welfare in 2004, the Reserve Bank worried that it might trigger a spending spree which would bring an end to the economy's winning run. But families saved the cash by ploughing it into the mortgage. Greedy they might have been, but they were also over-geared.

WHAT BINDS a society? Good ones know how to skirt between the extremes of anarchy and dictatorship. Anarchists don't trust governments; dictators don't trust people. In a democracy we will always be cursed with politicians who dislike something about the people. The good politicians are the ones who can spot a public flaw and attempt to moderate it, but without insulting the public along the way. The bad ones see something in themselves that is superior to the people, and seek to impose it on them. In between, there are, simply, politicians who cater solely to the electorate's whims.

Paul Keating tried to change Australia; John Howard returned it to what it was. The simplicity of this thought attracts both sides of the Keating–Howard cultural wars. But to sustain this line of thinking the Keating fan club and the Howard huggers have to ignore, together, the thing both men agreed on: deregulation.

Yet the Keating–Howard economy has made Australia something else again. The old checks and balances, between Sydney and Melbourne, between capital and labour, between old and young, no longer apply. Prosperity has created the means to unify and pacify the nation. But prosperity has also increased the distance between people. Deregulation has created enough wealth to insulate most of us from the tedious job of getting to know our neighbours. The only conversations we have in common are property prices and the disturbing shift in the weather pattern. The rest of the time we engage in the monologue of materialism.

Howard's strength is that he never underestimated the public. It is also a weakness, because his deference to public opinion meant he was less likely to lead it. But did the people really want leading, or to be left alone? As prosperity spread, it was clear that Australians had reduced the checklist of things they wanted government to do for them, and their sense of what governments should be held accountable for. Howard had lost seven frontbenchers in his first term, then rewrote the code of conduct for ministerial behaviour in his second term to reduce the risk that any subsequent scandal would lead to a sacking.

He had so altered the concept of government responsibility by his third and fourth terms that the children-overboard affair, the absence of WMD in Iraq, and the evidence of the AWB's double-dealing of the oil-for-food program became exercises in semantics. Howard had to say, in effect, that the government was duped in good faith, by public servants; by intelligence officials; and by the monopoly seller of our wheat. He may be have been right in each case, but the national interest demanded a government with a better grasp of the facts. And yet voters didn't mind these lapses, because their concern has always been the hip pocket.

Australians are, essentially, apolitical. This is both their strength and weakness. There is something to be said for the self-interest of the modern electorate. It keeps governments honest to an extent, because it compels them to be prudent economic managers. No amount of ideology can connect a citizen to the mainstream of society better than a decent job. But affluence also breeds complacency.

A nation that is raising one in five of its children in households without a breadwinner has less reason to be satisfied than it might think. The danger of the Howard era is that, economically speaking, this is as good as it gets, and that the next generation will awake to find it has a permanent underclass in its midst.

Perhaps it is a coincidence, but Australians only began rioting in years 14 and 15 of the longest decade. The 2004 election year began with Australian Aboriginals fighting pitched battles with police in Sydney's Redfern. Barely 12 months later, we witnessed our first white riot when the young unemployed of Sydney's Macquarie Fields housing estates went on a rampage. Then came Cronulla, at the end of 2005. All this crankiness came at a time when most voters had never felt wealthier. In Redfern and Macquarie Fields it was the outcasts throwing the Molotov cocktails. In Cronulla it was the middle class that rioted over race, and it did so while waving the flag. Even so, Australia under Howard is demonstrably more unified than it had been under Keating.

Howard has been, above all else, a brilliant politican. He took the pulse of the nation, and found that the longer he ruled, the more comfortable he was with the electorate's contradictions. He bent more to them than they did to him, in the end, because they assured him that they were as conservative as he was.

Howard also harnessed the power of repetition. Each election campaign was reduced to a single issue so he could be heard above the noise — Keating in 1996, tax .eform in 1998, border protection in 2001, and interest rates in 2004.

But framing political debate in this way must inevitably diminish the public conversation. With Howard, the electorate learned how to put out its hand, and to take prosperity for granted. Taxes were raised not to pay for government services, but to appease those voters who were threatening to change sides.

The talkback caller who encapsulated the Howard era was a grey voter named Terry from the Melbourne bayside suburb of Bonbeach. It was 4 September 2001, a week into the *Tampa* standoff, and a week before New York's twin towers were toppled. Terry came to praise Howard and to plead for a handout:

> *Terry*: I'm just calling to say congratulations on your firm stand regarding the asylum-seekers and as an ex-Navy member I was proud of the seaman-like manner in which the boat people were transferred from the *Tampa* to *HMAS Manoora* without apparent injury to anybody. And finally, and from a selfish point, as a Korean War veteran I'm wondering if any decision is to be made regarding the Goldcard for Korean veterans over 70.

We no longer blink when some guru of globalisation dubs us the 'miracle economy'. Yet this praise blinds us to what we have lost. The boom of the past 15 years has not secured social cohesion. Instead, it has encouraged a mass outbreak of social climbing. Deregulation has taught Australians to see their self-worth through bricks-and-mortar and the size of the bribe they can extract from government. Avarice is the new black, and the political system has sanctified it with the term 'aspirational voting'. But those who have too much cash to be tempted by any further handouts want what politics cannot deliver: a republic and reconciliation with our first citizens. The open economy has flipped the clichés of the Australian character. Egalitarianism is now the motto of the haves; capital gains, the mantra of the punters.

The nation's property obsession is its Achilles heel. Keating left office in 1996 with 53.8 per cent of household wealth tied up in bricks and mortar. By 2004, Howard had raised the share to 64.1 per cent. 'I haven't met anybody yet who's stopped me in the street and shaken their fist and said: "Howard, I'm angry with you, my house has got more valuable",' he explained in July that year.

He was right at the time, but he won't be right for all time on this issue. The capital gains tax is the defining economic blunder of the Howard era. Recall why Keating didn't hear the economy collapse until it was too late in 1990? Voters didn't notice higher interest rates whilst their properties were rising faster in value. Recall, also, why the public lost faith in Keating's economic policies even after the recovery was assured? House prices flat-lined between 1990 and 1997. The next recession, whenever it strikes, will have something to do with the household debt binge that Howard sanctioned when he told voters they could pay less tax if they took their money as capital instead of income. You can bet your house on it.

Keating on Howard/ Howard on Keating

IT SEEMS RIDICULOUS NOW, but Paul Keating and John Howard were on good terms during a critical period in Australia's economic history in the 1980s. Keating says that he enlisted Howard to his economic-reform mission, and that Howard, in turn, encouraged him 'behind the scenes' on the path of deregulation.

Keating's stint as treasurer would be informed by Howard's. Howard had power, but didn't use it, because he was stomped on by Malcolm Fraser. Keating would push his prime minister, Bob Hawke, not the other way around, and he would have Howard as an ally across the chamber. When people today bemoan the convergence of the main parties on economic policies, what they probably don't realise is that the source of this understanding came from the unlikely political partnership between Keating and Howard.

Labor colleagues were puzzled that Keating could be on good terms with Howard, just as they couldn't figure out why, a decade on, he had befriended another Liberal, Jeff Kennett. Howard went as far as playing de facto mentor to Keating. He had advised the new Labor treasurer to move his young family to Canberra, warning that the job would keep him away from home for long periods.

Howard confirms their closeness on policy with an anecdote on the GST. In June 1985, Keating was preparing to release his white paper on tax reform, which contained the so-called Option C for a

12.5 per cent consumption tax. Keating called Howard, then deputy opposition leader, to his office to offer him a leak.

'He handed me the document,' Howard tells me. 'He said, "Hang on to it for an hour, I haven't handed it to some of my colleagues yet". And we were, quote, "working together". I can remember a cartoon in *The Herald*, it was him and me dancing together on tax.'

The symbiosis couldn't last; they were political rivals, after all. The explosion came in March 1986, when Howard was six months into his first go as opposition leader. Liberal MP Wilson Tuckey had been baiting Keating in parliament about his private life. Tuckey was out of line, but Howard didn't mind because Keating lost his cool. He called Tuckey, amongst other things, a 'loopy crim'. Tuckey kept goading, suggesting, incorrectly, that Keating had fathered an illegitimate child. 'You stupid, foul-mouthed grub ... you piece of criminal garbage,' Keating roared. The electorate's sympathy was with Keating, but this was the first time they'd seen this side to his character. The lesson the coalition drew from the encounter was that Keating had a breaking point.

Keating blamed Howard for unleashing Tuckey. 'The cost of this to Mr Howard is going to be very expensive,' Keating told the media afterwards. 'From this day onwards Mr Howard will wear his leadership like a crown of thorns and in the parliament I will do everything to crucify him.' It would be personal from here on, for both men. Keating won the early skirmishes. He exposed the counting error in Howard's election tax-policy in 1987. When Howard lost the Liberal leadership in May 1989, Keating claimed the kill for himself. Yet Keating confessed to me during the 1990 election campaign that Howard was the best the Liberals had. Howard remained on Keating's radar after everyone else had written him off.

THE RIVALRY BETWEEN Keating and Howard had crossed into each other's period in office. Howard was the one who annoyed Keating the most when Labor was in power. In retirement, Keating remains the most coherent critic of Howard, even after you discount for the bitterness. But they still surprise. When I asked each what they thought was wrong with the old Australian economy before they got their hands on it, they replied like identical twins. Neither would know that the other answered the question in this way, so the similarities are indeed eerie:

Keating: The fact that we had the highest per-capita income at the turn of the 20th century, people believed this was our natural inheritance. There were three economic waves in the 20th century: 1904 to 1929; 1947 to 1974; and 1982 until now. The second one finished in the middle of the Whitlam government with the OPEC price rises, and I don't blame the Whitlam government for not recognising that. But you can in the following half-a-dozen years, when things got to a very low ebb, you can then start to, I don't think unreasonably, say that the government, which was Fraser's, and the bureaucracy completely failed to bark.

Howard: The Fraser government was essentially a continuation of the Menzies–McEwen approach. We were only in opposition for three years, and all of those senior ministers then felt that, okay, Whitlam was an aberration and all we had to do was get back into office and it would come good. They failed, in my respectful view, to understand how dramatically the world had changed in the first five years of the '70s; it was just amazing, the world turned itself on its head, just as it has socially turned itself on its head in the first five years of the '60s. In the first five years of the '70s, [we had] the oil shock, the breakdown of the Bretton Woods agreement, the pushing through into industrialised economies of equal pay for women. I mean that wasn't a bad thing, but it had a significant economic effect. The pressure was all building up and we didn't have the mechanisms to handle it. We had wages breakouts, and we had high tariffs and all that, and we needed change.

Keating and Howard remade Australia by stealing the other party's supporter. Keating had a very un-Labor love of private enterprise. He turned enough Liberals into Labor voters in the 1980s and early 1990s to change the nation. He is still switching votes from beyond the political grave. Labor achieved its greatest swings at the 2004 election in wealthy Liberal seats in the capital cities.

Howard had a very un-Liberal love of blue-collar Australians. He converted Labor's upwardly mobile working class into Liberal voters in the second half of the 1990s. This group, the handymen and the entrepreneurs, will miss Howard most when he is gone, because the next generation of politicians are technocrats; they don't appear to share his empathy for voters without tertiary degrees.

Howard and Keating are the most substantial leaders of their generation. Their 20-year argument still resonates today because it goes to the heart of the Australian character, the dichotomy between open and closed. The flaw in each man's make-up is that they see themselves as the nation's conscience, and deny the other their due in shaping how we live, work, and think about ourselves. But that's their political egos speaking. Politicians can't abide equals, which is why the people remain the true arbiter of these debates. If you could clone the perfect leader, he or she would have a dash of both men: a visionary who understands that his or her profession is politics.

HERE ARE Keating and Howard unplugged from their interviews with me, about themselves, each other, and the nation:

On leadership:

Keating: I invented talkback radio for politicians. And I always talked up to the community. I think the great mistake of Howard is to always talk down to people; you know, let them eat cake, the Marie Antoinette view of the world. I tried to include them into the problem, to try and explain it to them.

Howard: I always felt comfortable and at home with them [the Australian public], but I feel more comfortable and at home with them each passing year. I feel I understand them, and my respect for them has been very high and it grows. There is an enormous amount of common sense. The Australian electorate is very bright. Hawke, as distinct from Keating, did respect the electorate. I think, on occasions, Keating didn't. It is a fatal mistake for a politician to think that he is brighter than the electorate.

On each other, part I:

Keating: They didn't know what he stood for. He had this thing running for him: Honest John. In fact, it was meant as a putdown, meaning Dishonest John.

Howard: I have a view that some of these cultural issues that Keating grabbed hold of when he became leader were not things that he felt all that deeply about. I don't recall Keating saying a great deal about the republic or the flag or Aboriginal affairs before he became leader, certainly not while he was treasurer. He was obviously always proud of his Irish-Catholic background, but with the other things it struck me that a lot of it was as much a way of galvanising people in his own party as it was an expression of his authentic beliefs.

On the region:

Keating: I think I can say that we left behind a legacy in structure of a kind the Howard government will never leave behind. In fact, whenever Prime Minister Howard goes to an APEC meeting, he goes to a structure invented by his predecessor government in Australia.

First of all, they couldn't have developed APEC, they couldn't have developed the ASEAN regional forum, and they couldn't have done the Indonesian treaty — any one of those things, structural things. And to have actually connived in to the destruction of the third item is an act so recreant to the duty of a prime minister as to warrant the highest national sanction.

If I had lost the treaty, I would have been traduced by the Tories up hill and down dale for un-Australian activities, for being unpatriotic, you had to be incompetent, and yet this has happened at the hands of the erratic president Habibie and complied in by Prime Minister Howard without cost. And it just proves again that there is one rule for the Tories in Australia and one rule for Labor. They'd still be going on about it.

Howard: [The treaty was] completely and utterly useless. [But APEC] helped quite a lot, and the APEC structure has proved to be quite good for a whole range of reasons, and it proved to be a very valuable forum post the 11th of September. The shadow of Keating hangs over them [Labor], this extraordinary sort of thing he had about his relationship with Suharto, the bapak factor. It's very, very strange.

Keating: The IMF ransacked Indonesia, and the Indonesians wanted Australia to intercede on their behalf. Had I won the 1996 election I would have bailed president Clinton up over the behaviour of the US Treasury in what they had proposed. Indonesia was left without help, and it is that matter more than anything else that Indonesia holds against Australia, that fact that they lost five or six years of economic growth and a massive increase in attendant poverty just made them so sour on Australia and the United States, more so than Timor. And why do I think that? Because I know that. That may not be apparent in the Australian press, but the Australian press don't reflect what goes on inside Indonesia.

Howard: We helped Indonesia in '97, we gave them an IMF bail-out. I came through Jakarta in October '97 on the way home from a CHOGM meeting, and we gave the Indonesians quite a bit of help. It was complicated when Suharto went. Suharto's sudden collapse, I think, surprised a lot of people, us included. And then along comes Habibie, who is totally mercurial and unpredictable.

On a republic:

Keating: Essentially, Howard scuttled the republic, and he did a very foolish thing. I rang him [in June 1995] and I said, 'Look I'm bringing down this model', and the first thing he said, he interrupted me, one sentence into the call, he said, 'I hope it's not for an elected president', I said no, it's not, it's an appointed one. 'Oh good', and then on went the call.

By John Howard's connivance in seeking to put the wrong question to get the wrong answer, the option for the appointed president — who was chosen by a two-thirds majority of both houses of parliament, in other words not chosen by any one party — collapsed.

And Howard then held a party at Kirribilli House in which he invited all the people who opposed the referendum to celebrate its defeat. Not only did he cost the country the republic opportunity, and its date with history, but he has now almost certainly set up the conditions for the wrong model, and will conservative Australia in the future thank him for it?

He would not ask the threshold question of whether the public thought Australia should be a republic.. He knew he could defeat the thing by dividing the forces. Had my question been put and agreed to, the political system would then have an instruction by the community to come up with a model. That he chose not to do. What I think he has now saddled us with, unless there is someone prepared to argue the alternative, is an elected president eclipsing the power of the prime minister and the cabinet.

Howard: One of Keating's mistakes — it wasn't a mistake, in my view, that Hawke made — but Keating felt he had to fight and destroy something in order to [change something]. That's one of the reasons, in my view, why the republican referendum went the way it did. Okay, I called it, but he sort of forced the issue. That doesn't mean to say that it won't come back and it won't happen. When you make change you have got to change it for the right reasons, and he tried to get people to change with a sense that what had gone before was wrong, and was invalid. But people weren't just going to buy that, and they thought, well, bugger that, it's not —there might be a case, but that's not the reason, there is nothing wrong with what we've done in the past.

I felt a lot of Australians were uncomfortable with zealous multiculturalism and zealous republicanism. A lot of Australians can accept that we ought to become a republic because it is the next most logical thing to do, but they won't accept that we ought to become a republic because what's gone before is inferior and we really should be ashamed of all that so-called subservience, without understanding that it is all part of the continuity of our history. Keating made a terrible mistake, effectively, in saying if you weren't an Australian republican you weren't a true-blue Australian. And that was just so offensive to a lot of conservative people, both Labor and Liberal.

On refugees:

Keating: The erection of arbitrary and parochial distinctions between the civic and human community is always the stock-in-trade of scoundrels. If you take the spectrum with Hitler at the extreme end, and Hanson at the soft end, and the Le Pens in the middle, all along that line there is one thing in common to every one of them, and that is citizenship. Who's in and who's out, who is worthy enough to be a member of the civic community, and who in the human community deserves to fail the test. And when people like John Howard say, with a wink and a nod, that the country is for all of us, he always meant for some of us, and that meant not for those members of the human community whose language, culture, and origins were not suitable in his terms. Countries which cut across the human spirit so blatantly never triumph from it. And Australia will pay a price for 2001, for Tampa, for the detention policy, for the whole thing. It has diminished us.

There is a view around now: well, we're getting on with Indonesia again, the prime minister has a relationship now with President Yudhoyono. The Indonesians hold us in contempt for these policies, but importantly in quiet contempt — and so do many European states. Like a lot of bad things, they don't come costless. When the prime minister gives up the role as binder and healer, and gets into the business of segmentation and dark-heartedness, then communities lose the guidance that a good government should provide them.

It was Labor's policy that people should not wander around in Australia as soon as they arrived. Rather, they should be scrutinised. There's all the difference in having a process which is about testing people's claims and one which is tantamount to a penal structure, and that's what he and [Philip] Ruddock set up. You've got to remember this: the boats weren't coming to Australia when I was prime minister because the Indonesians didn't want to send the boats onto to us. We had at that stage a co-operative relationship with the Indonesians. That evaporated after president Suharto's decline. That's where the critical change came from, to be met by a brazen attitude by the Howard government.

Howard: Keating and the Labor Party seem to forget that it was the Keating government that brought in mandatory detention. So when they denounce that they are really denouncing part of their own policy. He can't seem to accept that the Australian people across the political spectrum wanted us to take a strong stand against illegal immigration.

Measured by the depth of our relationship with Indonesia, China and Japan, to nominate but three of the very large countries in Asia, these constant references to a golden age of Keating in the context of our relations with Asia lacks any credibility.

On each other, part II:

Keating: I don't think they [John Howard and Peter Costello] are perfectionists; they're not quality snobs. Whether constructing a moulding for my house, or working out a colour, I try and do it with the same kind of intense calibration I brought to the public task. Maybe that's a character thing, maybe you have to have this in your character to do this.

Howard: To be a successful political leader, in my opinion, you have got to identify with a certain strand or current in Australian life, or several. And you can say that, you can certainly say that of Menzies, you can say that of Hawke, others can make a judgment about me, but I guess I've had some success in doing it. Keating, I couldn't quite see. I mean who did he identify with, he identified with the arts? Not really. I mean he did, I mean he identified in terms of saying what they wanted to hear.

He had this fascination for Empire clocks, and France. I'm not denigrating that at all. I think there is a part of him that is hard to identify. He is not really part of the sporting thing about Australians. I don't think Paul has any great feelings there. I mean he was quite a good swimmer, wasn't he? He didn't seem to understand much about rugby league, for example, for a Labor leader coming from western Sydney.

On change:

Keating: Of course, lesser lights in politics will attack people who make changes. As Howard did, suggesting you had earned the right to be relaxed and comfortable when, in fact, the only way they could be relaxed and comfortable was because of the security given to them by the Labor Party. But no country can afford to be relaxed and comfortable. The pace of technological and trade change in the world is so profound that now the half-life of policies has just got shorter and shorter, and anyone who tries to pretend otherwise is just kidding people.

Howard: I do think he misunderstood the deep attachment that Australians have to what I call the traditional culture of this country, the whole combination of things. It's the pride in history, the whole ANZAC thing. Not saying that he was insensitive to that, but he was less sensitive to it than Hawke. Hawke was always more careful. Hawke understood those things better. See, even on something like the republic, Hawke's view was that, if I remember it, I don't know whether it is still his view, his view was, well, you leave things as they are while the Queen is alive. He just saw it as a very gradual, and I remember him being asked about the flag, and he'd say we need to be very careful about changing that flag, people fought under it. He had the feeling.

On Australia:

Keating: The problem for Australia is that John Howard has attitudes from my father's generation — not my father's, but my father's generation. People who are now in their eighties. And at the wrong moment in history the country ended up with someone driving ambitiously in reverse.

Howard: I think the country is incredibly confident and self-assured. It believes in itself, it feels affluent, it feels that it matters, their kids have got opportunities, and they think the country stands for something in the world. But they also think that we've also hung, and we ought to continue hanging on to, a lot of the things that we had in the past. For want of a better expression, we have recovered the orthodox sense of what it means to be Australian.

Acknowledgements

Thanks to Bronwen Colman, Anna and Lukas Ziaras, and to Henry and the gang at Scribe for sacrificing so much time to whip this book into shape. The following friends, colleagues and co-conspirators also deserve naming and shaming for hearing me out: Gabrielle Chan, Diane Colman, Joel Deane, Christopher Dore, Margaret Easterbrook, David Forman, Nina Field, Joe Fulco, Lynne Gallagher, Michael Gordon, Fiona Hando, Nick Harford, Susan Horsburgh, Bonois Hugelot, Jeff Jenkins, Kate Legge, Stephen Lunn, Richard Paddington, Fiona Pie, Allison Sloan and Katrina Strickland. Finally thanks and much appreciation to Susan Grusovin, David Luff and Arthur Sinodinos for getting your respective bosses to talk to me, and to *The Australian* for giving me the time off to write. Oh, and to Thomas and Nicola: there, I've named you both.

Notes

The main interviews for this book were conducted with Paul Keating on 6 June and 20 June 2005, with Jeff Kennett on 27 June, and with John Howard on 22 August. Keating gave me access to his personal files, whilst Howard supplied additional comments via email. The quotes drawn from these interviews are recorded in the book in the present tense. All other quotes referred to will be noted in the normal way below. A second interview with Howard was conducted on 9 December, for *The Australian's* book *The Howard Factor*, MUP, 2006, which *The Australian* kindly allowed me to quote from for this book as well.

Where I rely on information from an article I wrote, only the newspaper, headline and date are shown. All other newspaper sources are presented with the author mentioned first. I don't repeat the references to the budgets, and other political documents such as *Fightback!*, because it is clear from the text which year the relevant information is drawn from. Where I refer by date to a quote from a speech or media interview, I don't repeat it below, for the sake of brevity. I also rely on notes and transcripts I made at the time.

The detailed federal election results for 1993, 1996 and 1998 are taken from the Australian Electoral Commission's CD-Rom. The details for 2001 and 2004, and the national votes since 1949, are from the website www.aec.gov.au

The Newspoll tables are from www.newspoll.com.au

The various tax cuts auctions that have plagued national affairs, which are referred to in this book, are summarised in a table at the end of these notes.

Chapter 1: 'De-spiving Australia'

p. 6: '… the slaughter of 40 million confused moths' 'Fatal beacon lures confused Bogongs' *Daily Telegraph,* 3 November 1988

p. 6: 'Home loan rates to soar', *The Adelaide Advertiser*, 17 November 1988

p. 11: 'The numbers game of economics …' Australian Bureau of Statistics catalogue 5206.0; time series spreadsheet Table 2 seasonally adjusted, www.abs.gov.au/ausstats/abs@.nsf/lookupresponses/00efa54cb5a3fd98ca2 568fd007d97b1?opendocument

p. 12: 'What about interest rates? …' 'Sorry, sold out', *The Sun*, 11 July 1989. The breakdown of households was based on data supplied to me at the time by the ABS.

pp. 15–16: 'Six months later, Keating received …' Ian Macfarlane's comments as cited in David Uren, 'Risk that rates will rise, says Reserve', *The Australian,* 14 December 2005

p. 17: 'Down-trodden and anti-establishment …' 'Paul sums up Pies' plight', *The Sun,* 24 March 1990

pp. 17–18: '… Keating boasted how Labor had won …' *Hansard,* 6 December 1990

p. 19: 'Alfred Deakin …', as cited in Paul Kelly, *100 Years, The Australian story*, Allen & Unwin, 2001, p. 100

p. 19: 'Greed, when it led to recession in the past …' The wages share I use is the ratio to non-farm GDP. I downloaded the table from the Reserve Bank website, www.rba.gov.au/Statistics/Bulletin/G06hist.xls

p. 20: 'I feel for the decent people …' 'Jail the spivs', *The Herald Sun*, 22 November 1990

p. 21: 'Snapping the inflation stick', Paul Keating's speech to EPAC, 22 February 1991

Snapshot #1: 'You're terrible, Muriel'

p. 23: 'The cinema is normally the last place …' The box office numbers are from the Australian Film Commission's 'What Australians are watching' tables, www.afc.gov.au/gtp/wcboshare.html

p. 24: Lawrie Zion, 'You're terrific, Muriel', *The Australian,* 18 September 2004

p. 25: '… Australia had become a 60–40 society'. These are my calculations, using ABS catalogue 6202.0.55.001, Labour Force spreadsheet,

www.ausstats.abs.gov.au/ausstats/abs@archive.nsf/Lookup/CA256B7300
1F0708CA256DF90001DF62/$File/6202002.xls

Chapter 2: Placido Domingo versus Fangio

pp. 27–31: Paul Keating's Placido Domingo speech, as cited in Michael
Gordon, *A Question of Leadership*, University of Queensland Press, 1993
p. 30: '… Paul Kelly wrote' 'Down but never so dangerous', *The Weekend
Australian,* 24–25 November 1990
p. 32: '… Keating supporter dared me' 'No holds barred in this verbal
orgy', *The Herald Sun,* 3 June 1991

Snapshot #2: Jumping the Picket Fence

p. 39: 'In 1991, Generation X …' The figures for women with tertiary
degrees were supplied to me by the Productivity Commission in
December 2004
p. 41: For the detail on Generation W, see my first book, *Faultlines: race,
work and the politics of changing Australia*, Scribe, 2003
p. 41: 'Meanwhile men were undergoing …' ABS catalogues 6105.0 and
6310.0.
pp. 42–43: 'But there is another side to the story …' OECD research
report H200302, May 2003

Chapter 3: King Jeff

p. 47: ' … Victoria was a basket case.' See ABS catalogue 3105.0.65.001,
'Australian Historical Population Statistics'
p. 47: 'Victoria's share of the economy …' See ABS catalogue 5220.0. I use
the current price series for the state shares of the national economy on
advice from the ABS, and for growth, I use the chain volume measures.
p. 48: '… Kennett as a topple-toy' 'Jeff insists on volunteers', *The Sun,*
18 June 1988
p. 48: The car phone transcript was published in *The Sun,* 24 March 1987
pp. 51–52: 'You are the most gutless politician …' As cited by Tom
Ormonde, 'Kennett's furious outburst', *The Age*, 29 October 1993
p. 52: 'If you can't get a girl …' As cited by *The Age,* 'Kennett under
attack for "girls" jibe in Parliament', 20 March 1997

Snapshot #3: Keating as Book Critic

p. 57: 'He worried about light, germs, cancers, drafts ...' John Edwards, *Keating, the inside story,* Penguin, 1996, p. 17.

pp. 57–58: 'Without the heat of battle ...' Don Watson, *Recollections of a Bleeding Heart,* Random House, 2002, p. 225.

p. 58: 'The man who had kicked, scratched ...' Peter Walsh, *Confessions of a Failed Finance Minister*, Random House, 1995, p. 251.

p. 60: '... but now he was tired' Watson, op cit, p. 25.

Chapter 4: Keating as de facto Opposition Leader

p. 62: '... the nearest thing this country had to the mafia' *Hansard*, 2 April 1992

p. 68: 'It was 20 May 1992 ...' Neal Blewett's cabinet diary, as cited by Stephen Lunn and myself in 'Keating's hand held door open', *The Australian,* 28 August 1999

p. 71: 'It was Hewson's set-piece reply ...' *Hansard*, 20 August 1993

p. 71: 'Don Watson observed ...' *Recollections of a Bleeding Heart*, p. 248.

pp. 74–75: 'I had no intention of drawing ...' As cited in Sue Dunlevy, 'Hewson sorry over gaffe', *The Herald Sun,* 19 October 1992

Snapshot #4: Super Pensioners

pp. 77–78 and 80–81: 'Alarm bells are not supposed ...' This section is based on a series of articles for *The Australian* and *The Weekend Australian,* including 'Convicted MP's $1.4 million super double-dip from jail', 22 March 1999; and 'Silence of the rorts', 27–28 March 1999

p. 81: The final Bill O'Chee quote, about 'George Megafuckhead', was published in my 'Reality Check' column, 29–30 July 1999

Chapter 5: Cut Down by Women, and Tax

p. 85: '... how the GST would apply to the birthday cake' As cited in John Howard's interview with the Nine Network's 'Midday' program, 14 August 1998

pp. 88–89: 'Hewson explained five years later ...' John Hewson, 'Now is not the time to panic', *The Australian Financial Review,* 21 August 1998

p. 90: 'Peter Costello thought ...', Shaun Carney, *Peter Costello: the new*

Liberal, Allen & Unwin, 2001, p. 174.
pp. 91–92: 'Keating chose a formula ...' Paul Keating, Address to the
National Press Club, 22 July 1993

Snapshot #5: The Beatles versus Gladiator
pp. 98–99: 'Men, in turn, are the reason that the nation no longer feels as
equal ...' Customised tables supplied to me at *The Australian* by the ABS
in May 2005, based on the census in 1981 and 2001. The calculations are
my own.

Chapter 6: 'Rednecks with Blue Collars'
p. 105: 'Indigenous groups threw fuel on the bonfire ' As cited in John
Gardiner-Garden, 'The Mabo debate: a chronology', Parliamentary
Library, 14 October 1993, pp. 9–10.
p. 106: 'Fischer's most incendiary offering ...' As cited in Peter Rees, *The
Boy from Boree Creek*, Allen & Unwin, 2002, p. 195.
pp. 106–7: ' ... backyards might be open to native title claims' As cited in
Michael Harvey and Michelle Coffey, 'Kennett Mabo storm',
The Herald Sun, 20 July 1993
pp. 111–12: 'Keating had given voters fair warning ...' Paul Keating,
speech, Redfern, 10 December 1992
p. 117: 'Fischer has softened ...' The Tim Fischer quotes here, and in
subsequent chapters, are drawn from a series of interviews with me in
2003 for a cover piece in *The Weekend Australian Magazine,* 'The man
who tried to retire' 27–28 September 2003. This quote was published at
the time; the subsequent quotes on Hansonism are published for the first
time.

Snapshot #6: The Most Popular Nation on Earth
p. 120: 'Hawke went joke for joke ...' Stephen Mills, *The Hawke Years*,
Viking, 1993, p. 157
p. 121: 'What grabbed the president ...' Bill Clinton, *My Life*,
Hutchinson, 2004, p. 736.

Chapter 7: All the Way with Jakarta
p. 122: 'Clinton took credit for himself ...' Clinton, op. cit., pp. 560–61
p. 122: '... Keating described the epiphany' Paul Keating, *Engagement:*

324 THE LONGEST DECADE

Australia faces the Asia–Pacific, Pan Macmillan, 2000, p. 86.

p. 125: 'Hawke played the French card ...' Bob Hawke, *The Hawke Memoirs*, William Heinemann, 1994, pp. 501–2.

pp. 127–28: 'An example of the collective wisdom ...' Andrew Markus, *Race: John Howard and the remaking of Australia,* Allen & Unwin, 2001, p. 100.

Snapshot #7: Australians as Warmongers

p. 134: John Birmingham's *Quarterly Essay*, issue 20, 'A time for war', Black Inc, 2005, got me thinking about the new Australian militarism.

p. 135: 'Cultural enemies ...' *The Sydney Morning Herald* said in its editorial of 8 September 1999 that 'Australia, however reluctantly and without waiting for others, must lead the way — in force.' In his interview with John Howard on 2UE radio on 6 September 1999, Alan Jones said: 'Even if the UN agreed to send in some kind of peacekeeping force, are we to sit around and wait a month or more for that to happen?'

pp. 138–39: John Howard's statements welcoming the each new Indonesian prime minister can be found on his website, www.pm.gov.au

Chapter 8: The Search for a Contest

pp. 146–47: 'The Paxtons.' As cited in Mark Davis, *Gangland,* Allen & Unwin, 1999, p. 13

p. 147: 'A report to the government from the Bureau of Industry Economics' As cited in 'Jobs lost in recession "gone forever",' *The Australian,* 19 May 1994

Snapshot #8: The Long Decade

p. 153: 'Three years later, on Anzac Day ...' Stuart Rintoul, 'Long walk to freedom', *The Weekend Australian Magazine,* 11–12 June 2005

p. 154: Australian of the Year, full list at www.australianoftheyear.gov.au/recipients-aoty.asp

p. 155: 'Initially, Long divided people ...' Ashley Browne, 'Tony Shaw — Still telling it in BLACK & WHITE'; and Sam Newman, 'Sledging was just as bad in my day', *The Age,* 5 May 1995; B. A. Santamaria, 'A slur on good sense', *The Weekend Australian*, 20–21 May 1995

p. 158: 'Ceding about the same height disadvantage ...' As cited in Robert Craddock, 'Waugh takes no nonsense', *The Herald Sun*, 23 April 1995

p. 158: 'What Waugh actually said …' As cited in 'Waugh of words with Ambrose', *The Age*, 22 October 2005

Chapter 9: More Bypasses than Lazarus
p. 161: 'The day after the 1984 election …' As cited in Paul Kelly, *End of Certainty*, Allen & Unwin, p. 178
p. 165: 'Howard placed the apology …' Greg Sheridan, 'I was wrong on Asians, says Howard', *The Weekend Australian*, 7 January 1995
p. 168: 'Robert Garran …' 'Howard leaves GST door open', *The Australian,* 2 May 1995

Snapshot #9: Castlenomics
p. 177: The calculations of housing wealth are mine, based on the Treasury's final estimates for 'Australian net private wealth' published each year in its 'Summer Economic Roundup'. I've used Table A1(c): Real private sector wealth at market value.

Chapter 10: The End of the Beginnning
p. 187: 'Both sides had been warned …' As cited in Alan Wood, 'The Phoney Debate', *The Weekend Australian*, 3–4 February 1996

Snapshot #10: Envy Lines
p. 190: 'So toxic was the feeling …' Pamela Williams, *The Victory*, Allen & Unwin, 1997, p. 157.
pp. 190–91: 'Think of the 150 electorates …' I drew up my electoral income ladder in December 2002, using customised tables from the 2001 census supplied to me at *The Australian,* and relied on them for *Faultlines*. I adapted them again for this book, this time going back to the 1993 election. The best analysis of why the Howard battlers are a furphy can be found on Peter Brent's website www.mumble.com.au
p. 191: 'The two-income family became the dominant group …' Based on customised tables from the 1986 and 2001 census supplied to me at *The Australian* in November 2002
p. 192: 'This is deregulation's underclass …' Customised tables from the 2001 Census. 'The Missing Breadwinner', *The Weekend Australian*, 10–11 July 2004.
p. 194: 'About one in three people …' The overseas-born populations for

the capital cities at the 2001 census were: Brisbane 22 per cent, Adelaide 24.7 per cent, Melbourne 30.3 per cent, Perth 33.2 per cent and Sydney 33.4 per cent.

Chapter 11: Guns and Budgets
p. 202: 'Treasury confessed in 2005 …'From the Treasury 'Economic Roundup Autumn 20005, www.treasury.gov.au/documents/987/PDF/03_macroeconomy.pdf

Snapshot #11: 'Please Explain'
p. 210: 'Hanson's tiff with Mahathir …' As cited in Trudy Harris, 'Hanson lashes Malaysian PM over moron tag', *The Australian*, 2 December 1996

Chapter 12: Unmaking the Keating Society
p. 215: '… bring the pendulum back to the middle' John Howard, interview with the ABC '7.30 Report', 4 September 1997
p. 216: 'I got angry …' Interview with author April 2002
p. 216: 'He made the case early in his term …' John Howard speech to the Victorian Liberal Party, 11 May 1996
p. 220: 'Harradine told the Senate …' *Hansard*, 8 July 1998
pp. 221–23: '… from the floor of the Wondai RSL' John Howard, speech 25 June 1998
p. 224: 'The demographic tide began moving …' The interstate migration figures come from unpublished ABS tables supplied to me at *The Australian*, December 2004

Snapshot # 12: Hip Pockets and Hypocrites
p. 231 'Labor's package failed …' This paragraph was drawn from an anecdote I included in my chapter for *The Australian's* post-election book in 1998, *Future Tense*, Allen & Unwin, 1999

Chapter 13: The 'Government Salvation Tax'
p. 237: 'I am not like the leader of the opposition …' *Hansard*, 17 October 1885
p. 246: 'Stricken with stomach cancer …' 'Colston told to prove he's close to death', *The Australian*, 4 May 1999

p. 253: 'The GST was officially an orphan …' 'Bastard Child', *The Australian*, 1 July 2005

Snapshot #13: The rise of the McMansion
pp. 255–56: The data for foreign debt to exports are drawn from ABS catalogue 5302.0. Time series spreadsheet Table 35, www.abs.gov.au/Ausstats/abs@.nsf/lookupresponses/eb526df7b5d0e18cca 25701100819cd8?opendocument
p. 255: 'Geoffrey Blainey warned …' *The Sun*, 2 March 1990
pp. 256–57: 'The household debt burden …' Tables supplies by the Reserve Bank of Australia
p. 258: 'The Australian Taxation Office was $700 million in the black …' Taxation statistics 2002–03 Table 7, personal tax, selected items for income years 1993–94 and 2002–03
p. 258: '… then $2.4 billion' Australian Taxation Office, 'Compliance Program' 2005–06
p. 259: 'The suburban castle …' The ABS supplied the raw, unpublished tables from its survey of income and housing for 1994–95 and 2003–04. 'After the house party ends', *The Weekend Australian,* 18–19 February 2006

Chapter 14: Howard as Warrior
pp. 264, 268–69 and 272–73: 'As he boarded …' The stories of the asylum-seekers are drawn from interviews in August 2004, which formed the basis of two articles published in *The Weekend Australian,* 21–22 August 2004, 'Truth's tortuous journey'; and 'Ali find refugee at last'.
pp. 266–67: 'He was wrong …' The final asylum-seeker numbers were supplied to me by the Minister for Immigration's office in 2005. The data for the *Tampa* and the *Aceng* were supplied by the United Nation's High Commissioner for Refugees.
p. 273: 'The Anglo-Celtic-Continental …' ABS catalogue 3412.0 'Migration, Australia' 2003–04. My calculations are from table 5.5. The ABS media release 20 September 2005 also points out another Howard record '… almost a quarter (24 per cent) of Australia's resident population at 30 June 2004 were born overseas … the highest since Federation.'
pp. 275–76: 'It began innocently enough …' The chronology for the

Cronulla riot was taken from *The Weekend Australian,* 17–18 December 2005

Snapshot #14: In the Right Place at the Right Time
p. 279: 'Clinton felt it necessary to explain …' The off-the-record Clinton speech on 10 September 2001 was leaked to me 12 months later at *The Australian* for the feature article 'The foresight saga', 10 September 2002
pp. 282–83: The summary of the oil-for-food scandal is drawn from the transcripts of the Cole Inquiry, 16 January 2006

Chapter 15: A Quarry with a View
pp. 285–86: 'The 1960s are recalled …' See Australian Gallup Polls
p. 286: 'Labor pollsters Hawker Britton …' Bruce Hawker, question and answers, Fenner Conference, Canberra, 24–25 May 2004.

Here are the tax scales, from *Fightback!* to John Howard's GST deal with the Australian Democrats. These tables compare the offers in the original documents with what happened after reality set in.

One Nation. Paul Keating's L A w tax scales, as they were meant to apply from 1 January 1996. (The rates as they were before the 1993 election are shown in brackets.)

$ 0–5400	00	($0–$5400	00)
$ 5401–$20700	20c	($ 5401–$20700	20c)
$20701–$40000	30c	($20701–$36000	38c)
$40001–$50000	40c	($36001–$50000	46c)
$50001+	47c	($50001+	47c)

What happened after the election promise was broken.

$ 0–5400	00c
$ 5401–$20700	20c
$20701–$38000	34c
$38001–$50000	43c
$50001+	47c

Fightback! Mark I. The tax scales as John Hewson wanted them to apply from 1 January 1996

$ 0–7000	00
$ 7001–$20700	16.2c
$20701–$50000	30c
$50001–$75000	36c
$75001+	42c

Fightback! Mark II cancelled the tax cuts for the top two rates, but brought forward the proposed date for the middle-income tax cuts to 1 October 1994.

$ 0–7000	00
$ 7001–$20700	16.2c
$20701–$40000	30c
$40001–$50000	46c
$50001+	47c

John Howard's 1998 election tax package as it meant to apply from 1 July 2000:

$ 0–6000	00
$ 6001–$20000	17c
$20001–$50000	30c
$50001–$75000	40c
$75001+	47c

What it became after the GST deal with the Australian Democrats:

$ 0–6000	00
$ 6001–$20000	17c
$20001–$50000	30c
$50001–$60000	42c
$60001+	47c

Index

Australian Taxation Office, 258
Australian Tourism Industry
  Association, 74
Australian Wheat Board (AWB),
  282–4, 297

baby boomers, 11, 41, 42, 99, 102,
  263, 292
Bali bombings, 139, 260
Bali, package tours to, 131
banks, 14, 20, 21, 44, 67, 183, 258
Bannon, John, 16, 44
Barnett, David, 290–1
battery hens, 285
The Beatles, 103
Beattie, Peter, 44, 220
Beazley, Kim
    1998 election, 234, 241–3
    asylum seekers, 115
    East Timor, 135
    Howard, 227
    Keating, 41
    One Nation Party, 220–1
    politics of prosperity, 231–2
    mentioned, 202, 293
beer excise, 251
Berlin Wall collapse (1989), 58–9,
  123
bin Laden, Osama, 279
Bishop, Senator Bronwyn, 143–4
Bjelke-Petersen, Joh, 104, 224, 237
Blainey, Geoffrey, 255
Blair, Tony, 149, 281–2
Blewett, Neil, 68
'The Block' (TV show), 260
boat people *see* asylum seekers
Bogong moth story, 6
Bond, Alan, 9, 20, 154
Borbidge, Rob, 220

Boucher, Trevor, 143, 257
Bowen, Lionel, 182
Boxing Day 2004 tsunami, 139
Bracks, Steve, 44, 54, 55, 56, 210
Brennan, Sir Gerard, 104, 106
Brereton, Laurie, 190
Bretton Woods agreement, 303
British Empire, 29
Brumby, John, 51–2, 54
budgets *see also* current account
  deficit
    1988, 7
    1989, 11
    1990, 11
    1993, 94–6, 113, 141–3, 199, 240
    1995, 96, 186
    1996, 185, 198–9, 199–206
    1997, 184, 238
    2001, 262–3
    2004, 234
    2005, 231
    budget calculations, 186
    budget lock-up, 230–2, 234
    GST figures in, 253
building societies, 20
bulk billing, 64
Bureau of Industry Economics,
  147
Burke, Brian, 44, 108
Bush, George Herbert, 59, 120,
  122, 132
Bush, George W., 125
    Howard, 120, 197, 278–9, 280,
    281
business interests, 238–9 *see also*
  lobby groups; small business and
  self-employed
business tax system, 257

Victoria
  1993 election, 86–7
  budget deficit, 50
  Cain, 44
  dairy industry, 53
  economy, 18–19, 22, 46, 47
  Hansonism, 223
  Keating's recession, 12, 16–17
  Kennett *see* Kennett, Jeff
  Melbourne, 18, 194, 224, 254
  share of national economy, 47,
    56
The Victory (Williams), 181, 190
Vietnam war, 134, 280, 285–6
voters *see also* public opinion
 (opinion polls)
  1993 election, 90
  Asia-first accusation, 124–5
  aspirational, 204, 299
  the battlers, 190–1
  castlenomics, 177–9, 190
  'comfortable and relaxed',
    165–6
  compulsory voting, 83
  defecting, 41, 190–1, 304
  downward envy, 146, 193
  grey voters, 262–3, 295, 298
  GST debate, 34–5
  Honest John Howard and,
    167–8, 170, 187–9, 305
  interest rates equate recession
    for, 143
  Keating and, 51, 62, 152, 170,
    187–9
  One Nation Party supporters,
    212–13
  partisan and swinging, 102–3
  racism, 110–11, 213
  small-target strategy for, 170
  WW (white and on welfare),
    191, 193

wages
  explosion, 13–14, 15
  national wage increases, 170
  penalty rates and leave
    loadings, 88–9
  profits and, 40
  share of, 19–20
  for women, 39–40
  workplace agreements, 67–8
Walsh, Peter, 58
Waluwarra/Georgina people, 229
Warne, Shane, 157
Washington, George, 28
Watson, Don, 57, 59, 60, 71, 109,
  130, 154
Waugh, Steve, 154, 158–9
Western Australia
  1993 election, 86–7
  Burke, 44
  Court, 52
  Keating's recession, 16, 20
  native title, 109, 113, 217
  Perth, 18, 194
  royal commission, 180–1
  share of national economy, 47
White Australia policy, 131
Whitlam, Gough
  1975 election, 177, 188
  four-year term referendum, 182
  Fraser, 9
  GST, 236
  Keating, 232–3
  Racial Discrimination Act 1975
    (Cth), 113
  recession (1974–75), 8–9